WILD

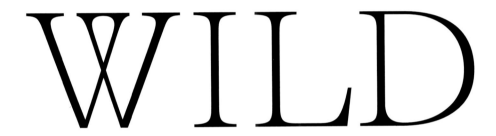

WILD

The Naturalistic Garden

**NOEL CLAIRE
KINGSBURY TAKACS**

Planting – the way plants are used and arranged – is changing. Private gardens, public parks and other public spaces, even some corporate landscapes are increasingly sporting wildflower meadows, prairie plantings, or perennials and ornamental grasses in great naturalistic sweeps. Sometimes these creations are remarkably like what might be seen locally in open countryside; at other times they are more like a conventional garden that has somehow overflowed its boundaries and spread an exuberant but definitely designed and styled plant mix over what in the past might have been staid mown lawn, stiff perennial borders or dreary evergreen shrubs. Grasses and other plants formerly considered too low-key for ornamental use are often fundamental to these novel plantings. Large, colourful flowers tend to be missing, and instead there are more understated colours and a more subtle interplay between plant shape and form. There is none of the regular spacing of conventional planting, and usually little bare earth to be seen between plants; if there are any straight lines they are there to contrast with and thus emphasize the romantic softness of the vegetation.

Many in the garden and landscape fraternity know what is going on, and among the public, there is a general feeling that the new style of planting is a good thing – that it is somehow more sustainable, better for the environment and wildlife, perhaps lower maintenance. Nevertheless, the details of the species used, their organization and layout are mysterious. In this book we want to throw some light on this transformation – to define what makes this wilder-style planting special and different to what went before, to explain its importance, to clarify its different brands and styles, to tell something of its history and the personalities behind it and, above all, to explain its aesthetics and emotional appeal.

← A meadow incorporating many
non-native species as well
as local wildflowers at
Le Jardin de Berchigranges,
in eastern France, illustrates
the very best contemporary
wild-style planting design.
It also incorporates the most
ecologically dynamic and
therefore 'wildest' of planting
styles, clearly shown to be
intentional by the meticulously
maintained lawn grass in the
paths. The creative tension
between 'wild' and 'cultivated'
is what gives a spark to
some of the most skilful
naturalistic gardens.

Urban Naturalism

A good place to start to understand what is going on is New York's High Line, the best-known example of this new trend (see pp.132–9). This linear public park, two storeys above the ground, has been a game-changer in the way it has transformed how people view plants in public spaces. Every day, thousands of people experience plants used in ways they have never seen before; indeed, in many cases it may be the first time they have ever really looked at plants. Designed by Piet Oudolf, the Dutch garden designer who is seen by some as the founder of the new movement in planting (although he is only one among many proponents), the High Line is clearly ornamental but much wilder, freer and more complex than people are used to seeing, especially at this height above the ground. Indeed, some of those who climb up the steps on to the steel platform probably think that they are looking at wild vegetation, or a re-creation of it: grassy meadows, and woodland with a rich ground flora of ferns and sedges. Naturalists, or anyone familiar with the wild places around New York City, would never be fooled; they understand immediately that this is an artistic creation.

The fact that some people might be convinced of the natural authenticity of the High Line and others not at all is perhaps evidence of its strength. This is a place that encapsulates a particular feeling that many city-dwellers have – a yearning for something natural in an environment far removed from nature. However, most of those city-dwellers do not want real nature, with its mosquitoes and ticks and flies, in the city, nor do they want real natural plant life. Real nature is difficult for many to read: sometimes too wild, sometimes too dull, too untidy, too difficult to make sense of. The High Line offers a safe alternative – nature tidied, nature organized (if only just a little), nature tamed ... but nature nevertheless. Perhaps we should refer to this version of the new style of planting as 'naturalistic', implying a natural inspiration but not necessarily an ecological function. A genuinely ecological planting would have the density of a natural plant community, with absolutely no bare soil visible, and be dynamic, with a constant waxing and waning of the component plants over the years.

Plantings by Piet Oudolf in other US public parks, such as New York's Battery Park or Chicago's Lurie Garden (see overleaf and p.265), are similar to but subtly different from the High Line, for they have more of a sense of organization – the plants are more likely to be grouped, so the overall effect is more garden than nature. The fact that Oudolf's plantings of summer-flowering perennials and grasses (see pp.20–7) are similar to conventional plantings has undoubtedly made his work the most accessible of many practitioners and the most comprehensible, hence the crown bestowed on him by the horticultural media. Others might object, saying that his work is naturalistic-lite and not 'ecological' at all, in that it does not relate to the ecology of the site or aim to develop a self-sustaining ecosystem. It is, however, undeniably naturalistic in that the plants are either identical to, or very similar to, wild species, so the qualities and proportions of plants (no double flowers or huge flower clusters) are maintained. Do the insects mind? Many probably do not, for however the plants are arranged, bees and other pollinators are buzzing around, making the most of the bounty made available by the flowers. Around 200 wild animal and insect species are to be found in New York City, a powerful reminder of just how much biodiversity can be found in urban areas. Other naturalistic practitioners, however, might stress that these plantings could do a lot more for biodiversity, and that the level of maintenance the High Line receives constantly disrupts it as a habitat.

← Designed by Piet Oudolf,
the Lurie Garden in Chicago's
Millennium Park is an example
of extensive, large-scale
planting. As with many such
projects, there is an extensive
network of paths for the public
to walk through. While this is a
very stylized version of nature,
its rolling topography and plant
selection (many native to the
Midwest) provide an artistic
representation of the regional
landscape to an urban population.

In Europe, urban naturalism is exemplified by the *heemparken* ('home/habitat parks') of The Netherlands – public parks that use Dutch native plants in a naturalistic way. The *heempark* concept is one of the oldest in the world of nature-inspired planting, dating back to the 1930s and the life of Jacobus P. Thijsse, a teacher turned early environmental campaigner, and founder, in 1905, of the Society for the Preservation of Nature Monuments in the Netherlands. In a country that had made the defeat of nature almost a pre-condition of its physical survival, he campaigned for the preservation of what little remained of Dutch nature. From the 1960s onwards, a growing environmentalist movement began to face down the engineering and agricultural lobby that had long dominated the nation's land-use planning, and an increasing number of wilderness areas or habitat restorations has been the result.

In the Amsterdam suburb of Amstelveen, three areas – the Dr Jac. P. Thijssepark, De Braak and the Dr Koos Landwehrpark – are a hybrid of nature and cultivation. The particular process of maintenance employed here is crucial to their visual and ecological diversity and to their popularity with the public. Much of the parks is managed on a cyclical basis, so that every ten years or so the heather-dominated vegetation, which tends to suppress all smaller plants, is stripped off, and the bare peat sown with seed of the kind of wildflowers that typically grow on newly exposed surfaces. Over the next few years, other species move in and overshadow them, and the process continues until the heathers succeed in another complete take-over. In nature, the heather would then eventually be replaced by tree seedlings, and forest would be the end result of the process that started with the bare peat – 'succession', in the jargon of ecologists. Management prevents this from happening here, and instead the process is restarted, again and again. Much conventional garden maintenance aims to keep plantings looking the same, more or less, from year to year. Nature does not work like this, and while the management of the Amstelveen *heemparken* aims too at keeping everything looking the same, it is done in a cyclical way, so that the various early, dynamic stages of vegetation development are embraced.

For city-dwellers in particular, one of the great things about these new plantings is the opportunity to appreciate the change of the seasons (see p.265), but more naturally and with greater subtlety than is indicated by the

stiff and brightly-coloured tulips of convention or the masses of daffodils sprawling along roadsides. The spring flowers look more like what you might expect to find on the forest floor when hiking in the woods: small anemones, crocuses, daffodils half the size and twice the elegance of the usual park planting. Come the autumn and winter, much remains standing, particularly the seed heads of the late summer perennials and grasses. Low winter sunlight can create a surprisingly warm glow when it strikes the endless variants of russet seed heads and dying foliage, and be unexpectedly bright when backlighting the seed heads of the taller ornamental grasses.

Biodiversity is one of the drivers behind the new planting – prompted by the feeling shared by many people that humanity, having destroyed so many natural environments in the making of its own, has an obligation to repair some of the damage. More convincing than moral obligation for many people, however, is the sense of sheer joy engendered by the sight and sounds of wild nature in the city. There is increasing evidence that nature, and green plant life in particular, has a highly beneficial effect on human beings, with positive impact not just on mental health but physical wellbeing, too. In bringing more nature into the city, we are helping ourselves as well as the rest of creation.

Domestic gardeners across the industrialized world have been gradually 're-wilding' their patches over the last few decades, driven by the desire to see their gardens not merely as attractive displays of flowers but also as places to appreciate visiting birdlife, butterflies, bees, salamanders. The re-wilding of the garden is an opportunity, too, to be more relaxed about maintenance, less fussy about getting rid of every weed, to ignore the blackspot on the roses or the caterpillars on the vine.

Before looking further at how we bring nature into the garden or park, we should look at what we are leaving behind – traditional ways in which parks and gardens were planted and, in many cases, still are. Plant use in gardens has traditionally been very directed, precise and controlling. Such planting reached its peak in the nineteenth century, when an explosion of gardening interest in the newly industrializing countries of Europe, North America and, indeed, anywhere that was subject to the impact of Western-defined modernity, resulted in a planting style that emphasized the vibrantly colourful, the geometrically ordered and the completely human-orientated set of aesthetic values. All of this was fuelled by the global distribution of plant species that the age of European empires enabled, and was made possible by cheap labour and cheap coal, the latter for heating the greenhouses that made the growing and mass-production of warm-climate species possible in cooler regions. Everywhere, it seemed, had South African pelargoniums to bed out in spring, European box bushes to clip and Himalayan rhododendrons as a backdrop.

Bedding plants bought and set out every spring, to flower colourfully in summer but to be disposed of in autumn, perennials manured and staked to rigid perfection, hedge and topiary sculpture regularly and precisely trimmed – these were the elements of the nineteenth-century garden that continued to dominate through the twentieth. The latter decades of the twentieth century, however, saw a rebellion against all this. The nineteenth-century legacy was increasingly denounced as unnatural and unsustainable, in part because it was supported by an extravagant use of fertilizers and pesticides. New agendas arose, in particular the idea, which would have seemed quite alien to previous generations, of gardens as refuges for wildlife. Behind these concerns – which, in some ways, were profoundly moral, even ideological – were pressing practical issues, notably the rising cost of labour: no longer could armies of workers be employed to cut, prune, weed and stake. The fact was, wilder, softer, more natural planting cost less.

During the first two decades of the twenty-first century, ethical concerns have risen in volume, and sustainability has come to dominate the agenda. To the need to reduce irreplaceable inputs (water and fertilizer) and harmful outputs (pesticides, waste plastics) has been added another powerful argument, that of carbon capture and storage. Plants and healthy soils sequester carbon, and the denser the growth, the more carbon is put out of the way. The second decade of the present century saw a variety of approaches reaching maturity and acceptance and others being developed. Crucially, a style once limited to specialist interest in a few of the most advanced economies has leapt across borders: there is now interest in sustainable gardening in Argentina, Brazil, Lithuania and Ukraine, to list but a few of the emerging markets where grasses and perennials are beginning to capture the imagination of park managers and private gardeners.

Above all, there is interest in China, home not just to one of the world's most dynamic economies but also to truly incredible levels of plant biodiversity. Planting in these emerging economies tends to be focused on native plant species – selecting plants that not only look good but also convey something of the character of the wild flora of the region, thus helping to promote a conservation message as well as local patriotism.

Sustainability has been a major factor in changes taking place across the globe. Planting design was once driven by the desire to replicate an ideal of nature ordered, and gardening was, to a large extent, about changing the environment to suit the plants. Central to what we should perhaps call the 'New Planting', in contrast, is the desire – or perhaps, more appropriately, a recognition of the necessity – to choose plants that suit the existing conditions. This is based on the realization that however difficult the situation (within reason), nature has a beautiful wild plant flora for that environment. This awareness is key to the most important aspect of planting sustainability – water preservation. It is perhaps the curse of horticulture that the region that drove its nineteenth-century golden age was the well-watered northwest corner of Europe. That same region pioneered the twenty-first-century natural style of planting, with the knowledge that it is imperative today that design and management of planting styles do not need water during the dry seasons that are part of most climates around the world. Naturalistic planting also embraces the creation of attractive gardens and landscapes on post-industrial rubble, in wetlands or on barren, sandy soils. The New Planting aims to root its creations in the environmental reality of California, New Zealand, Brazil or wherever the practitioner is, rather than trying to recreate some romantic northern European ideal.

As the New Planting moves from its largely northern European point of origin it has to face the challenge of public acceptance: will people like it enough in the local park, would they have it in their gardens? This can be a challenge, as cultures vary enormously in their attitudes to wild nature – or, at least, wild nature all year round. Dry climate zones, in particular, present a problem: they are lively enough in spring, with flowering shrubs, bulbs and often brightly-coloured annuals, but during the dry season, when plants are essentially dormant, the rather subtle grey-green of low shrubs and yellow

← The Priona Garden, in the eastern Netherlands, was one of the most talked about European gardens in the 1990s, largely because of its rejection of conventional plant management. The wholeplant lifecycle was embraced, in particular the appearance of dying foliage and seed heads. Its creators, Anton Schlepers and Henk Gerritsen, were inspired by natural plant communities and wanted to bring something of the wild into the garden, using both native and non-native species.

of grass seed heads can be a visual low point that is hard to sell. This despite the fact that any dry habitat tends to look more interesting in its dormant season than moister environments, which are far more likely to have minimal off-season visual interest (see p.233).

The success of any planting depends on a good knowledge of the plant species used, in particular how much they spread over time, their lifespans and how they compete with each other. What we are seeing in naturalistic planting is a new way of looking at plants. Piet Oudolf's photography of his own work made us look at seed heads, dying foliage and autumn decay in a new way, and influenced the work of a number of professional garden photographers, in particular the Dutch painter and photographer Marijke Heuff. A number of other Dutch practitioners, now departed to rewild the Elysian Fields, also made a big contribution here, including Rob Leopold and Henk Gerritsen. Leopold developed and popularized mixes of annuals and the use of wildflowers in gardens, all marketed through a highly innovative seed company he founded. Gerritsen became quite famous for his combinations of bolting vegetables, wild-flowers, perennial seed heads and hedges clipped into *avant-garde* shapes. These practitioners and promotors were part of a wider movement that was particularly strong in The Netherlands, involving the growing of native plants and the making of wildlife-friendly gardens and public spaces. They have encouraged us, the public, to see beauty where we did not see it before. We are also being increasingly taught that a certain amount of wildness, perhaps what in the past would have been called disorder, is part and parcel of the garden as wildlife habitat.

Naturalistic and Ecological Planting: A Gradient of Styles

There are so many different approaches to the New Planting that the field may seem as confusing as those swatches of myriad paint samples that interior designers and decorators thrust at their clients. One way to help understand the range and diversity of the movement is to follow it historically; another is to imagine a gradient between two extremes and to explore nature-inspired planting in terms of where it sits on this line.

Most of the work of the Dutch designer Piet Oudolf might be positioned at one end of the gradient (see, for example, pp.20–7). A possible reason for the success of Oudolf's commercial work is that it is not too unfamiliar, not too wild or challenging of established norms. His landscapes, with grass seed heads waving in the wind and bold clumps of perennials, look natural to many people; his skill is in capturing a kind of stylized vision of nature. The spacing between plants is relatively conventional, so there are gaps where, at least in winter and spring, bare earth is visible. Plants are usually grouped, with a block of at least a square metre or so filled with individuals of the same species. The natural look here is an entirely stylized aesthetic one: it is 'naturalistic' but not 'ecological'. Moreover, the planting is relatively forgiving of change over time, for as plants grow and spread and seed, and to some extent shuffle around, the overall appearance of the planting does not change too dramatically. Its good looks are not dependent on the geometric precision that dominated traditional planting design.

Now let's imagine something quite different – a wildflower meadow, an American prairie or a Himalayan meadow. The ground is completely covered, no bare earth is visible, and if you, or even many ecologists, were to try to count the number of plants within a given area, you might well scratch your head. Most of the plants are grasses and so relatively quietly coloured, but between them are flowering plants, standing out not just because of their flowers, but also because of their very different leaf shapes and textures. This planting will be almost indistinguishable from a natural habitat. It will be genuinely ecological, in that plants will be continually seeding, spreading, dying, moving; every year will be different. It will be dynamic, with its own processes of change and development, over which human control will be quite minimal.

The latter, truly ecological style is dominated by practitioners using locally-native wildflowers and other species, but it does not have to be; indeed, the future is likely to be dictated by attempts to create increasingly elaborate and visually striking mixtures that combine locally-native and introduced plant species (see p.145). This will be partly driven by the desire to provide seasonal interest for as long as possible, and partly by the recognition that geological and biogeographical history has dealt us an uneven hand. Eastern North America, for example, is relatively poor in species for calcareous soils but has a rich acid soil flora; Europe's balance

→ The author's former garden in early summer, with a range of species selected for fertile, moist soils. The selection was intended to be highly decorative but also to minimize maintenance by eliminating space for competing weedy species. The blue is Siberian iris (*Iris sibirica*); the pink is bistort (*Persicaria bistorta*).

of flora diversity is the opposite. Work by two academics at the University of Sheffield in England, James Hitchmough (see pp.104–9) and Nigel Dunnett (see pp.170–7, 224–31), is strongly multicultural in this regard: South African red hot pokers (*Kniphofia* spp.) thrust orange-red flower spikes out of combinations of European meadow and American prairie plants, and the magenta splashes of central European pinks (*Dianthus* spp.) illuminate a prairie planting a good month or two before its main flowering season.

Thinking about planting on a gradient from the more 'cultural' to the more 'natural' is a good way of focusing attention on a range of issues: the combination of plants, the types of plants chosen, the role of other garden elements, such as hard landscaping or hedging, and, crucially, how much maintenance intervenes to manage the inevitable changes that happen as plants grow, seed, spread and die. In this book we start with more strongly and obviously designed gardens and proceed, gradually, to the wilder looking ones, where natural processes have a larger role in shaping what we see.

The New Planting Style: A History

The first attempts at naturalistic planting involved setting out garden plants (not native species) into semi-natural habitats in parks and large gardens. A number of adventurous gardeners tried this in the late nineteenth century, notably William Robinson, an Irish journalist whose ideas about wild gardening helped to popularize the English cottage garden, and Ernst Graf Silva-Tarouca, a self-taught dendrologist from what is now the Czech Republic. These gardeners were not very successful, largely because there was little understanding of what we now call plant ecology. Some of Silva-Tarouca's plants still survive in the woods of his estate near Prague, whereas one of Robinson's legacies is the aggressive spread of some notoriously invasive species, such as Japanese knotweed (*Reynoutria japonica*).

Nothing much more happened until the 1970s, when two developments began to disrupt the ordered world of the garden border. One was essentially about habitat creation, the making of wildflower meadows in western and central Europe and prairies in the United States. Some people, very often with a background in the relatively young science of plant ecology, set about creating habitats modelled on natural ones, as part of a movement more concerned with nature conservation than with garden-

← Founded in 1977, the partnership of Oehme, van Sweden was very influential in breaking the mould of planting design in the USA. Although its work today looks highly ordered and not at all naturalistic, it was in its time revolutionary, largely because of the plant material used (grasses and perennials) and the rejection of the elements of classical garden culture that had become clichés, such as orthogonal geometry and clipped shrubs.

making or landscape design. Nevertheless, the latter two fields rapidly began to benefit, as more and more people appreciated the wild beauty of these re-created habitats and the wildlife they attracted. Meadows and prairies were, in some ways, easy to sell, with a wide range of colourful species when in full flower; both also have strong romantic associations. However, their period of glory can be short, that of meadows especially.

This desire to create habitat tended to go hand in hand with a growing interest in using locally native plants. In the United States, the growing awareness of the dangers of invasive alien species and of the need to support biodiversity with plants that are part of the food chain led to an almost explosive growth of interest in growing native plants. This interest was helped immensely by the region's rich flora, which includes both a strong spring showing – species of dog's tooth violet (*Erythronium*), wake-robin (*Trillium*) and *Phlox* carpeting the forest floor – and a very diverse late summer grassland flora, in particular the innumerable members of the daisy family: goldenrods (*Solidago* spp.), yellow sunflowers (*Helianthus* spp.) and the pink shades of coneflowers (*Echinacea* spp.). The role of one highly innovative landscape design practice, Oehme, van Sweden Associates, must be mentioned here. Although its work today can hardly be described as naturalistic, its informal use of grasses and perennials was, in the 1970s and 1980s, little short of revolutionary. Its impact can be likened to a dam burst, allowing a flood of new ideas, practices and planting philosophies to develop rapidly – and, crucially, to be taken seriously by those outside the profession.

The other development that took place in the 1970s began from another direction: the softening and blurring of what had once been the rigid certainties of conventional garden-making. In England and, a little later, in The Netherlands and Sweden, gardeners working on a domestic scale began to develop a planting style that allowed, even encouraged, self-seeding and enabled plants to merge, interpenetrate and sprawl over and into each other. The English writer Margery Fish, who created the garden at East Lambrook Manor in Somerset, was a notable exponent of this, while Beth Chatto promoted the idea, obvious to us now but not in the 1970s, that gardeners should try to match the ecology of their site with the ecological requirements of the plants they grew, choosing drought-tolerant plants for dry soils, for example. Her own garden in Essex, one of the driest parts of England, became a popular destination for gardeners from all over the world, many drawn by her books, all of which focused on linking plant and place.

This relaxing of strict gardening practices began to occur in Germany as well, but on a different scale and in the public sector. New city parks, often the legacy of a summer flower show, began to be laid out with ambitiously large and complex planting schemes that were ecologically based and intended to be long-term, sustainable and wildlife-friendly. They were also meant to look as good as possible for as long as possible.

The first decades of the twenty-first century have seen a proliferation of naturalistic and ecological planting design. The German plantings began to be formalized through a system of Mixed Planting matrices, which enabled landscape designers and others to buy plantings by the square metre. Researchers, who often combined academic experimentation with a personal passion for gardening, including Wolfram Kircher (see p.103) and Cassian Schmidt (see pp.152–9), led this innovative form of standardization. Gifted designers with good plant knowledge then took the methodology further, developing site-specific plant combinations – a good example of this group of innovators is Bettina Jaugstetter (see pp.160–3). A similar development has occured in the United States, where prairie creation as habitat restoration is morphing into the making of 'designer prairies' at the hands of garden designers such as Larry Weaner (see pp.290–7).

As the earlier habitat recreations began to mature, other more sophisticated and aesthetically-driven versions began to appear. Some adventurous practitioners began to explore the middle ground between habitat creation and the merely aesthetically naturalistic, notably James Hitchmough and Nigel Dunnett, who have tried creating plant mixes that have genuine ecological dynamism but who are not focused on working with regional natives. Indeed, these two researchers have firmly set themselves against the 'natives-only' movement, arguing that this limits their ability to create plantings with what Hitchmough calls 'the wow factor', necessary if they are to be accepted by the public. Both have adopted a very experimental approach, casting their nets wide to develop sophisticated layers of planting that aim to integrate

← One of the annual mixes created by Nigel Dunnett for the Olympics held in 2012 in London. The mixes enable local government and other clients to create colourful and pollinator-friendly short-term plant communities.

16

spring-flowering species into combinations of summer-flowering perennials. When London hosted the Summer Olympics in 2012, the two men were offered a golden opportunity to show off their work and create a legacy for the future in the Queen Elizabeth Olympic Park, working in collaboration with garden designer Sarah Price.

The strongest design input in the United States, moreover, comes not from those who restrict themselves to natives but from practitioners who may use a majority of them but are also open to non-natives for particular purposes; these designers include Bernard Trainor (see pp.46–53) and Sean Hogan (see pp.36–9), who both work on the West Coast. Native plants may create an ecology, but non-natives can add the spice or drama that a local flora lacks: late-flowering American daisies jazzing up northern European gardens, or Asian-origin clematis in a California garden. Here we should mention a young partnership between a landscape architect and a horticulturist, Thomas Rainer and Claudia West, who have begun to apply a German methodology of creating blended plant combinations to native-heavy plant mixes in the American Mid-Atlantic region. Better known as promotors and educators, many practitioners eagerly await the maturing of their first projects.

Increasing numbers of gardeners, amateur and professional, have made spaces that reflect these new ways of thinking. It is common now for designers and garden-makers to see themselves as working in partnership with nature, which in practice means allowing plants to make certain design decisions themselves, resisting the determination to control the exact location and lifespan of everything in the garden. In many cases this is easier to do on a domestic scale, where the garden-maker has only themselves and their immediate family to keep happy. Britain and The Netherlands, with strong traditions of independent and adventurous domestic garden-making, have tended to take the lead here.

Nature-inspired Planting: The Visual Qualities

Successful plantings appeal to our visual senses for the same reasons that natural environments such as wildflower meadows appeal to us, so it makes sense to try to understand their visual qualities together. How does naturalistic and ecological planting work visually, and why is it beautiful?

When we look at wild vegetation or its human-created cousin and see it as attractive, it is often because it combines two apparently contradictory aspects: complexity and simplicity. Frequently, there are few visually prominent elements, hence the simplicity, but they are distributed in a way that is very complex – there is no pattern or predictability, but instead a semi-randomized distribution. There are areas where one species tends to be at a high density, but others where it is less common, and there is a constantly changing gradation between the two. Even if there are only three prominent species in a mix, their distribution patterns change relentlessly. There is a frequently quoted design slogan, 'less is more', which helps to explain why an effective planting is often one that has only a few visually prominent elements. Here, the constantly changing distribution of a few elements provides interest – its lack of predictability engages our attention, even if only subconsciously.

Among these limited elements, grasses reign supreme – often literally, as they have a flexible strength that enables them to survive autumnal storms and stand tall, while the softer perennials around them collapse. Grasses were first promoted by Karl Foerster, an extraordinary figure whose career

as a grower, plant breeder and writer earned him a position as an important cultural figure in the Weimar period (1919–33) in Germany. (The circle of artists, writers and gallery directors he was part of has even been christened 'the Bornim circle', after the village where he lived.) Grasses provide continuity and visual stability to many of the best examples of the New Planting, as they should – they are the matrix in the meadows and prairies that inspire the movement.

It follows, then, that attractive, nature-inspired planting involves a lot of repetition and a limited number of elements, which may be prominent because of their colour or their structure, and which give the entire scene a visual unity and coherence. Having established this unity, their semi-random pattern of distribution also creates a certain sense of rhythm. The strong difference between sunshine and shade should also be mentioned here. Naturalistic planting in open habitats almost inevitably involves a lot of grasses and many fine textures, the exceptions being those harsher environments in which low, hummocky sub-shrubs dominate. Grasses do not flourish in shade, however, where the look is quite different. Woodland plants grow more slowly, compete with each other less, have coarser and bolder textures than grass, and are more likely to form clumps with stronger and more contrasting shapes.

There is another level of complexity that also engages. At first sight of a naturalistic planting, we appreciate just a few elements – but when we look more closely, and there are plant species we did not see at first, along with, quite possibly, patterns and distributions that operate on a more local level. A wildflower meadow or prairie is the best place to appreciate this impact on our eyes and minds, as close inspection reveals a myriad species, offering the onlooker a constantly shifting mix of plants as they walk through the area. The more we look, the more there is to see. Nature-inspired planting should reward our attention at first and then hold it, continuing to repay our notice as we walk and explore – for plants have evolved into many different forms, and it is these that we are looking at when we cast our eyes

→ Spikes and spires, umbels,
   daisies, buttons — structure
   and tonal depth (the range
   between light and shade) are
   often perceived subconsciously,
   but they are no less important
   for that. This planting
   at Schau- und Sichtungsgarten
   Hermannshof (pp.152–9) is
   worth analyzing on this basis.

over vegetation. Strong forms, such as upright flower spikes or dramatic foliage, seize our attention. Their absence can render even a rich and diverse vegetation dull, but too many can be over-stimulating and make the whole seem too busy and fussy. Those who have waterside areas to plant have to be particularly careful in this respect, as there are so many striking, lush foliage plants that thrive in these locations, including big-leaved umbrella plant (*Darmera*), giant rhubarb (*Gunnera* and *Rheum* species), as well as many competing colours, such as magenta loosestrife (*Lythrum*) and yellow ragwort (*Ligularia*). The most visually effective planting has a sense of balance and harmony, often expressed through a majority of quiet, unemphatic forms and a minority of strong ones.

As we become accustomed to looking at wild plant habitats as well as gardens, we can begin to judge the latter on the basis of how effectively they evoke nature. Of course, opinions will differ greatly on how much a given garden really resembles a natural habitat. It must be said, however, that some of the most effective and popular nature-inspired plantings are those that offer some sort of idealized nature. The reality is that however beautiful a wild habitat may be, there will always be extensive areas that are dull and uninteresting, especially to the non-expert. Good planting minimizes this. It concentrates those aspects of the wild that we find stimulating, bringing together forms, textures and colours that spark off each other. There must also be a quiet background, however, and it is this that perhaps distinguishes some of the most effective nature-inspired planting from its traditional forebears. Meadow and prairie habitats, consisting mostly of green or, later in the year, sandy-brown grass, forms a visually quiet matrix for the colours and shapes of the wildflowers that grow in it as a minority element. Such a low-key medium serves to highlight the more striking elements but also creates a sense of harmony and rest.

Simplicity and complexity, visual prominence and understatement – it seems as if nature-inspired planting is dealing in paradoxes. Perhaps this underlying creative tension is a major part of its appeal.

'A plant is only worth growing if it looks good when it's dead.' So says the garden designer Piet Oudolf, who has done more than anyone else to raise the profile of planting design in general and nature-inspired planting in particular. The comment was made as a joke, but it illustrates one of the reasons Oudolf's work has become so successful: he uses plants that have presence and character for months after their main flowering season is over. The designer's enormous success also owes much to the fact that his work bridges traditional ways of organizing the spatial relations of plants and more naturalistic design; it is comparatively orderly, easy for non-gardeners to 'read', and does not challenge too many ideas about what a garden or park planting should look like. It is a stylized, carefully planned vision of a wild plant community.

The display in autumn and early winter at the Hauser & Wirth Gallery at Durslade Farm in Somerset, in southwest England, is an impressive array of grass and perennial seed heads and fading foliage. The reduced colour range means that the eye focuses on subtle tonal differences, but it is the forms that are the main interest. Walking along the broad paths that separate wide areas of planting, one can admire a huge range of seed head shapes, from hard, defined spheres and spikes to soft, almost cloud-like sprays of tiny heads. The darker, more defined shapes are usually those of flowering perennials whose moment of glory may have been several months earlier, while the paler, less defined shapes are ornamental grasses, many at their best in autumn and winter.

'I am not a colour gardener', declares Oudolf, rejecting a major aspect of conventional thinking about putting plants together; instead, he has always focused on structure. He uses a special vocabulary to describe the categories in which he thinks about plants: balls, spires, umbels, plumes and curtains. Stronger, more distinctive shapes are not necessarily better, as the length of time they hold their form is also important. This focus on 'post-peak performance' guarantees that an Oudolf planting looks good well into the winter. The down side is that spring and early summer interest can be low, although there are spring bulbs planted at the Durslade gallery. Oudolf has drawn up a separate bulb

Oudolf Field

Hauser & Wirth
Somerset

plan for the garden, as well as a plan for summer perennials.

The visitor's first sight of the main part of the planting is from the east-facing terrace at the back of the main exhibition galleries. The viewer faces a rectangle of around 6,500 square metres (1.6 acres), with a slight rise towards the far side. From this key vantage point, its rectangular shape strongly resembles a painting – something that stands alone, rather than being part of its surroundings. There is a central axis, but most visitors leave it to walk around the wide grass paths between the perennial beds. 'In a large garden I like to lead people from one ambience to another', Oudolf says.

Plants are grouped into blocks in which many individuals of the same cultivar grow together, clearly separated from the neighbouring block. In this regard, the planting is relatively conventional, bearing little relationship to the work of most other naturalistic planting designers, including nearly all those in this book. Seen from afar, however, the impression is of flowing drifts of grasses and perennials, with everything repeated several times over. This repetition creates a subtle sense of rhythm and a strong sense of unity. As Oudolf describes it, 'this garden is meant to have a meadow feeling, nothing higher than the hips, but with a feeling of enclosure and intimacy from the taller, robust plants at the sides.' Movement is important, too, and enhances the meadow-like feel; by the end of the summer, most of the plants are tall enough to catch every breath of wind, so are almost never still.

There is one area at Durslade of what Oudolf calls 'matrix planting': by combining a dominant base planting of (usually) a grass with a minority element of flowering perennials, he neatly imitates the basic ecological proportions of a meadow or prairie. In the Sporobolus Meadow, the versatile and horticulturally predictable North American grass prairie dropseed (*Sporobolus heterolepis*) is used for the matrix. Oudolf uses different variations of block planting and intermingling in his work, but he believes that the latter is much more difficult for garden staff to manage, as it is less easy to interpret, especially if plant knowledge is limited. Rather than having his design end in 'tragedy', he favours the block planting approach wherever there is any doubt about the levels of future management. The matrix planting technique is a good compromise, however, and is perhaps one of the most significant innovations of his work in the 2010s.

The best way to think of Piet Oudolf as a designer is to see him, first and foremost, as an artist. Unlike most successful designers, he does not run an office or have assistants. His work is

very intuitive, based on using a range of plants he knows intimately and, in many cases, has grown commercially. In the 1980s he set up a nursery in order to obtain enough plants for his own design work, as they were unavailable in wholesale quantities from Dutch nurseries at the time. By analogy, an artist might have an intimate knowledge of materials, be it paint, bronze or marble, but then have to make or quarry these individually.

The considerable number of plant species and cultivars used in the Durslade planting – around 100 – is typical for an Oudolf project of this scale. This is far more than most designers use, and the immediate reaction may be that it goes against that well-established design slogan, 'less is more'. But consider what this diversity actually covers: a range of plants that in many ways have a similar aesthetic. Much traditional planting

design was based on the use of relatively 'artificial' plants: double flowers, bright colours, variegated foliage etc. Virtually none of this appears in a Piet Oudolf design, and almost every plant used is either part of the same gene pool as its wild ancestors or, if not, is a cultivar selected for flower colour or some other distinct characteristic, and so has the same proportions and relations between leaf, stem and flower as its wild predecessors. The range of plants may be wide, but the range of visual stimuli is kept within bounds. The senses are not overwhelmed, which means that subtleties of form and texture are more easily appreciated. In this way, the design's visual qualities are like a distillation of a natural habitat. Aesthetically pleasing wild places, such as wildflower meadows, are impressive because of the repetition of a limited number of elements, which may be

a repetition of species or of particular growth forms or flower shapes.

The Oudolf planting palette has been refined over many years, with additional commissions in North America (see pp.132–9). His work is not necessarily site-specific; the plant mix at Durslade would work equally well in Chicago or Berlin. Having been selected for continental climates, there is no winter greenery, and there is almost nothing that exploits the particular potential of the mild climate of southwest England.

This is planting design as art. As a publicly accessible site and a model of plant selection for both gardens and larger projects, the Durslade garden has proven very popular, as well being a useful learning resource for amateurs and professionals. Inspired by natural growth forms and habitats, it is naturalistic, but in its stylizing of nature it is but the beginning of our journey.

An aerial view gives a good idea of how the repetition of certain plant clumps is used to guide the eye of the viewer on the ground. Such repetition is normal in natural environments, and the subtle use of it in naturalistic planting is a big part of the style's distinctive visual appeal. The somewhat different character of the two beds on either side of the path, left of centre in the photograph, is now readily appreciated: they involve a matrix of the grass prairie dropseed (*Sporobolus heterolepis*) with emerging clumps of flowering perennials, rather than the block planting used in the other beds.

Autumn at the Hauser & Wirth Gallery sees repeating clumps of ornamental grasses and perennials create a powerful sense of rhythm. Varieties selected for durable seed heads ensure a long season of autumn and winter interest, and make the most of the low-angled sunlight typical at this time of year. Certain species have strong autumn colour – a rarity with perennial, as opposed to woody, plants. An example here is the acid yellow of Arkansas blue star (*Amsonia hubrichtii*). The arrangement of the plants into single-variety blocks emphasizes plant characteristics that might well be lost if they were more blended. Each block may not be perceived as especially attractive on its own, but the aesthetic impact comes from seeing many planting blocks in combination. However, this approach does depend on a majority of species possessing a distinct and attractive winter identity.

↑ Yellow clumps of Arkansas blue
  star (*Amsonia hubrichtii*)
  mark out a rhythm across
  Oudolf Field, looking back
  towards the main gallery.

↓ Joe pye weed (*Eupatorium maculatum*) stands tall,
  distinctly higher than surrounding plants.
  Disparities in height are one of the visual tricks
  that designers use to add interest to plantings.
  Its dead stems are not especially noteworthy except
  for their height, which can be useful in places
  as an effective silhouette.

← The dark umbels of ice plant
  (*Hylotelephium spectabile*)
  are renowned as one of the
  most reliable winter seed heads
  in contemporary planting.

↓ → Wispy Mexican feather grass (*Stipa tenuissima*)
  is a grass species popular for its light, ethereal
  nature, an effective contrast with hard, dark,
  defined shapes like the seed heads of coneflower
  (*Echinacea pallida*). This grass and perennial
  combination works with many species.

GRONINGEN,
THE NETHERLANDS

KEMPKENSBERG BUILDING
PUBLIC GARDEN

DESIGNER:
LODEWIJK BALJON LANDSCAPE ARCHITECTS

An imposing modern building stands alone, exuding a powerful presence. Associated with it is an urban garden where we might expect the kind of formulaic planting that often accompanies modern buildings: stretches of grass and evergreen shrubs with the occasional tree. But here there are swathes of colourful perennials, with bulbs in spring and grasses in the autumn; areas of meadow grass seem to merge into the perennial planting at several points.

The Kempkensberg Building houses government offices and some 2,000 people who work in them. Opened in 2014, the 1.1 hectare (2.7 acre) garden surrounding it displays a remarkable commitment to quality public space and to supporting biodiversity. According to landscape architect Lodewijk Baljon, the brief stipulated a colourful garden and a water feature that 'should be open to the public 24/7, complementing a recreational facility where there is a pavilion with a cafe and meeting rooms.' The site abuts a small historic park, the Sterrenbos, laid out first in 1765.

The City Garden is best understood in the context of Dutch urban planning, which is particularly skilful at developing a sense of locality and intimacy within a larger city environment. It follows in the tradition of the most influential Dutch planting and garden designer of the twentieth century, Mien Ruys (1904–99), who created many urban gardens in the 1950s, with an emphasis on making city spaces as garden-like as possible.

The City Garden has a main path that reaches across the site and links with the building entrance. Walking along it, there is a strong sense of being in a garden, rather than in a park – not just because of the very diverse and ornamental nature of the planting but also because of a series of yew hedges and ivy screens on metal frames that divide the area. These function primarily to break the force of the winds that sometimes hit the building and are then directed downwards.

They also create a very strong visual impression, one that produces a greater sense of intimacy than is normal in public spaces. For those familiar with such classic English gardens as Sissinghurst or Great Dixter (see pp.282–9), they evoke the tall yew hedges that break up those gardens into a series of what are often called 'garden rooms'.

The City Garden is, in large part, a roof garden: the central area planted with perennials is built over an underground car park. The perennials have a 40-centimetre (16 in) substrate depth, with twice this for the trees. The trees are all 'multistem', with several trunks

Groningen City Garden

emerging just above ground level and then tending to grow away from each other. This evokes the appearance of trees in traditionally-managed coppice woodland, where wood is harvested and stumps allowed to re-grow. Baljon explains that 'multistem trees are more in scale with perennial planting. If they start to lean in the wind they are more resilient [than single trunk ones], and they can develop a distinctive character.'

The planting has been designed to make the most of the relative openness of the space, with a particular role for grasses, whose almost constant movement contributes an added aesthetic dimension. 'We have a similar combination of plants repeated throughout the area to encourage a sense of movement', explains Annemieke Langendoen, the company planting design specialist, 'which complements the curves of the path. Plants flow through and around the hedges.' Most of the planting uses perennials in small groups, and these

groupings may be repeated, so that there is a certain amount of intermingling.

The size of the groups tends to be related either to the character of the plant or its lifespan. Varieties with a strong character, such as the very upright feather reed-grass (*Calamagrostis* x *acutiflora* 'Karl Foerster') are more likely to be scattered, as one plant can impose itself on its surroundings decisively; the same is true of short-lived species such as the evening primrose (*Oenothera macrocarpa* 'Silver Wings'), which when it dies will leave as small a gap as possible, but which is also highly likely to self-sow its progeny into new locations. Certain varieties are massed in larger groups, either because they make more impact this way, as does low-growing blue-hair grass (*Koeleria glauca*), or because they are near a path. Langendoen wanted to use certain plants 'in groups around paths more than in the middle, to make a stronger impression', and mentions sedum (*Crassulaceae*), commonly known as stonecrop, and yarrow (*Achillea*), both of which have flat heads that look more effective when repeated within a defined area. The more overtly 'designed' gardenesque planting in the main part of the garden segues into less intensively planted areas of meadow grass with wildflowers at the periphery of the site, helping to integrate these edges into the wider landscape and to maximize the value of the project as a wildlife corridor to and from the adjoining green areas.

The ongoing management of public landscapes such as the Groningen City Garden is often problematic. In this case, the contract for the landscaping was contingent on the design team offering a twenty-five-year maintenance contract that would ensure the future quality of the planting. The future of naturalistic and ecological planting will depend heavily on the willingness of those who commission such plantings to commit to the training of staff gardeners who will develop a good understanding of the particular plants used.

The garden of the Kempkensberg Building links a historic park, the Sterrenbos (to the left), with a meadow area and lawn (upper right). High-impact planting can serve as a useful transition between different types of habitat or landscape features in urban areas, and can act as crucial wildlife corridors.

↑ → Broad masses of perennials in the garden are
generally broken up with lighter grasses. Planting
nearer the paths is typically lower growing. The pink
perennial is ice plant (*Hylotelephium spectabile*)
in flower (see p.27 for the winter seed head);
when blooming, it attracts butterflies and other
pollinators. The grass on the left is Korean feather
reed-grass (*Calamagrostis brachytricha*), a medium-
sized Asian species that is popular with designers,
as it retains its looks over a long period.

→ Feather reed-grass (*Calamagrostis* x *acutiflora* 'Karl Foerster'), blue Russian sage (*Salvia yangii*) and yellow coneflower (*Rudbeckia fulgida*) are three of the most widely used perennials in this style of planting. A common characteristic is the fact that that they remain distinctive for several months after flowering.

↓ The hedges in the garden serve as functional windbreaks as well as being an effective way of breaking up space. They evoke the hedges in traditional English gardens and therefore help contextualize the garden for its many visitors.

↓ Lower planting along the paths is practical and helps visitors feel secure. Taller grasses behind, such as switch grass (*Panicum virgatum*, left), are a strong autumn feature, with red-brown foliage and distinctive seed heads. White *Anaphalis triplinervis* and yellow coneflower (*Rudbeckia fulgida*, right) are the ideal height for path edges.

← Feather reed-grass (*Calamagrostis* x *acutiflora* 'Karl Foerster') can be clearly seen here in its role as a rhythmic element, along with blue clumps of flowering asters. Effective repetition is key to successful naturalistic planting. The hedges guide the eyes of passers-by while never actually blocking views.

→ Water bodies are a popular feature in urban naturalistic landscape projects, as they create a further layer of interest and can be a very important additional habitat.

↓ The seed heads of Turkish sage (*Phlomis russeliana*) are not just imposing but physically resilient and long-lasting. This plant has many of the characteristics of an ideal low-maintenance landscape plant, with yellow flowers in spring and weed-suppressing evergreen foliage. The multi-stemmed trees are typical of those used in the project.

A boldly contemporary house sits astride a ridge above the city of Portland, Oregon, surrounded by lush green scrubland, looking as if it had been inserted into a pre-existing natural environment. Look closer, however, and the range of shrubs, small trees and other vegetation is too diverse for it to be completely natural. Most of the planting is a dull green, but other foliage colours include the silvery-grey that often occurs in environments experiencing regular drought. Flowers bloom in the spring and, to some extent, the summer, and while some are deliberately chosen for their rich colours, they are mostly muted. There is a lower layer of vegetation, some grass-like plants, a few perennials and, in the shadier areas, ferns. A green roof is planted with low, grey-leaved plants. It looks like a good place for birdlife; indeed, the owner, John von Schlegell, who, with his wife, Frances, commissioned the 4,000-square metre (1 acre) garden, is an avid birder.

Portland is noted for its gardens, both public and private, but this one differs from most because it faces up to the realities of the local climate. 'People come to Portland, and they know about the rain', says the garden's designer, acclaimed plantsman Sean Hogan. 'What is less well known is the several months of dry summer weather. We have, in fact, a Mediterranean climate.' Water is (currently) plentiful, so most gardeners irrigate. Many of the gardens for which the city is famous are rich in perennials that are dependent on water throughout the summer.

For those who want to grow native plants, there is a problematic paradox: the region is, naturally, dense coniferous woodland, so local ground flora tends to be shade-loving and unsuitable for many garden or public situations; but native sun-lovers (plants of rockfaces or dry prairie habitats) go unattractively dormant in the summer. The answer, suggests Hogan, is what he calls 'Willamette Valley iconic … a nativesque planting palette … a sense of regionalism and evoking what used to be here. A lot of the valley would have been grassland and savannah, and north and east slopes, where this garden is, would have had ponderosa pine, garry oak, shrubs like flowering currants, garrya, madrone.' To replicate this type of planting, Hogan uses 'around 70 per cent western North American natives, but coastal species rather than interior – essentially, Mediterranean climate plants, tolerant of dry summers, mostly from our part of the world but some from other places with a dry summer climate'. Most of these are evergreen shrubs, which will look good in summer even if not flowering. Hogan has an encyclopaedic knowledge of the flora of western North America, and his nursery, Cistus, just outside the city, grows an amazing range of species, native and non-native.

Von Schlegell Garden

Mediterranean climate regions typically contain shrubby species that either re-sprout after one of the fires that are part and parcel of life in these areas or regenerate from seed. The former can be hard-pruned, and Hogan suggests that 'these are chosen for prominent positions like path edges', while renovation planting will occasionally be needed elsewhere.

Diversity is the key to building interest in a situation in which many plants look very similar. Species of *Yucca* are useful as counterpoints: these North American natives have a form that is dramatically different from much of the rest of the planting here. As Hogan points out, 'there are not many spiky plants in Mediterranean climates', and yet these and other steppe and desert plants are often used in gardens in dry summer climates, as designers find them irresistible; the few that appear here are in pots.

A key plant, here and in an increasing number of gardens in the region, is the Pacific madrone or madrona (*Arbutus menziesii*) and the related manzanitas (*Arctostaphylos* spp.). These are small trees and shrubs with distinctive silvery leaves and rich cinnamon-coloured bark, well-displayed through an open, bendy branching habit. These species are icons of the regional flora, but are easily killed by soil disturbance (including transplanting) and by irrigation during the dry season.

The colours of the house are picked up by the planting. The red cedar cladding naturally combines greys and oranges, which Hogan describes as 'the colours of the West: mahogany oranges – the colour of the bark of the *Arbutus* and manzanitas – and the blues, which you see in the leaves of some of the manzanitas, dark glossy greens, the golden of the grasses … Green is not a summer colour here, as it's a dormant time. With the first rains in October and November, the bulbs emerge, the grass turns green, shrubs like the currants [*Ribes* spp.] flower; but during the dry summer the bones of the garden and the colours of the evergreens have to work. We make dormancy work for us.' As with the flora of the Mediterranean itself, many locally native species are aromatic, and the release of their fragrant oils on a hot day, as one brushes against plants, is part of the experience of this garden.

Greens are important on the cool northern side of the house, where there are ferns and several species of *Araliaceae* shrubs, notable for their dramatic hand-shaped leaves. Some courtyard spaces around the house have been developed with spring and early summer plants that have strong, saturated flower colours. Just as in a natural habitat where different aspects and levels of shade are home to different plant species, micro-habitats can be an important way to differentiate spaces and provide a sensory experience of garden exploration.

With a muted colour palette that is one of its design strengths, this garden is far more realistic for the place than most Portland gardens, which are increasingly unsustainable. It should be seen as a vision for the future.

→ A green roof will dry out far more quickly than normal soil, and plants are smaller. Here, various sedum species are creatively blended with other plants, segueing into the surrounding garden vegetation. The green-silver blend is typical of drought-tolerant vegetation; given the short flowering season typical of this type of environment, foliage should always take priority in design considerations.

↑↓→ Drought-tolerant evergreens make for a very sustainable garden, but key to their visual interest is a wide range of foliage colours and textures, as well as growth forms that fill spaces effectively. Species of the iconic local manzanitas (*Arctostaphylos*) are particularly useful (e.g. the broad-leaved, silvery shrub, below right). Ground covers such as wire vine (*Muehlenbeckia axillaris*, top), which perform the visual functions of lawn, despite not being particularly suitable for walking on, are also useful for what designer Sean Hogan calls 'negative spaces'.

Von Schlegell Garden

The 110-metre (360 ft) driveway leading to garden designer Phillip Johnson's house overlooking a vineyard near Woodend, Victoria, in eastern Australia, is an exuberant botanical journey, stocked exclusively with Australian native species. Grass trees (*Xanthorrhoea* spp.) tend to seize the attention first, with their enormous heads of fine leaves radiating out from the top of the stem. At a lower level, there is hummocky, grey foliage of the kind familiar from many water-stressed environments around the world, and an assortment of shrubs with an array of foliage textures and colours. Low-growing plants wend their way over rocks or find places among taller species. Flowers are few, but those that are found here are bright and, in many cases, prominent, such as the dusky red flowers of kangaroo paws (*Anigozanthus flavidus*), held on tall, upright stems, and the ivory-coloured spikes of white-plumed grevillea (*Grevillea leucopteris*).

Since the late 1990s, Johnson's work has been strongly centred on water – understandable in a dry climate – water that is sourced and managed as sustainably as possible. Rocks play a big part, too, and the planting is firmly Australian. The observer might ask why Johnson uses natives confidently, while other designers clearly feel more reticent (see pp.78–83). The answer possibly lies in scale: Australian flora may offer more plants for situations where a planting is seen at a distance rather than nearby.

Garden and landscape design in Australia presents something of a paradox. The native flora is spectacular and is increasingly widely used in gardens and public landscapes. There is a thriving network of enthusiasts who use native plants and who disseminate information about how to grow and propagate them; this group is one of the most impressive non-academic native plant research networks in the world. The Australian nursery industry has been busy selecting cultivars, promoting them, and – as other dry climate zones around the world expand – exporting plant selections. Yet there is surprisingly little naturalistic planting design in the country. 'So many

of my colleagues mimic English gardens', says Johnson, and many Australian gardens feature English plants. Despite political and cultural attempts to cut the apron strings with the mother country, in the garden and landscape world, the process has been much delayed.

There is also the question of Australian plant communities as sources of inspiration. The Antipodean landscape can be spectacular, as can individual plants, but the 'stuff in the middle', the plant communities, are arguably not, or offer great spectacles only for brief periods. There is very little among Australian natural planting to compare with seductive environments in more temperate countries, such as wildflower meadows, prairies or forest floors covered in bulbs. As in many stressful

Phillip Johnson Garden

environments, a few hardy species tend to dominate over vast areas. Moreover, plants often grow in ways that dilute the impact of their most visually striking qualities: colourful flowers may be scattered, or attractive foliage may appear only at the top of a leggy bush. There are also relatively few native species of herbaceous perennial in Australia. The genus that has been most successfully developed commercially, including for an export market, is *Grevillea*, which has plenty of species with a low, compact or ground-covering habit for domestic or urban landscape situations.

Johnson wants to change all this. 'My vision', he says, 'is to re-connect people to nature through this incredible flora ... I look at how plants grow in the wild and then try to achieve that in the garden, with both individual plants and in combination ... Western Australia is

a particular inspiration: there are some incredible plants there. ... I'm trying to use them over here in the east, though the soils are very different here.' The country's most visually spectacular flora is that of the southwest, with its Mediterranean climate; that region's plants have tended not to thrive in the southeast, where summer rainfall and humidity can cause fungal diseases. Nevertheless, a better understanding of their needs is making the inclusion of western plants in eastern Australia more common. Examples are species of *Banksia*, with their huge flower heads and leaves that look like they are cut out of felt, and the intensely colourful species of featherflowers (*Verticordia*) and blue *Leschenaultia*.

'Native species', Johnson points out, 'have huge advantages. They can survive very harsh conditions, such as incredible heat ... I only irrigate a few times to establish, and usually never again.' He is experimenting with growing plants in different gravels and rock mulches, an effective visual backdrop that also 'has many advantages, such as fire protection around houses; they help with water percolation and can be good seed beds.' Such beds are useful for the regeneration of annuals, particularly the daisy family (*Asteraceae*), which can make a colourful lower storey below the shrubs for a brief season after rain.

This particular planting has an upper storey of young rusty gum trees (*Angophora costata*), which over time will change conditions at ground level, with inevitable losses; realistically, many plantings (not just here) include relatively short-lived species that are an important part of the picture in the first decade but decline later on. 'Plantings are dynamic', says Johnson, 'and it's important that long-lived structural species are always included. I'm using this driveway to showcase our flora, to be proud of our vegetation.' In light of the continent's extreme environment, which with climate change may present ever greater challenges, the use of tough native flora seems sensible, quite apart from the fact that it includes so many attractive species and diverse regional floras that deserve to be celebrated in their own right.

The garden at Woodend catalogues the extraordinary potential of native Australian plant species for horticulture – if ways can be found to use and manage them in designed landscapes. The nursery industry has made a good start with some ground covers, such as *Acacia baileyana* 'Prostrate' (see p.40). Australian flora is particularly strong on varied and well-defined plant forms, as Johnson's planting illustrates. This extends to trees such as the Queensland bottle tree (*Brachychiton rupestris*), with its distinctive trunk.

← → A key plant for an effective focal point is *Xanthorrhoea glauca*, one of the grass trees, an iconic species of the Australian bush (also overleaf). Plants with this form tend to seize the attention and have long been used by designers to draw the eye – like the agave or cordyline in an urn, so beloved by Northern Hemisphere designers (see also the yuccas, p.63). However, too many in one space rapidly distract and are easily read as chaotic and restless. The red flowers are kangaroo paws (*Anigozanthus* 'Kings Park Federation Flame' and *A. flavidus*), among the very few perennials in Australian flora and useful for variation in form.

Phillip Johnson Garden

43

There is a feeling of botanical exuberance in this northern California coastal garden, as succulents spill out of low shrubs, and mound-forming evergreen perennials and low ground-cover plants crawl and ooze out from under larger plants and into whatever spaces they find convenient. The plants are taking over, but in a way that is intentional and managed. The strong feeling of diversity seems very Californian.

This is landscape architect Bernard Trainor's own garden, a sloping 6,000-square metre (1.5 acre) site with enough mature native trees to cast some shade and provide different habitats. As is often the case with designers, Trainor's own space is somewhat different to the gardens or landscapes created for clients. 'In my work, everything has to be planned on a schedule. We have to co-ordinate with architects and engineers ... my own garden is a great contrast. I'm doing things more intuitively, there are fewer drawn plans, I'm working with seasons rather than schedules. It's gardening with no rules – a dynamic, living art and science project, and very personal to me.'

The exuberant diversity here is, indeed, very different to much of Trainor's commissioned work, which is strongly focused on sensitivity to place. 'If you can't always tell what I've done, that's fine,' he says. 'I want my gardens to connect seamlessly with surrounding plant communities, to look as if they're meant to be.' He talks about the 'existing vocabulary' of the natural landscape and the importance of working with that, and he resists using the word 'replication', preferring 're-interpretation': 'One could argue that trying to 'replicate' California imprisoned by a suburban fence can look ridiculous, so I see cultivated gardens having a broader artistic range in their design ... Perhaps my own garden does not really represent the main body of our work, but it does inform some of our smaller garden design work, where people appreciate a higher level of diversity.'

Much of Trainor's work involves properties in relatively undamaged natural environments, where clients want to preserve as much nature as possible.

It is not so much about recreating or restoring but shoehorning in, with minimal disturbance; and where there is disturbance, repairing and covering over the traces. This is illustrated most sharply, and on a practical level, by the California live oaks (*Quercus agrifolia*) that are often such a vital part of the scenery; their root systems are very sensitive to disturbance, and they can also be killed by irrigation during the drier summer months. The same applies to the manzanitas (*Arctostaphylos* spp.), which are some of the most visually striking native shrubs of the region. Respect for the environment here is not just a visual issue, but a practical one.

Fundamentally, though, Trainor's work is about developing home landscapes that respect the sense of place – what

Bernard Trainor Garden

could be dubbed 'visual ecology'. Part of this may be about replacing habitat damaged in construction, but it segues into an approach that involves choosing garden plants that look appropriate or that describe transitions from the domestic and designed to the natural and spontaneous. In some cases, this can mean using native grasses like prairie junegrass (*Koeleria macrantha*, also known as crested hair grass) as lawn grass substitutes. Junegrass's somewhat bumpy appearance makes a statement about it not being a lawn, but grown as a monoculture it is not really natural, either. Elsewhere, plant choices seem to take an element from the natural environment and then emphasize it, as with the South African-origin restios (*Restio paniculatus*), the stiffly and elegantly upright foliage of which seems to be a distillation of the form of native bunch grasses.

At the other end of the spectrum, in situations too small, too domestic or too suburban to be any kind of natural landscape, Trainor's own garden is leading the way to a more intensely aesthetic approach to planting design. One danger of the mild and generous coastal northern Californian climate is that of being able to grow too much and ending up with a discordant botanical chaos of competing forms, colours and textures. Trainor, wisely, uses only two basic plant shapes – mound-formers and rosette-shaped succulents – and builds plant combinations around them. California natives would mostly be among the first group, while the second are nearly all 'exotics'. The former root the garden in its place, the latter add range, diversity and surprise. Together they make for very effective occupation of space and enable a pattern of layering.

'I try to use a palette of plants from similar climates', Trainor says. 'I'm using South African, Australian and Mediterranean basin species. I'm trying to use fewer resources. In my own garden I'm very selective with irrigation, and I don't use an automatic system. There are some areas of the garden that are seven or eight years old and have never been watered, but there is a problem with summer deciduous plants, which many people find disturbing, as they don't expect plants to drop their leaves at this time.'

Over the ten years he has been making the garden, there have inevitably been changes, some of which Trainor accepts might make this particular plant mix too dynamic for use in some client gardens, particularly the self-seeding of certain plants, such as some of the *Echium* species. The growth rate of some of the succulents has surprised him: he has become very conscious of the slow rate of growth of some iconic California natives, such as the manzanitas. 'I feel I walk in the middle between garden-making as design and gardening as a science', he says. Sensitivity to aesthetics and awareness of growth over time, and how it needs to be managed, complement each other in the development of a new climate-appropriate style.

Bernard Trainor Garden

← ↓ Succulents thrive here, and their varied and sculptural forms, textures and colours provide a year-round visual richness. They are most effectively used in combination with less emphatically attention-seeking plants, such as rosemary (*Salvia rosmarinus* 'Tuscan Blue', below) and other sub-shrubs and creeping plants, which provide a restful 'negative space'. Agaves such as *Agave attenuata* 'Nova' (p.49) are good focal points, here used with discretion. Very effectively contrasting is the bunched linearity of restio foliage – this (p.49) is *Thamnochortos insignis*.

↖ ↑ Rosette-forming *Aeonium* species are particularly prominent, especially *Aeonium davidbramwellii* (above right). Spire-shaped or conical flower heads are a good contrast to the predominantly mounded forms of many of the plants here, such as the vivid blue of Pride of Madeira (*Echium fastuosum*, above left).

↑ The yellow sub-shrub *Phlomis anatolica* 'Lloyd's
Variety' makes a prominent splash during its flowering
season, quietening down to a silver mounded form for
the rest of the year. This kind of planting, here
featuring cultivars of *Aeonium* and *Kalanchoe* (also
pp.52–3), among many other succulents, offers a high
level of visual intensity; contrasting leaf colours
are visually striking, while growth habits combine
to make a very effective and complete ground cover.

← ↑ The open gravel-covered areas with occasional low
planting or spreading plants coming in from the
side, blurring the boundaries between borders and
hard surfaces, recalls the approach used by Olivier
Filippi (pp.124–31) in a similar climate zone.

Neither setting nor contents make this a typical Spanish garden. It is located high in the Sierra de Guadarrama mountains at an altitude of around 1,600 metres (5,250 ft), where the trees are the typical oaks and ashes of northern and central Europe. Lush in spring, with pastures of grass and wildflowers, this is nevertheless a harsh environment, with long, cold winters and dry summers.

The garden has been created on land surrounding a derelict water mill (now the house). It is very simple, with bands of dark evergreen foliage clipped into swirling organic shapes, along with a number of birch trees and a few flowering perennials. It is also small, just over 500 square metres (5,400 sq. ft), sheltered by walls low enough to peer over at around 1.5 metres (5 ft) high, and in many ways very unexpected. 'Unexpected', because this is a national park, with a generally wild environment and little human habitation, and because this being Spain, a typical garden might be expected to be much more formal and classical. Created by designer couple Miguel Urquijo and Renate Kastner as the garden of a holiday home, this is an example of an emerging trend in Spanish gardens. In one way – the dominant use of clipped foliage – it continues a long tradition, but in other ways, notably its lack of classical geometric formality, it is a complete break with the past. Its location in a relatively high-altitude mountain environment disconnects the visitor from preconceived, stereotypical notions of Spain, so this little garden can be appreciated with an open mind. The birches and the use of heather (the winter-flowering *Erica* x *darleyensis*) as one of the key elements make the garden feel rather Nordic. The heather and the main evergreen component (yew, *Taxus baccata*) are cut so as to resemble the way shrubs on exposed clifftops by the sea or in high mountain regions are sculpted by the wind. 'Here, in this region, higher up, on the mountain tops around here', explains Urquijo, 'you will find plants sculpted by the wind like this, gorse and broom species kept low by very strong winds. Also, on Minorca and many other places in the Mediterranean, you can find wild shrubs shaped like this by the wind, and grazing by animals can make similar shapes in different plants, such as species of *Phillyrea* [an olive relative occasionally used in Mediterranean region gardens], *Pistacia lentiscus* [mastic trees], and wild olive.' These shapes worked well for this particular client, 'who had travelled

Water Mill Garden

widely. He had ideas of gardening from the East, he wanted something organic, oriental.' In addition, 'We needed something very stable, that would look good all through the year, so the garden had to be built around form … this has to be worked at over the years, especially when you consider continuous masses, not individual topiary, things that money can't buy.'

So, although in some ways this garden may appear to be very 'artificial', in that regular clipping has created its living sculpture, it is completely natural in inspiration, drawing on the forms that plants take in environments exposed to powerful winds. Because these environments are widely distributed, and because the character of the plants that survive in such environments tends to be similar (tightly branching, with small, tough leaves), there is something universal about this garden. It is worth noting that the clipped foliage of Japanese gardens is derived from the same ethos: both the idea of clipping and the asymmetric aesthetic are inspired by the form of wind-sculpted shrubs on the rocky coasts of Japan.

It took Urquijo some eight years to achieve the wind-sculpted effect he wanted here. Faster results can be expected in more climatically generous environments, or with faster growing plants. Various species of the *Phillyrea* that he mentions are being used by him and other designers to create organic, flowing forms in gardens in Spain. They are a logical progression from the classical, Italian-derived formality that has so dominated traditional garden-making here, and so can be understood and accepted culturally; the methodology (clipping) remains the same, but the aesthetic is completely different. The shift from classical orthogonal geometry to forms that relate not just to nature but also to abstract sculpture mirrors a wider shift in the arts.

Among the sculpted evergreen shrubs and gravel are a limited number of flowering perennials that offer a brief flurry of spring and early summer interest: irises, pinks (*Dianthus gratianopolitanus*), and the silvery leaves of a groundcover perennial *Stachys byzantina*, which, although evergreen, is very much brighter and bolder earlier in the year. Behind the house is a small, more traditional garden of lawn and box balls, and behind that a meadow of native wild grasses and wildflowers, very similar to what might be expected further north in Europe.

Here is simplicity, and the evocation of plant growth in natural, exposed environments. There is much to appeal to those who like a controlled and managed look, yet at the same time the aesthetics are completely different to traditional ways of achieving this.

↑↓ A native species of heather (*Erica carnea*) and yew (*Taxus baccata*) are clipped in a version of plant sculpture that subverts the art of traditional clipping, imitating bushes sculpted by low wind and grazing animals. The silver foliage of *Stachys byzantina* and *Dianthus gratianopolitanus* contrasts with those darker green species. This lean but very restful garden evokes the vegetation of the nearby mountains but also gives a nod to Japanese gardens. Birch trees (*Betula pendula*) cast a gentle shade.

↑↓ Although the garden is walled, the line of the wall is broken by the birch trees that link to trees outside of it. Most naturalistic planting in rural areas aims to connect the garden to its surroundings, fostering a conceit that the garden is simply an extension of what is beyond the wall.

↑ A wildflower meadow flourishes on the far side of the wall. Managed traditionally with a mid-summer hay cut, this is home to a number of wildflower species that are sensitive to fertilization and other intensive management practices of modern agriculture. While distinctly wet earlier in the year, it dries out and dies back during summer. Traditional meadows such as this have been an important model for naturalistic planting throughout Europe. The trees are ash, pollarded to provide dry season fodder for livestock.

Water Mill Garden

Jo Wakelin's 2,000 square metre (0.5 acre) garden in the Central Otago region of New Zealand's South Island is dominated by its surroundings: mountains that reach up to 2,000 metres (6,500 ft). There are no obvious boundaries, and the garden, as she notes, 'may be under an acre, but I feel like I've got thousands of acres'. She feels she has 'a very strong connection to the landscape around, my place of standing – *tūrangawaewae* in Maori'.

The plants of Wakelin's garden blend in with their surroundings through their form – gently curved hummocky shapes, generally organized into rounded planting borders – and their colours: muted greens, greys, fawns. The bleached grass of the surrounding pasturelands, the grey rock, the occasional dark-leaved evergreens are all echoed in the garden, the forms and colours becoming more tangible here, as if the vast landscape has been distilled down, concentrated.

'It's very dry here', says Wakelin. '250–400 millimetres [10–16 in] of rain a year, six to eight weeks with no rain, often above 30° C [86° F] in the summer and minus 10° C [14° F] in the winter ... It's a tough climate, and it's very windy.' She adds that the soil is a 'low-nutrient gravelly glacial outwash'. Inputs are minimal: no feeding, no pest control and, crucially, no watering, although there is a large pond that provides a somewhat damper habitat for some native species such as the dramatic clumps of New Zealand flax (*Phormium tenax*), which is one of the iconic plants of the South Island. Local stone plays an important part in the garden. One low mound of stones forms a shape that echoes that of the surrounding borders: 'it mimics the early goldminers' tailings, piled rock by rock during the gold rush in the 1860s. I also built mine rock by rock!'

New Zealand's flora is very singular, particularly visually. There are few species with prominent or colourful flowers, but many with distinctive foliage colours and strong shapes; nearly all are evergreen. Many of these species are used extensively in landscape design elsewhere, particularly in Britain and France, where the climate is roughly similar; indeed, Britain has seen a growing New Zealand aesthetic across its public spaces, since the 1990s, particularly with the popularity of spikey species of *Phormium*. Here, in a harsh steppe habitat, the range of native species that will survive is limited, with relatively muted colours and forms.

Wakelin is a teacher of horticulture at a local college, and passionate about the ecology of the region. When she started the garden in 2005, there was a strong

Jo Wakelin Garden

urge to use only regionally native plants. She has done a lot of what she calls 'eco-sourcing' – collecting the seed of wild plants such as the Kōwhai (*Sophora microphylla*), an extremely attractive small tree that grows in the vicinity, in an effort to get more people to grow them in gardens. However, she describes herself as 'a bit of a magpie', and loves the colours of exotics. The result is a garden in two halves: one dedicated to native plants and one to non-native exotics. The latter area is closer to the house, while the former forms the bridge between landscape and garden. 'I decided to try to keep them separate', she says. 'I trained as an ecologist. I cannot bring myself to combine them.'

Although Wakelin consciously rejects European models of garden-making, it is, ironically, a British gardener who helped shape her thinking about what to do here. Beth Chatto (1923–2018) was possibly the most influential gardener of the latter part of the twentieth century in Britain, as she introduced the idea, now perhaps obvious, of choosing plant species on the basis of the existing garden habitat. Her gravel garden, created on the site of a former car park and part of a larger overall plot, was possibly the most influential garden of the period. Wakelin is one of many who are inspired by its selection of drought-tolerant plant species and by the aesthetic of low-growing plants scattered across a gravel-mulched soil. The gravel garden comes into its own in severely water-stressed situations. Gravel mulching helps stop water loss from the soil, keeps roots cool, and creates a visual linking element that can flow from one part of a garden to another. It is also a very good backdrop for showing off foliage shapes and colours.

The visual appeal of dry gardens like Wakelin's revolves around a set of shapes and colours that are essentially year-round features. A surprising range of species flower throughout the summer until the autumn, many of these being common Northern Hemisphere border species such as stonecrop (*Hylotelephium spectabile*). The fact that plants from stressful environments are generally evergreen provides continuity, although Wakelin notes that 'seasonal change is hugely rewarding in this garden, especially given that I don't soften the effects of summer by watering. Without supplementary watering, I feel connected to the larger climate cycle I live within. Autumn rain comes, and the plants respond. I think it actually intensifies the seasonal pleasure in the garden for me, compared to an earlier garden where I did water.'

Pragmatically blending a love of colour with a strong sense of local identity and a commitment to growing local flora, this garden succeeds visually by making a seamless connection between its dramatic surroundings and an ornamental version of ecologically-appropriate planting around the house.

← ↓ This is a garden that uses the forms and textures of exposure-tolerant plants to create an oasis in a majestic but harsh landscape – without the planting looking at all out of place. The low hummocks of false dittany (*Ballota pseudodictamnus*, also p.62, centre) are typical of plants adapted to dry environments. Yellow Jerusalem sage (*Phlomis fruticosa*) and the pink flower structures of *Euphorbia myrsinites* illustrate two variations on this theme, and lavender (*Lavandula angustifolia* 'Pacific Blue', below) is a well-known example of this plant form. Among grasses, the tussock form is also typical of dry habitats; here, the native silver tussock (*Poa cita*) grows around the pool.

Jo Wakelin Garden

61

← ↓ → The planting here achieves harmony largely
through variations on the low sub-shrub
form. Occasional contrasts, such as the
yuccas (*Yucca filamentosa* and *Y. gloriosa*
'Colour Guard', right) — make the most of
a dramatically different environment and
tune in to a sub-conscious association with
desert habitats. The tight green cushion is
Euphorbia spinosa. *Nepeta tuberosa* (below)
is a drought-adapted species with spikes
of intense colour that provide interest in
early summer but die back later. The silver
foliage of many of the plants here is an
adaptation to reduce water loss; the silver-
leaved plant with yellow flowers is woolly
sunflower (*Eriophyllum lanatum*, right).
Rusting metalwork, remnants of the area's
mining history, are used as focal points.

Jo Wakelin Garden   63

Block Planting vs. Intermingling

Planting design on anything larger than the small garden scale has traditionally favoured grouping individuals of the same species or variety to create blocks of flowers or foliage. This is, of course, completely unnatural, as plants in nature rarely grow in single-species blocks of colour, foliage or form. This style of planting does enable clear graphic effects to be created, and it has worked well for formal artistic effects, for example the work of early twentieth-century writer and garden designer Gertrude Jekyll. It is not surprising, then, that many of those who want to embrace nature within a garden context will reject such an approach, instead creating mixtures made up of individuals of different species, similar to what occurs in wild settings. However, this has not always been the case. ¶ Whether to group or to mingle goes to the heart of the division between those who are primarily concerned with creating the *effects* of nature and those who want to create something more like a genuine ecology. Mingling plants actually presents a lot of challenges to the gardener, so it is not surprising that until the 2010s very few practitioners did this. Those who did were the 'real' ecologists, primarily interested in recreating natural habitats rather than making anything principally aesthetic. In Europe, wildflower meadows attracted the most attention; in North America, it was tallgrass prairie. Christopher Lloyd made meadows an important part of Great Dixter garden (see pp.282–9), while in the United States, practitioners such as Larry Weaner are using prairie plantings as a design element (see pp.290–7). ¶ One of the main challenges involved in intermingling plant species is their competition for space, light and nutrients; stronger ones inevitably displace weaker ones, so skilled maintenance is required to manage these outcomes, by people who know the life cycle and lifestyle of individual plants and can readily tell one plant from another. In the early days of naturalistic planting, from the 1970s to the 1990s, such plant combinations were often seen as messy by a public that was only familiar with group plantings, at least in public spaces. The breakthrough in popularizing naturalistic planting came in large part from practitioners who skilfully used block planting of species that evoked natural habitats mostly from association. James van Sweden and Wolfgang Oehme formed a highly successful partnership in the United States and started to use perennials and ornamental grasses in the late 1970s to create dramatic and yet soft and romantic compositions in their public work, and a scaled down but still very graphic version for their private commissions. Oehme (1930–2011) had been trained in Germany and was above all else a plantsman; van Sweden (1935–2013) was an architect. Very different in personality as well as in their training, the two nevertheless enabled and inspired a younger generation to work with perennials and native plants, and stimulated huge innovation in the nursery industry. The contrast with the shrub- and annual-dominated style of the time was enormous, with a limited number of species used to evoke a stylized natural environment. But ecologists soon pointed out that there was not necessarily much difference between these plantings and their predecessors in terms of how much they supported local biodiversity or their real ecological functioning. ¶ Oehme and van Sweden's work broke the ice, however, and opened many eyes to the possibilities of the new style. At the same time, in northern Europe, Piet Oudolf's work in public parks and publicly accessible private gardens also helped change perceptions. Both practices made featured the autumn and early winter look, promoting the beauty of seed heads, big grasses and fading foliage (see pp.20–7). In the early 2000s, Oudolf began to experiment with intermingling, including 'matrix' planting, in which one species, usually a grass, forms a dominant matrix, with a minority of more decorative species dotted into it. This form of planting offers great advantages in weed control and an aesthetic that can effectively highlight a limited number of species. At the same time, researchers in Germany, followed by others in Switzerland, the Czech Republic and Britain, began to develop plant mixes that gave a more genuinely natural look. They could do this with some confidence, because by now much had been learned about the behaviour of the plants involved. ¶ Intermingling plants in this way creates something of the complexity of natural environments, where many species and a great number of individuals occupy an area that only a handful would in a conventional planting; at its best, it conveys something of the softness and the romance of wildflower meadows or prairies. It can, however, deteriorate, and it is crucial to choose the right plants in the right combinations – if too many short-lived species are used, for example, gaps will result, and if there are too many aggressive self-seeders, they will tend to dominate over time. ¶ Despite these challenges, there are very real reasons to believe that the trend towards greater intermingling of plants, as opposed to block planting, will continue. This natural style packs maximum seasonal interest into a space, and if the species mix is well chosen, a dense, weed-suppressing mesh of very attractive plants can result. Moreover, functional applications, such as green roofs and sustainable drainage systems, work best with a blend.

'We wanted it to look as if the house had been slotted into a wild landscape, as if this patch of forest was just there, and the owners had fallen for it and built', says Xanthe White of the garden she designed around a house on a 1,000-square metre (0.25 acre) plot in the suburbs of Auckland, on New Zealand's North Island. The climate verges on the sub-tropical, so luxurious, leafy vegetation is to be expected, and plants like palms and tree ferns are common in this climate zone. The green canopy is echoed in lush green ground-level planting. White says that 'we like to be the invisible hand, we don't want people to notice what we have done'. Much of her work is ecological restoration, or re-wilding, the creation of native plant communities which will be largely self-sustaining. 'We can't garden all the work we do, we have to act as catalysts', she says. So 'we do sequence planting', by which she means mixes of species, some of which will grow quickly and then die out and others of which will develop much more slowly but be there for the future.

Having a perspective that sees planting as much in time as in space is normal for ecological restoration but not necessarily for garden-making, even within naturalistic design. Many of the habitats favoured by garden designers are inevitably time-sensitive – tree seedlings will inevitably take over meadow and prairie habitats for example, unless weeded out or continually cut back. The natural vegetation of the North Island is, however, multi-layered forest, so this is what Xanthe and her team plant. 'We embed some things that will take a long time to establish. They are placed well back but they could potentially become legacy trees.' Mamaku is named for the black tree fern (*Cyathea medullaris*) that is the garden's theme plant. There are young palms too, the native nikau palm (*Rhopalostylis sapida*). 'In time', White explains, 'they will become legs and form a canopy garden, way up above.'

To many, the garden at Mamaku, including a courtyard that makes use of the fact that the house has been sunk into a slope, might look a bit like what they might find in a local nature reserve; but in fact it is, as White explains, 'very composed compared to nature; we have to make it an appropriate scale'. She describes nature as 'controlled chaos … but as we pull into more intimate spaces, the level of control becomes greater and more artful.' Nature has an embedded complexity in this climate, where there is so much variation in foliage size and texture, tree ferns being the most imposing. 'We look at the forest and try to work out how to compose it. It just looks green at first, but the more you look, the more you realize is going on … but there comes a point when all the complexity becomes one.'

Mamaku

What she is describing is common to most natural habitats, which involve a great many species and much complexity that we do not normally appreciate – we see a totality, and only appreciate what makes it up when we move in to take a closer look. In designing her larger projects, White describes how 'we begin to make plantings more composed as we get nearer the house' – visually more striking and with groupings rather than intermingling different species.

The impact of this garden is made by relatively few species, which makes for a look which is graphic and simple to read, but this does not mean it is ecologically simple. As with all Xanthe White gardens, there are small ground-cover plants shoehorned into odd spaces, which over time will spread and find their own niches. The species chosen need to look good over long periods – examples include mat rush (*Lomandra tanika*), an Australian grass-like plant, or the native New Zealand wind grass (*Anemanthele lessoniana*). The effect is reminiscent of a forest edge situation, where more light hits the forest floor. Indeed, White explains that 'for garden inspiration we tend to look at forest edges, transitions between more open and forested areas'. Across the globe, these transition zones are nearly always very diverse, as plants of shade and of more open conditions tend to co-exist as well as share spaces with others unique to this zone, inspiring naturalistic designers.

Given the graphic nature of much New Zealand vegetation, the problem of public perception of it as 'untidy' is possibly less than for many other regions. However, White is well aware of the need to convince people who have a lesser appreciation of the wild than she does, to enable them make sense of what they see and feel more positive about wilder-style planting. Sometimes this can be achieved with architectural elements: 'If clients don't want things too wild, we can always put in a white wall, to make them feel as if everything's OK.' She also develops plant combinations that can be sold as 'a cocktail'. These are similar in concept to the perennial plant mixes with which European naturalistic designers are working. 'Plant cocktails are developed for particular situations', White explains. 'Each may contain up to twenty species, arranged mosaic fashion. It looks simple but is actually very complex, and it's a way of convincing people to do complex things.' Mixes are rarely repeated, as they need to be kept fresh, and White wants to stay ahead of other designers who are also using this methodology.

Mamaku is one of those gardens that is designed to look 'undesigned', with an approach similar in many ways to the results achieved by large-scale re-wilding in its ecological integrity, but also one that produces an easy-to-read, intimate landscape for human users.

↓ → The site's split-level construction allows a perspective on the garden's signature black tree fern (*Cyathea medullaris*) that differs from our normal ground-based view of these plants. The understorey (below) is dominated by mat rush (*Lomandra longifolia* 'Tanika') and several fern species.

← ↑ ↓ The brown seed heads of *Lomandra* provide contrast to the green environment. Muted shades and the dominance of green are typical of the New Zealand flora, in which bright flower colours are relatively rare. Contrasts in texture come from the native grass pheasant's tail (*Anemanthele lessoniana*, below). The young nikau palms (*Rhopalostylis sapida*) will grow tall and become an imposing part of the design. The use of grasses and grass-like plants here is a reflection of their importance in the New Zealand flora of open habitats.

Mamaku

Walled gardens are a distinctively British space. There are several thousand across the country, most of which have become ornamental gardens, with only a few still used for their original purpose – the growing of food for country estates. The results of this conversion from practical function to ornament illustrate changing ideas about planting design and the conundrum of combining modern needs and ideas with a sense of history. The approach at the Cambo Estate, in Fife, southeast Scotland, is strikingly contemporary, with roots in continental European practice. Elliott Forsyth, who was Head Gardener at Cambo from 2000 to 2018 (succeeded by Fay McKenzie), took the garden in a direction inspired by Piet Oudolf (see pp.20–7 and 266–73), German parks and natural habitats.

Cambo's walled garden is big (1 hectare / 2.5 acres), with a more uneven terrain than most, and, unusually, it has a stream running through the middle. The various perennial plantings are planned either to evoke particular habitats or to be at their best during particular seasons. This is very much a summer garden, but with a good winter follow-on from grasses and perennial seed heads. The first impression is that of traditional British herbaceous borders that have somehow morphed into something else. There is a lot of colour, and the plants often form quite big clumps (there is little that is meadowy and fine-textured here), but the plantings feel immersive, as the paths are narrower than those that usually front typical borders. The plants are different to those in the traditional border palette, the colours less intense, and texture plays an important role. Ornamental grasses play a major part in the visual linkages from area to area, as well as in providing continuity from one season to another. The walls bound our experience of the garden, while the paths through the various plantings take us on a journey, the outcome of which never feels quite certain.

One of the most spectacular groupings is the late-flowering double border, which feels like a very broad interpretation of a traditional double border, all the more effective for being on a slope so that the visitor looks up at it as they approach. Big grasses such as silvergrass (*Miscanthus* spp.) are combined with a wide variety of later-flowering perennials, including asters, bee balm (*Monarda* spp.), hardy sage (*Salvia* spp.), and that mainstay of the 'new perennial' garden, the statuesque Culver's root (*Veronicastrum virginicum*). There is also a steppe-themed bed, where drought-tolerant perennials flower earlier in the year; a naturalistic potager; early-flowering borders; and a cut flower area. Outside the walled garden is a newly renovated woodland-edge area.

Cambo Gardens

The Walled Garden and the Prairie

From summer to autumn, the impression is of a romantic haze of perennials and grasses, interspersed with numerous elderly apple trees and the occasional low box hedge – reminders of various past lives for this space. A key word that Forsyth uses again and again is 'diffusion' – the repeating of particular plants across space in concentrations. 'I associate this with Hermannshof (see pp.152–9), and linearity or block planting more with Oudolf', he explains. 'I see myself as developing a balance between them. This balance changes from planting to planting, depending on how natural I want the border to be and how much initial impact I require. This also supplies range. ... Susan, my wife, is an artist, so I have learned a lot about art theory from her and have applied it in the garden.'

Forsyth's enthusiasm for wide borders and drifts of perennials and grasses has been backed up by plenty of personal research. He has travelled to Germany several times, visiting famous perennial gardens such as Weihenstephan, Munich's Westpark, Maximilian Park in Hamm (in northern Germany), and his favourite, Hermannshof, in Weinheim, Baden-Württemberg. He is one of the few British gardeners to have really engaged with German planting design.

One of the better established experiments is the 'naturalistic potager', which occupies a central position in the walled garden and combines ornamental vegetables, tender perennials and annuals. According to Forsyth, 'We used around 2,500 plants selected from a tight palette of around 150 different varieties, but 5 to 10 per cent every year are new trial plants. ... We laid it out expressing a different theme every summer, and it acted as an experimental area. Ideas tried out here feed back into other parts of the garden.' He goes on to explain how this worked in practice: a plan on paper, 'with every plant position marked', is prepared the previous winter. 'I then drew a grid over the top, corresponding to a grid set out in the garden, so that locations on paper can be transferred quickly and exactly.' Key to the success of the potager was that 'when you look across, you don't see the paths'. This is one of the effective visual tricks of the German park perennial planting style – the illusion of a solid 'meadow effect' of planting. The potager shows that the naturalistic style can be flexible. Its particular, visual appeal can be adapted to work with annuals and bedding plants as well as with wildflowers and perennials.

Having created a planting plan on the ground, Forsyth would constantly monitor it; usually it would be satisfactory for several years with nothing more than routine maintenance. 'Once borders get to around seven years old', he says, 'we find that some species have out-competed others or grown beyond their allotted

space, changing the balance. And some have seeded too much, so the planting loses detail.' Replanting of up to three-quarters of the area then tends to follow, to bring back the balance and intention of the earlier years.

A 700-square metre (7,500 sq. ft) area outside the walled garden is planted up as a North American prairie. This has not been sown, as have nearly all experimental prairies, but rather planted out with plugs (plants grown in trays, where each occupies a cell around 25 millimetres across and 50 millimetres deep (1 × 2 in). This allowed Forsyth to have more control over the distribution of plants than when prairies are sown. Care was taken to ensure that the plants and combinations were as stable and attractive as possible. From late summer to mid-autumn, the prairie is a very colourful place, and very

popular with pollinating insects. The non-American visitor might feel transported to the Midwest, while the Midwesterner would immediately notice the very low proportion of grasses. For this is an ideal vision of a prairie, a flower border version of one. As a spectacle, it is very successful, with a wide variety of flower shapes and a colour range that is narrow enough to keep it cool and sophisticated – predominantly the blues, violets and whites of various *Aster* varieties, and the yellows of coneflowers (*Rudbeckia*) and sunflowers (*Helianthus*); otherwise, there are a few dull pink flowers, and the occasional flash of scarlet.

Forsyth is one of the few naturalistic gardeners concerned with colour theory. 'In my approach to combining colour, it's important to understand how a colour would be mixed using primary colours.

This helps me to understand the colours it contains – which will harmonize, which are missing, and which will contrast. I often use three to four colours and a range of tones when designing. I give each colour a percentage as a guide, but I don't stick to it rigidly ... I also like to add a subtle bit of discordance to avoid it looking too safe. So in a cool scheme, I may use just a touch of red here and there to enliven it.'

Cambo's shoehorning of old and new, its sophisticated layout and its combination of technical and artistic approaches to planting design make this a very exciting garden, especially since it illustrates what can be achieved in a cool summer climate zone, with many of the plants grown here being many degrees of latitude north of where they would grow naturally.

↑ → Perennial plantings in the old walled kitchen garden fill
spaces that are often similar to the old borders, where
plants were looked 'at', but they then break out into more
fluid forms, inviting the eye to look over, often to more
distant plantings. Old fruit trees and hedges break up the
space and link to the trees on the other side of the wall.

↓ The role of grasses has become one of the defining characteristics of naturalistic planting. Whereas flowering
plants are best seen in direct sunlight, grasses often
look their best back-lit, as here, with golden oats
(*Stipa gigantea*).

→ The scarlet spikes of red bistort (*Persicaria
amplexicaulis*) find their way into many naturalistic
plantings. It flowers for a long summer-to-autumn
period and is vigorous without being aggressive. It also
has a habit that enables it to attractively fill space
sideways. Its solid, clumping form provides some weight
to plantings with more ephemeral elements. The white
here is *Eupatorium fistulosum* 'Album'.

→ (Overleaf) The prairie at Cambo is outside the walled
garden, with views out to the house and other estate
buildings. At its glorious, butterfly-attracting peak
in September, the spikes of white burnet (*Sanguisorba
canadensis*) make a strong impact with several species
of blue aster (*Symphyotrichum*) and yellow prairie
coneflower (*Ratabida pinnata*), as well as sunflower
(*Helianthus*) and *Rudbeckia* species. A few taller
clumps of joe pye weed (*Eupatorium maculatum*) stand
dramatically taller (see p.26 for the plant in its
winter state).

Cambo Gardens

It feels as if the flowering perennials sweep all around us, at a height that (in late summer) makes us feel truly immersed. In a relatively open landscape, there are no clear boundaries to this garden, allowing our attention to be completely absorbed by the spectacle of the planting. There are some taller grasses, but on the whole there is a harmonious similarity of height, which helps to emphasize the form and texture of many of the plants here. We are led around by gravel paths, over the edges of which the planting seems to seep; here and there is some obvious self-sowing into the gravel, particularly by the elegantly narrow flower spikes of foxglove relative *Digitalis ferruginea*.

There are, in fact, two gardens here – one a luxuriant celebration of perennials that look their fulsome finest in late summer, the other leaner, surrounded by rock that indicates its past as a small quarry; the vegetation is lower and dominated by tough-looking, tussock grass-like plants, which maintain a year-round presence. In spring, bulbs flower profusely among the grasses and sedges, although this area does not have a real 'high season', as various bulbs come and go throughout the year.

This roughly 6,000-square metre (1.5 acre) garden just outside Melbourne, created by Australian designer and garden television presenter Michael McCoy for some clients who are also near neighbours, is an example of what has become the global 'new perennial' approach to planting design. While it looks very much like an Oudolf garden (see pp.20–7), only looser, given the evident self-sowing, McCoy describes his primary influence as having been a lecture given by the American landscape architect James van Sweden (see pp.146–51). He describes how at a conference held in 1989, 'a thousand plus Australians sat there and were implanted with imagery that we couldn't shake off. We'd never seen anything like those big-scale perennial plantings ... It was at least ten years before we heard of Oudolf', he adds, 'who took it all to a whole new

level, an extra nuance beyond the big blocky look of Oehme van Sweden.'

'I love these huge expanses of repeated undulating mounds of perennials', says McCoy. 'My aim is not nicely graduated heights in a two- or three-metre wide border; we're taking perennials *en masse* and treating them as an undulating surface, rather than the traditional vertical presentation in a border.' There is one dramatic form in the perennial garden, however: the very neat shape of beaked yucca (*Yucca rostrata*), whose perfect starburst of narrow radiating leaves 'is always the star of the show in people's photographs'. Rather to McCoy's chagrin, one thinks: 'They were a client suggestion, and I'm very reluctant to get in the way when a client shows initiative.'

Stone Hill

Their inclusion is, of course, a matter of opinion, and many might feel that such strong forms can make a useful focal point among soft textures and forms.

The main perennial garden here peaks in late summer, but as McCoy notes, 'it does need some irrigation to achieve this. Even with that, everything in there is mildly stressed, so we only use things that perform to at least 70 per cent capacity when under that kind of stress. There are some species that can't cope, and we've had to drop them.' The quarry, on the other hand, receives at least minimal water and has quite a different aesthetic. 'It's a largely evergreen matrix, within which there is a range of bulbs that flower in flushes, and low-growing, self-grooming things like *Euphorbia myrsinites* [myrtle spurge], which produces early yellow-green flowers above silver foliage. This represents the other extreme to the perennial garden and what I do if I cannot provide water. I would rather go to a low, stable-height matrix of drought-tolerant plants, with a seasonal thrill largely through bulbs – about 70 per cent matrix – and minimize the seasonal volume change.'

At Stone Hill, the Australian natives are conspicuous by their total absence – and this in a country that has a strong movement to encourage their cultivation. Other designers (see pp.40–5) firmly promote their use, but McCoy points out that 'naturalistic planting worldwide is driven 97 per cent by herbaceous plants. We in Australia have zero deciduous perennial flora, and using shrubs and sub-shrubs takes you to whole different aesthetic.' Most Australian natives are woody plants, 'and they are very difficult to integrate into mixed planting containing tall herbaceous plants'. Many are impossible to prune, and so like many plants of the Mediterranean region have limited lifespans; few natives have compact, garden-worthy forms, and those that do are often totally intolerant of being shaded. McCoy's opinion is that 'they would only work in a much sparser planting, with more open gravel. They would need different angles of visibility, to be seen sideways as well as from above, with a greater variation of density.' He says that he loves 'the ideas and images emerging from Olivier Filippi (see pp.124–31), and he thinks that 'there's some fabulous aesthetic models there that could lead the way with our natives. But to ask why I didn't think to include Australian natives in this garden is a little like asking why Picasso didn't include some Spanish tile-based mosaic in *Guernica*. They're just not of the same medium, or even the same language.' Such thoughts might be not be universally shared, as Phillip Johnson (see pp.40–5) is clearly confident with native only plantings.

McCoy has created here an accomplished perennial garden, but as he points out, planting design is a developing field. 'We are rapidly developing our ideas, and while I'm very happy with this garden, I've moved on in my thinking. By the time any garden of mine is ready to be photographed, it's likely that I'll have learned from it and evolved beyond it.' This is, indeed, an eternal problem with the making of gardens – and an oddly satisfying one.

← ↓ This consummate New Perennial garden illustrates
the importance of being able to view planting
in the round, liberated from the backdrops that
limited the viewing of the traditional English
border. Planting here reaches little more
than waist height for the most part, allowing
the viewer to see over the plants and enjoy
a continually changing series of combinations
and juxtapositions.

'Emergent' plants help to avoid uniformity in height. They occupy
only a small percentage of the total area, but by being at least twice
the height of everything else, they create drama. Yellow mullein
(*Verbascum olympicum*) and golden oats (*Stipa gigantea*) play this role
here. Emergents can be dramatically backlit, especially against a dark
background. At this latitude, the effect can be appreciated but will
be minimal, whereas at higher latitudes, with the sun lower, it can
be a striking part of a planting's aesthetic. Colours are, for the most
part, in a pastel range; limited palettes make the eye concentrate
more on subtle distinctions of form, texture or colour.

The quarry area of the garden has a leaner look, befitting a location with exposed rock and thinner soil. Grasses predominate, but with a range of muted colours for long seasonal interest: blue-grey fescue (*Festuca glauca*), mat rush (*Lomandra* 'Lime Tuff') and bronze-tinged sedge (*Carex testacea*). The purple is slender vervain (*Verbena rigida*). In spring, bulbs provide a colourful spectacle.

Wildside is a garden like no other. Located on the southwestern slopes of Dartmoor in Devon, in the southwest of England, its combination of mild, wet climate and acidic, well-drained soil allows an enormous range of plants to flourish. And flourish they do, in a series of micro-habitats across a 1.6-hectare (4 acre) landscape of miniature hills and valleys sculpted from what was originally a gently sloping field.

Although the botany at Wildside is exciting, Keith Wiley is first and foremost a man with an artistic vision. Wiley and his late wife, Ros, came here in 2004 with a huge collection of plants after working for many years at a neighbouring garden, The Garden House. The artistic sensibility and the language used to describe what he does should not be surprising, as Ros, who played a major role in developing the garden, was a talented artist and one of the few painters who has been able to capture the complexity and seeming randomness of naturalistic planting.

Sculpting the land with a mini-digger – 'my idea of bliss … you can play God', Wiley says – is about both habitat creation and place-making. Sun lovers can go on one side of a slope, shade lovers on the other, and given how the terrain constantly changes, some remarkable juxtapositions are possible, with exotic-looking rosette plants and soft, moisture-loving ferns in the same line of sight. The shaping of the terrain results in an entrancing network of paths by means of which visitors can explore in a random series of circuits. 'I like to think that the landscaping evokes the rolling hills of Devon, and gives a sense of there being a mini-landscape within a larger one.'

The shaping of the landscape also has an impact on how we see plants. 'The beauty of the banks is that they throw everything up, making it easier to see and appreciate small ground-level or woodland species.' They also make it possible to appreciate how some of the component species of the garden are happily self-seeding.

In a few places the view is larger, as with an area Wiley calls the Temblor Hills,

after a favourite region of California where rolling hills are echoed by the rounded shapes of savannah oaks. His Devonian interpretation involves using pruned conifers to evoke the oaks, beneath which is an intensely coloured carpet of rockery plants that evoke wildflowers, such as species of pinks (*Dianthus*) and pink star grass (*Rhodohypoxis* spp.) – in Wiley's words, 'a big effect in a small setting'. This approach – the developing of vignettes inspired by particular places – is rare in Western garden design, although it has a long history in the Japanese garden tradition.

A visit to Crete in 1992 was the first of many trips Wiley made to look at wild plant communities, and it was the beginning, for him, of a realization that gardeners have an enormous amount to learn from nature. One of Wiley's guiding

Wildside

principles came to be that 'the biggest set of gardening ideas on the whole planet is the countryside around us'. Travels to many different countries and habitats to see plants in the wild resulted in the development of a planting methodology that aims to capture the distribution patterns of wild plant communities, but without in any way copying particular habitats or necessarily even using plants from the habitats concerned.

Our perspective on the plants at Wildside changes over the seasons. Intimacy is all-important in spring, when bulbs and small woodland species dominate. Many of these have naturalized extensively here, blending and intermingling in a way not often seen. Wiley uses the language of an artist in describing how he puts plants together: first of all, 'careful placing of the shading magnolias so as to frame any pictures with their trunks', then a 'semi-permanent structure' of shade-tolerant plants such as barrenwort (*Epimedium* spp.) and hellebores, among which space is left for bulbs to flourish and, crucially, self-seed. It is this seeding that creates not just the

sheer quantity of spring-flowering plants here, but their naturalistic distribution. Application of composted leaves in the autumn, the leaving of enough space between larger plants, and patience are all essential for this to happen – especially the latter, as seedling bulbs take up to six years to reach flowering size. The result is a wonderful blending of familiar bulbs like species of daffodil (*Narcissus*), crocus and snowdrop (*Galanthus*), with less familiar wild cyclamen (*Cyclamen hederifolium*), dog's tooth violets (*Erythronium*), anemones, and some famously slow-growing and hard-to-establish species such as wake robin (*Trillium*). Most of these are in relatively shaded environments, where the competition of later-growing perennials is reduced.

Later in the year, the scale of vision needed to appreciate the planting becomes wider. Repetition of key species is a central part of all successful naturalistic planting, and it is achieved here particularly skilfully. Earlier in the year it is on a small scale, but later it works across the whole of this unique landscape, with some strong effects seen from the tops of the 'hills'. July offers repetitions of blue agapanthus and a variety of yellow-flowered species including tickseed (*Coreopsis verticillata*), creating a powerful complementary colour effect; from then on, grasses play an increasingly important role in generating a sense of rhythm, linking scattered parts of the garden. 'Many are very similar from a distance, so they are good unifiers', notes Wiley. Their long season helps provide a continuity into the winter, too.

The variation in elevation built into this garden makes it very different to most naturalistic planting, and it enables the place to work on two levels – what Wiley calls 'the big effect, something that grabs you emotionally' in combination with what he refers to as 'little corners'. The elevations also help create a strong sense of a world apart, whereas much naturalistic planting is often concerned with creating links with local landscapes. This garden is surely one of the most purely artistic visions considered here.

← ↑ ↓ Wildside's range of habitats allows for wet areas with damp-
loving plants like the leafy *Rodgersia aesculifolia* (p.84),
as well as sunnier areas. The miniature hills and valleys give
a feeling of intimacy. The planting is often multi-layered, and
many spring-flowering plants are naturalizing. Even forms of
dog's-tooth violet (*Erythronium*, above) and wake robin (*Trillium
kurabayshii*, left), both slow to establish, are regenerating.
The pruned trees (below) are part of a planting called the
Temblor Hills, after an area in California; the trees represent
the local oaks that dot a savannah-type landscape.

← (Previous) The upper part of Wildside has a more open character and is at its best in summer, with a mix of different cultivars of *Agapanthus* providing a combination of blues; yellows come from a variety of different species, mostly golden valerian (*Patrinia scabiosifolia*). Grasses contribute a meadowy feel.

↓ → One visual high point occurs in late July, after the main flowering season for most Eurasian perennials but before that for many North American prairie-origin plants. Many South African species are at their best now, such as yellow, orange and red *Crocosmia* (p.84) and blue *Agapanthus*. Various ornamental grasses serve to subtly separate and break up flower colours, enabling a wider range of colours to be appreciated without clashing. The trees (below) are *Cordyline australis*, a common ornamental in southwest England.

Gelli Uchaf (Upper Grove) is not an easy place to get to. Once you have found the house sign, there is still a 0.8-kilometre (0.5 mile) drive up a steep dirt track to reach the seventeenth-century Welsh longhouse and its 6,000-square metre (1.5 acre) garden.

The first reaction of the visitor is probably to look around to get a sense of where they are: on a shoulder of land with a wide view to the east and south, and the sense of more hill behind. The terrace in front of the house is a riotous tapestry of low ground-cover plants, and there is clearly a very wide range of species: the tight cushions of sea thrift (*Armeria maritima*), the silver-grey of sea campion (*Silene maritima*), the glossy purple of bugle (*Ajuga reptans*). This selection is unusual, although it should not be, as most garden centres sell a range of tough, low-growing plants, often marketed as 'alpines'; but they are rarely encouraged to cover ground, run into each other, and develop their own complex patterning. The range of different foliage colours, shapes and textures is striking, and these are more important than the flowers, as it is these other features of the plants that will predominate over most of the year. Elsewhere, there are clear signs of the passion for reusing materials that innovative environmentally-conscious gardeners go for: plants growing in old car tyres, and discarded plastic bottles full of water in the vegetable garden, as a way of moderating temperatures. The remainder of the planting feels equally full and generous, reflecting the owners' confidence in letting plants do their thing – an attitude the terrace well displays.

Julian Wormald is a retired veterinarian, and he and his artist wife, Fiona, have owned the property near Llandovery, in mid-Wales, since 1993, but only started seriously gardening when they retired here in 2005. Julian is very focused on how the garden works within its local environment and ecosystems, and he has a particular interest in pollinators.

There is a clue to the Wormalds' inspiration for their garden in the title of the website and blog that Julian has created – The Garden Impressionists. 'About the time we started to seriously garden', he recalls, 'we visited [Monet's garden at] Giverny, and it had a big impact – the massed, intermingled flowers, and the abundant insect diversity.' Local wildflower meadows, two of which the Wormalds manage, are also an inspiration: 'Increasingly we

Gelli Uchaf (Upper Grove)

are interested in how many plants from different countries can be grown within the same metre, spatially and temporally, a reflection of our experience viewing meadows.' Much of what the couple have achieved here is a result of their exploration of plant diversity, but in the context of encouraging plants to share space – a look that traditionally was seen as confusing but is seen now as merely realistic, in that this is what happens in nature. The mention of an Impressionist source of inspiration is interesting, as the conventional reaction to Impressionist brushstrokes from the conventional art world was similar to the reaction of some commentators on the new planting style. There is a parallel, too, with the dense and delicate brushstrokes of Monet and Pissarro as against the bold, academic style of the nineteenth-century artistic establishment.

Plant selection throughout the garden at Gelli Uchaf is limited by conditions that other gardeners might find challenging; summers are cool and winters sometimes very cold. The soil is poor and acidic, and this, combined with high rainfall that averages 1780 millimetres (70 in) annually, has guided choices towards shrubs that thrive in these conditions, such as rhododendrons, and woodland plants. Soil poverty is actually used advantageously, as it stops vigorous species growing at the expense of slower ones, allowing for more diversity. The evergreen foliage of the rhododendrons and other acid-soil plants is familiar, but the diversity of the ground layer much less so. One particular plant stands out: the bold, glossy leaves of a low, clump-forming variety of the fortune saxifrage (*Saxifraga fortunei*). Having the complete set of vegetation – from trees through shrubs and down to the ground flora – makes for a more holistic feel than is often seen when shrubs are grown as isolated specimens.

What the Wormalds call the Multicultural Magic Terrace Garden is one of the first things the visitor sees here, and one of the most innovative features. Developed on smashed-up concrete and shale from the house's restoration, it is completely covered in low creeping plants, most notably varieties of mossy saxifrage (*Saxifraga* spp. *Dactyloides* group) and rock knotweed (*Persicaria vaccinifolia*). Flowering starts off with crocuses, then some dwarf daffodils (*Narcissus* spp.), then grape hyacinths (*Muscari* spp.) and a small camassia (*C. quamash*), all of which self-seed to some extent.

'We thought about having lawn here, but that was when we were only coming up at weekends, and I did not fancy mowing it every time I came', says Julian. 'The original inspiration for this area was the Beth Chatto Gravel Garden, but it's morphed over the years. We learned a lot from a workshop you [Noel Kingsbury] ran here at Y Gelli on plant growth, and from James Hitchmough's

work on seeding' (see pp.104–9). The Multicultural Magic Terrace Garden was based on a series of single-species blocks 'inspired by Welsh flannel quilt designs, which Fiona is very interested in', says Julian. Quilts rely for their appeal on juxtaposing small areas of fabric that contrast and complement each other, but the reality with living plants is different, as they inevitably grow into each other, and as Julian says, the terrace garden 'has morphed into a much more naturalistic style over the years.' The thick mesh of low plants reduces weed growth and, in many cases, can be combined with taller perennials, such as asters and betony (*Betonica officinalis*), which are able to break though the ground cover and grow above it without taking over. This is partic-ularly important around the edges, where, later in the season, the appearance is more that of a conventional but densely planted border.

Although the climate may be very different, the substrate (soil might be too generous a word here) makes a connection with the Filippi garden (pp.124–31), where there are also many short, spreading species, and the development of alternatives to grass as a ground cover is a priority; a thin soil over limestone and building rubble are physically and chemically similar. The possibilities for thin soils in urban areas is obvious.

The Wormalds are passionate about insect biodiversity, and having a wide range of plants is probably the most important factor here in that respect, with what Julian calls 'multicultural, multi-layered plantings with perennials, bulbs and shrubs in order to maximise flower numbers throughout the year'. Not only does this increase the feeding opportunities for insects, it also creates a complex habitat, offering shelter to invertebrates and birds. 'Self-seeding

plants are important, too', says Julian – species that increase their own numbers, filling gaps and building up habitat.

As well as the garden, the Wormalds have two areas of wildflower meadow, one above the house – now an established hay meadow, which they maintain by cutting once a year – and wet meadows in the valley bottom below the garden, with a very different plant range. 'The upper meadow', Julian says, 'we graze very short with sheep in the winter and then take off a hay crop, which allows wildflowers to seed.' The wet meadow has required a lot of work. 'It was almost solid soft rush (*Juncus effusus*) three years ago, but we dealt with that through cutting and using a weed wiper ... now there are 120 species', he reports proudly. Paths cut through the meadows allow access and make for a very romantic impression, the final touch to a garden that integrates nature and art in varied and novel ways.

The lean soil around the rubble and stone of an old
farmyard limits the spread of the weedy grasses and coarse
wild perennials that often dominate in the western British
Isles. The result is a dense tapestry of spreading and
interpenetrating plants that vary from one small area to
another, and from year to year; the main season of interest is
spring and early summer (these photographs were taken in May).
Stony conditions (as with gravel gardens) prompt the self-
seeding of many species, such as various colours of columbine
(*Aquilegia vulgaris*). Low-growing species that propagate
sideways effectively fill gaps between paving stones.

↑↓→ A pink *Clematis montana* drapes itself over trees
overlooking the east-facing terrace (above). The low-
growing plants that flourish here include native species
such as white sea campion (*Silene vulgaris* subsp.
maritima), pink thrift (*Armeria maritima*) and blue bugle
(*Ajuga vulgaris*). Bulbs that need a summer baking, such
as *Allium aflatuense*, will thrive in stony environments.
The yellow flower is the Welsh poppy (*Meconopsis cambrica*),
a short-lived but self-seeding locally native plant.

Gelli Uchaf (Upper Grove)

95

A cursory look over this 3,500 square metre (0.9 acre) garden on France's Mediterranean coast would instantly remind any onlooker of the local vegetation – the maquis (scrubby, evergreen shrubs or small trees) and the somewhat lower and more ascetic looking garrigue ecosystems. The planting is bushy, to about head height, with dense growths of aromatic foliage, patches of bare gravelly ground, and a few smaller plants in the gaps. The limestone cliffs that overlook the garden help to set the scene: this is a garden that is supremely of its place.

'The client was interested in zero irrigation', says James Basson, who runs Scape Design with his wife, Helen, and who designed the garden in 2012, 'and in making it as relevant as possible to local landscape. They were very enthusiastic about plants and keen for us to try out as wide a range as possible.' James took the invitation seriously and used over 200 different varieties of plants, sourcing as much as he could from the catalogue of nurseryman Olivier Filippi (see pp.124–31). Some eight years later he is very open about the mistakes he felt he made. 'It was an early garden for us, working with this type of vegetation, and our biggest problem was that it was ex-agricultural land. It used to be used for growing flowers. It had been fed and treated for generations, and it was too rich.' This is the central paradox of Mediterranean zone garden-making. The most attractive and extensive range of native drought-tolerant plants are those of thin limestone soils, the vegetation known as garrigue. 'On a fertile soil', says Basson, 'when you start planting a Mediterranean garrigue-type landscape, everything just grows too quickly. Five years into the project we realized we had over-planted by 50 per cent. We had a lot of losses of plants competing with each other, and we had to massively prune stuff back.'

Now, much the wiser and with a string of gardens in the region under his belt, Basson has a refined strategy for planting an irrigation-free garden. 'You almost have to overplant. If you put in small plants that will mature without competing with each other, then it takes five years to look good.' Instead, he tries to devise 'a balance between plants that will be more or less permanent, and those which are essentially temporary. Ideally, we then maintain the garden in a direction where it's clear what we will keep and what can go.' Over time, the longer-lived species will almost inevitably displace the shorter-lived ones, although the latter are often able to re-generate from seed. Upright myrtle spurge (*Euphorbia rigida*), a sprawling spring-flowering, lime-green perennial, is a good example of the latter. It helps to create a sense of unity in

Les Cyprès

the garden, popping up everywhere but giving way to taller plants.

Planting in this garden involves thinking in layers: up to 30 centimetres, 30–60 centimetres, 60–120 centimetres (12 in, 12–24 in, 24–48 in), with the lowest layer becoming an underplanting to the taller in some places, in others opening out to become ground cover. The lowest layer plays an important role as an alternative to grass; there is no thirsty lawn here. The taller species are often variants on familiar Mediterranean plants: lavenders, species of rock rose (*Cistus*) and *Phlomis*, and rosemary – all very good at filling space with a mass of dense foliage that offers subtle variations in a spectrum from dark green to white-silver. Contrasting elements are provided by a limited number of species with rosettes of linear leaves, such as Algerian iris (*Iris unguicularis*), a classic regional winter-flowering species. These are few in number but make a big difference to what would otherwise be a relative uniformity of leaf shape and visual texture.

There is uniformity but still considerable diversity, thanks to the botanical enthusiasm of the original planting scheme. 'Now', Basson explains, 'we always choose three or four plants for a garden and use them widely, so they are spread throughout the landscape. Then we can interplant with huge diversity ... These theme plants will also provide seasonal continuity, with a lower layer of species that will change through the year.'

The maintenance regime established in the first few years is crucial to the long-term success of the garden. Fortunately, the Bassons have at hand Alejandro O'Neill (see pp.234–41), who runs a local garden design and management consultancy. 'He has a real eye for plants, he is very good with clients, and he communicates well with the gardeners. We call them artist-gardeners, as we set the system and then give them a game to play, the opportunity to manage creatively. Alejandro makes sure everyone is going in a thoughtful direction, as we don't dictate precisely.' The result is what Basson calls a 'dynamic landscape', which may develop in unpredictable ways. Pruning plays an important role. 'I used to think that low-maintenance gardening did not involve any pruning', says Basson, 'but Alejandro is very much into regulating the plant community through different ways of pruning, which gives the garden a good appearance in the summer, when there is nothing in flower and everything is a bit bland ... I used to leave things looking a bit shaggy, but he'll sculpt some and leave others to be scruffy, so the whole feel is of somewhere cared for.' Occasional replacement planting is foreseen, and part of the budget is kept back for 'refresher planting every few years.'

It has been said that with gardens, 'maintenance is half of design', and it is clear from the way this garden has developed that this is particularly true of Mediterranean gardens that have a high proportion of low, maquis-type shrubs. Design and ongoing horticulture are inseparable.

↓ Yellow *Phlomis* 'Le Sud' (also p.99 bottom left) makes bold splashes of late winter/early summer colour in plantings dominated by sub-shrubs. Their evergreen and mound-forming habit offers year-round continuity. The white flowers on tall stems (bottom) are asphodel (*Asphodelus albus*), a common Mediterranean perennial, which in the cooler season bears rosettes of linear foliage that are a complete contrast to shrubs. Radically different to most poolside planting, the scents of Mediterranean vegetation add another sensory layer to an enjoyment of the view.

← Zoysia grass (*Zoysia tenuifolia*) performs the
visual functions of a traditional grass lawn,
requiring very little irrigation. The bright
silver-white foliage on the right is dusty
miller (*Senecio viravira*), one of the best
grey and silver foliage plants available to
designers in Mediterranean climates.

←↑↓ A maquis habitat has relatively little
variation in overall plant form, increasing
the importance of its wide range of texture
and foliage colour. Occasional clumps of
linear foliage, such as the *Iris unguicularis*
(overleaf) make a good contrast, as do the more
irregular forms of herbaceous plants like the
red-flowered valerian (*Centranthus ruber*).

Mixed Planting and other Randomized Systems

Naturalistic planting is especially attractive on a large scale. The repetition of colours and forms over large areas is key to the visual impact of many natural habitats, and similar repetitive effects create a strong impression in a public or larger private landscape. The demands of public landscapes, in particular, are high: plantings need to look good for as long as possible, offer a number of different spectacles through the year, and be easy and cheap to maintain; a new demand is that they support biodiversity, particularly pollinators. ¶ Successful public projects inevitably involve some method of selecting suitable plants and organizing them so the results continue to look good year after year. Some of those working in this sphere have developed a systematic approach to planting, using a formula that enables large areas to be set out with minimum effort. Such a planting method has been most clearly promoted and supported in Germany, where investment in public parks has traditionally been high. Building on a long history of the study of plant communities in nature, German practitioners have created plant mixes that aim, however crudely, to mimic a natural plant community (see also p.153). ¶ The roots of this probably lie with Alexander von Humboldt, a nineteenth-century explorer and scientist with a uniquely holistic vision of the world, its climates and its lifeforms. Thanks to him, German-speaking cultures developed an emphasis on natural community and connectedness, in contrast to the more reductionist approach of English-speaking cultures, by which elements of nature are examined and understood separately. And just as nature can be analysed as a community, versions of it can be synthesized. ¶ The style used in an increasing number of German public plantings is called Mixed Planting, emphasizing the idea of diversity and combination. Mixed Planting involves a combination of plants, usually perennials but increasingly including shrubs, chosen for the constituent plants' ability to thrive in similar conditions and to co-exist for around ten years without major intervention. Species with different growth forms are chosen so that the mixture will mesh to cover the ground and reduce weed infiltration. The proportions of the component species may be very different in size, shape and vigour. Planting is at equal spacing and randomized, simplifying installation. The random look, which occurs in many of the plantings at Hermannshof, for example (see pp.152–9), creates a natural impression, even though natural habitats are not strictly random. The solidity of a well-developed Mixed Planting is witness to an effective replication of a natural plant community. ¶ Mixed Planting was developed in the 1990s and was launched commercially in 2000, with *Silbersommer* ('Silversummer'), a mix of perennials designed for dry, calcareous soils. Its development occurred at a time of increased interest in wildflower meadows in garden and landscape projects, and in the summer garden shows that are an important part of Germany's gardening scene. Some functional plant mixes were created, such as for green roofs and natural swimming pools. In some cases, the personnel involved in developing these mixes have been the same – notably, Wolfram Kircher of the Anhalt University of Applied Sciences, who has played a crucial role in all three developments. ¶ Since 2000, the number of commercially available mixes has grown. Produced by publicly funded bodies such as universities, they are trialled over a number of years and the results published in peer-reviewed journals. Nurseries have also begun to produce their own mixes, often for domestic gardens; these do not go through the same rigorous testing process. Site-specific mixes, combinations put together by designers or horticultural managers for particular places, have also been created. All the projects looked at here come under this label. ¶ Mixed Planting and the research that has gone into it have stimulated practitioners in the Czech Republic, Switzerland and, increasingly, the United States. There has been some impact in Britain, too, although the roots of the ways British practitioners, such as Nigel Dunnett, put plants together are arguably distinct, with much mixing of plants of different origins and a focus on combining particular colours or plant forms (see pp.224–31). The modular approach used by Dan Pearson at Japan's Tokachi Millennium Forest (see pp.164–9) adopts a different methodology that nevertheless creates a similar randomized look, as do the relatively unsystematic plant combinations being used around Sheffield by the city council (see pp.178–83). These projects look natural to most onlookers because there is no obvious arrangement of the plants. Over time, some species may increase and others decrease. The movement and fluctuation in numbers of short-lived species, which need to regenerate from seed, is particularly dynamic, and contributes to a feeling of spontaneity. ¶ Mixed Planting and similar randomized systems are a cost-effective way to fulfil aesthetic as well as floristic diversity requirements, essential for supporting biodiversity in urban areas, and offer scope for exciting and beautiful combinations. They are low-maintenance as well, although this maintenance requires a higher level of staff expertise than traditional parks management.

'Planting has to have the wow factor', says James Hitchmough. 'If it looks good on a calendar, then it's good.' There is no doubt that his 500-square metre (5,400 sq. ft) garden in Sheffield has plenty of 'wow' – it is an extraordinarily exuberant space. There is a lot of colour and a lot of striking foliage and strong shapes that many might describe as exotic. In fact, the exoticism or associations with distant parts of the world has much to do with the unfamiliarity of many of the plant species here, for this is no sub-tropical garden; it is in Yorkshire, perched high on a hill.

Hitchmough is Professor of Horticultural Ecology in the Landscape Department at the University of Sheffield, so perhaps the first thought on seeing his garden is to think, 'How nice to find someone who practises what he preaches.' Along with his colleague Professor Nigel Dunnett and designer Sarah Price, Hitchmough was the force behind the spectacular planting at the 2012 London Olympics, much of which still thrives as part of the Queen Elizabeth Olympic Park. He is passionate about public spaces and about how to bring colourful, life-affirming planting to parks, public gardens and housing estates. He always has plenty of stories about meeting intimidatingly large men with big dogs who are full of praise for the drifts of perennials and annuals that he and the rest of the Sheffield University team have managed to roll out around their city (see pp.178–83).

At home, Hitchmough says, 'I'm having fun. This is an opportunity to indulge a passion for plants without the pressure of having to produce results, which is always at the back of every professional designer's mind.' On one level, it seems like a very condensed botanical garden, such is the variety of forms and colours. There are South African bulbs, such as cheerfully red species of *Gladiolus*, long, narrow spikes of foxtail lilies (*Eremurus* spp.) from Central Asia, bright pinks (*Dianthus* spp.) and cool, spiky sea holly (*Eryngium* spp.). It's all very eclectic, but there is a rationale behind the apparent botanical madness. Hitchmough firmly rejects the idea that it is only appropriate to grow the native plants of a region. 'What interests me', he says, 'is how to apply the ecological rules that govern

what can be designed. These rules are universal and blind, and they don't distinguish between wild and cultivated plants, as in ecological terms these are one and the same. I am equally interested in native and non-native vegetation. We need more of both in urban places, and in many urban projects I work more with non-natives – there are a lot more of them.'

Much of Hitchmough's work is the selection and trialling of a huge range of plant species, sourced from commercial producers all over the world. The idea is to create mixes of these species that are long-lived, resilient and stable enough to be used in public spaces. His approach until now has been to look in detail at various temperate zone habitats around the world. 'I'm working my way through the world's vegetation. I've done North America, much of central Europe,

James Hitchmough Garden

I've looked at the montane landscapes of South Africa, I've been to Argentina, all the time looking for vegetation that is like what we want to create. An example we've tried might be a Himalayan yak meadow transported to Harrogate.'

'It's actually not just fun', he insists. 'This is a place to test ideas.' He moved to Sheffield in 2008, but 'the house was a wreck, so I didn't start on the garden until 2011.' There is a studio building, 'which I use as an occasional office, and as a store for garden furniture', three apple trees, a cherry and a hazel. 'There is quite a bit of shade, and I have to work around that, so there is a transition from full shade to full sun.' In many ways it is a very ordinarily sized and shaped town garden. Being up a hill is, he thinks, an advantage: 'There's good drainage and good cold air drainage; the coldest it has ever got has been -9° C [15.8° F].' The planting is denser and wilder than what is conventionally found

in gardens, which combined with often unfamiliar flowers and leaf shapes may leave some visitors disorientated; but a seating area makes it feel like a relaxed living space, too.

Hitchmough comes from a mining village on the outskirts of Newcastle upon Tyne, in the northeast of England. 'My parents had quite a large garden, where they grew lots of annual bedding every year', he recalls, 'like they were trying to compete with the council parks department.' That perhaps explains the exuberance of his own garden, the lack of fear in putting yellow, pink, blue and purple all together.

Looking more closely at the planting, there are a lot of elements that bring a sense of unity to what might otherwise be a botanical melange. Rosettes of strap-like foliage repeat a theme, and certain distinct shapes recur, like the reflexed pink petals of coneflowers (*Echinacea pallida*), or the red hot pokers of several *Kniphofia* species. Many of the flowers are held well above the foliage layer, examples of what Hitchmough calls 'emergents'. Above all, there is a key concept at work here, that of plant layers. This takes account of the fact that with perennials and bulbs, the earliest to flower are small, and latter ones are large or tall and upright. There need to be a lot of small early plants to make an impact, but not nearly so many of the larger later ones. 'I want to have it flowering all the time', says Hitchmough. 'The year starts off with masses of dwarf bulbs and species of shooting star (*Dodecatheon*), so it has to be cut back in autumn or winter to let light through ... If you did not have so many of these, you could leave the winter seed heads up for longer.' The density of the planting is crucially important; everyone concerned with contemporary naturalistic planting is very keen on this, as the more space you have filled with the plants you want, the less there is space for weeds. High plant density should mean that there is a complete ground canopy of vegetation by May.

This vibrant garden is clearly a lot of fun for its owner. More importantly, it is playing its role in helping guide some of the most innovative thinking in the development of planting mixes for the future: science and pleasure combined.

→ The dramatic yellow spike of a foxtail lily (*Eremurus*) is an instant focal point, though their rather exacting cultivation requirements preclude them from widespread use. Nevertheless, a small number of dramatically taller plants ('emergents') are good for visual drama. In summer, the planting changes as the shade increases beneath a hazel (p.104), with dramatically less flowering; most shade-tolerant plants are spring-flowering. Here, the blue African lily (*Agapanthus* 'Bressingham Blue') and pink *Tritonia drakensbergensis* are summer plants of sun.

↑ Incredibly diverse planting (also pp.108–9) reflects its creator's professional passion and illustrates how a large number of plants of different species can co-exist in a small space. In late summer, the quantity of linear and rosette foliage is greater than in 'normal' northern hemisphere naturalistic planting; this is a legacy of the flora of the regions being researched by Hitchmough, and may contribute to a tighter integration of plants. The rosette of wide strap-shaped leaves is giant red hot poker (*Kniphofia northiae*), with *Agapanthus* 'Bressingham Blue' behind, while the blue foliage in the foreground is caulescent red hot poker (*Kniphofia caulescens*).

→ Red *Gladiolus cardinalis*, one of a vast number of *Gladiolus* species from South Africa, nod to orange *Watsonia marlothii*. The linear foliage makes a very different visual matrix to that of most border plantings.

← The South African caulescent red hot poker (*Kniphofia caulescens*), which thrives in mild winter climates, is much valued by designers as a focal point plant. The bright pink at lower right is a Carthusian pink (*Dianthus carthusianorum*), a common central European species of dry meadows. It is a good example of a plant with a spindly habit, unsuitable for conventional planting design; in the denser environs of naturalistic planting, this gets hidden and only the flowers are noticed. It also often self-seeds well.

The famous gardens of the Cotswolds – Hidcote, Kiftsgate and others – shelter in its valleys, but the growing popularity of converting the region's fine stone barns and other agricultural buildings into houses has resulted in some more recent gardens being created on the level uplands, which have a much more open character and can be bleak in winter. Such is Hailstone Barn, where designer James Alexander-Sinclair has created a 1,200-square metre (0.3 acre) garden for a client for whom the property is a second home. The client wanted a naturalistic planting style and chose Alexander-Sinclair because he increasingly works in this style, after a long career in garden design with a focus on planting. Alexander-Sinclair, it should be noted, is a passionate gardener himself, which has given him an in-depth knowledge of the wide range of plants he uses.

The Cotswolds, a hilly limestone plateau in the southwestern part of central England, has an important place in early twentieth-century garden history. Several of its gardens became some of the most celebrated examples of a style loosely associated with the Arts and Crafts movement, fed by the English practice of global plant collecting and bolstered by an obliging climate for plants from a wide range of habitats. The English contribution to the naturalistic planting movement was, as a result, a pragmatic one, with little of the emphasis on locally native plants that has been a feature of the movement elsewhere.

Nevertheless, 'the garden has to have a conversation with the fields around it', says the designer, James Alexander-Sinclair, referring to the arable fields on the far side of a traditional drystone wall that surrounds the property. There are none of the high hedges that garden-makers have traditionally used in such locations. Much of the planting here has a fine, wispy character that evokes meadow wildflowers, although there are few grasses; indeed, in parts it looks as if a goodly selection of meadow perennials have escaped their normal grassy companions and set up on their own. At the same time, there are some firmer, more graphic shapes, such as globe artichokes (*Cynara cardunculus*) and the familiar early spring flowering Mediterranean spurge (*Euphorbia characias*), which help to anchor the eye as it sweeps across the garden.

'It's a tough environment', explains Alexander-Sinclair. 'It used to be a cattle yard. The Cotswolds have stony soil anyway, and a lot more stones must have added over the years, with the animals tramping them in … The planting process involved a lot of pick-axe work, so the plants grow up tough and slightly smaller than normal, forming stocky shapes.' Such a lean environment reduces the possibility of plants getting top heavy and flopping over. There is relatively

Hailstone Barn

little maintenance: 'A gardener comes in once a fortnight or so; the general rule of thumb is that if it looks untidy, cut it back, but if it looks good, leave it.'

The planting looks random because it is. 'All set out by my own hand', says Alexander-Sinclair. 'The plants were ordered and I set them out, walking around and scattering them – this is what I tend to do quite a lot, rather than doing a planting plan, which often tends to be a waste of time. Often you get on site and you change your mind, and it's always an additional expense for the client, so I gave up doing plans a long time ago.' Setting out plants is clearly a deeply intuitive process for the designer. 'I always do this on my own. It is really instinctive, so no one else can really be of any help, apart from carrying trays of plants around.' He refers to long experience of what he feels to be right in terms of putting plants together, at more or less equal spacing: 'Some things will outgrow their space and suppress their neighbours, but others fade away, and after a few years we will need to top up.'

'Randomization', he says, 'comes from not doing planting plans and trying to be naturalistic, rather than the old practice of planting in odd-numbered groups. Things don't plant themselves like that.' Crucially, however, the process is not totally random. 'It is about having two here, one over there, and another one in that direction over there; there are occasional repeated groups, but in different numbers, and there are lots of odd ones.'

Planted in 2015, with some replanting in 2018 to fill gaps, a clear dynamic seems to have evolved within the garden. One species in particular, the native common valerian (*Valeriana officinalis*), has thrived – unusually, as it is generally found in moister locations. It has almost-white flowers, which form the kind of pale haze that is not unlike the froth of many of the umbelliferous plants, such as cow parsley (*Anthriscus sylvestris*), that so dominate in the English countryside in spring and early summer; its presence helps to create a subtle, sub-conscious link to the local landscape. It is one of those plants that moves around, partly through seeding but more normally through spread of its rhizomes; not just advancing but often simultaneously advancing and retreating, a behaviour guaranteed to annoy conventional gardeners but which contributes greatly to the spontaneous look sought after by a naturalistic designer.

Inevitably with the dynamic plant combination at Hailstone Barn, Alexander-Sinclair is sure that 'every year is different, which I see as positive' – an attitude a long way from the relatively static organization of conventional planting, or even the careful spatial orchestration of designers such as Piet Oudolf (see pp.20–7). This Cotswold garden, in contrast, is much nearer what makers and owners of wildflower meadows or prairies say about their habitat restorations: complex, constantly-evolving and, at the end of the day, never entirely predictable.

← ↓ → The perennials used here are those found in traditional borders. Here they are let loose, but the colour impact — lime-greens, pale pinks and yellows, blue-violets and endless variations on not-quite-white — is similar, incorporating muted shades that look their best under grey skies and soft light. In early summer there is a high proportion of columnar flower head shapes, adding rhythm and theme: green *Euphorbia characias* (also pp.114–15), pale yellow-eyed grass (*Sisyrinchium striatum*), white lupins. Globe artichoke (*Cynara cardunculus*, below, and p.112 bottom) dominates its corner of the garden, with striking grey foliage that appears very early in the year.

The flat landscape of the northern Netherlands around the village of De Wilp seems a particularly appropriate site for a European prairie planting. The garden made by Lianne Pot is the most pragmatic, and possibly the most innovative, of the various prairie plantings made in Europe over the last decade, in that it aims to blend non-American species with 'genuine' American prairie ones. After having been a social worker for fifteen years, Pot became a garden designer and developed a particular love of grasses. She opened her specialist nursery in the year 2000.

Visits to Sichtungsgarten Hermannshof in Germany (see pp.152–9) introduced Pot to the idea of 'biotope', or habitat planting, while 'the prairie garden there made me want to visit the USA. So in July and August 2008, the family spent six weeks travelling across the prairie states. Back home, I decided to try to translate the prairie concept to the garden, and show people what is possible.'

First planted in 2009, Pot's 3,500-square metre (0.86 acre) garden offers visitors an immersive experience, as they wander along paths between massed perennials and grasses. It is clearly not a natural prairie, but neither is it a conventional garden. While there is a 'real prairie' area using only US Midwest natives, most of the planting is a mix of North American species and those from regions with a similar climate, mostly European. 'I would describe it as an artificial ecosystem of several designed planting communities – beautiful, durable, long-living', explains Pot. 'I wanted to combine grasses and perennials, not just prairie species, and do no watering and no feeding. And I wanted as wide a range of plants as possible.' A viewing mound on one side of the garden offers an opportunity to look at it from above. This is an unusual and quite valuable touch, as the height of some perennials, prairie species in particular, sometimes militates against our ability to appreciate them – we are simply not tall enough to see them at their best. Pot is aware of how important it is to manage how visitors see plant communities: 'I wanted people to walk through and look over several plantings: examples of height, of colour, and of special grasses with perennials.' Indeed, she describes the viewing mound as 'the heart of the garden'.

Whereas many concerned with naturalistic planting are overwhelmingly focused on the nature of what goes on inside the garden, Pot's attitude towards wider design issues is very clear. 'The garden has an open character', she explains, 'surrounded by maize or potatoes in this agricultural area … I wanted almost no hedges or trees, although there are some trees, making a connection with others in the surrounding area.' She describes the value of sight lines out of the garden into the landscape and the importance of maintaining an open character.

Lianne's Siergrassen

Prairie Garden

Pot relates that she 'had been a child in the country, and I think that was why I loved this style'. During the late 1990s she was inspired to try naturalistic planting by Ton ter Linden, an artist who over the course of a richly creative life has made three gardens, all of which have been open to visitors and have had a great impact on Dutch amateur gardeners. Having developed the nursery and prairie garden as a business, Pot is now finding an increasing amount of work as a designer and, significantly, is being asked by landscape architects to develop planting designs for their projects, particularly those that involve reduced maintenance.

The De Wilp prairie garden is built around a series of plant combinations, simplified versions of which are made available to customers who can buy modules made up of a chosen range of plants in the appropriate proportions. Some of these are named after key theme plants, for example 'Helenium', which is a relatively tall combination with white, orange and purple predominating; 'Gaura', a shorter range of plants with white, red and purple; 'Perovskia', with yellow/orange, blue and purple species. Interestingly, the theme plants chosen are not necessarily prairie species. Other mixes are named for dominant colours or for particular heights, such as the 'Tall grass prairie' mix, which – with plants of up to 2 metres (6.5 ft) – is for those who want the fully immersive experience.

Pot may, perhaps, have paid more attention to seasonal spread than many of those who have fallen in love with this planting style. 'We have some spring and early summer prairie perennials like *Pulsatilla* [pasqueflower] and *Camassia* species. But any small botanical bulbs are good, and more conventional garden bulbs like *Narcissus* [daffodils] and *Allium* too.' Camassias are one of the great success stories of early twenty-first-century garden-making. Tall, blue-flowered bulbs from open habitats in North America, they grow well in lush northern European grass with virtually no maintenance, and with an expanding output from the bulb industry they have become increasingly popular for late spring/early summer planting. They bring the sheets of blue that were traditionally associated with woodland edge species such as English bluebells (*Hyacinthoides non-scripta*) out into the open in a remarkably trouble-free way. At the other end of the year, the winter aspect of seed heads is particularly important and can mean that the prairie garden maintains its good looks until well into January.

The prairie garden continues to evolve and develop. Some planting inspired by the steppe, and therefore more drought tolerant, was introduced in 2018. In this intensely agricultural area of northwest Europe, Pot has demonstrated the essential pragmatism of the grasslands prairie garden, which is inherently open to new ideas and influences and has the capacity to show off naturalistic planting to a wide range of audiences.

↑↓ Clear winter light and the reduced palette of late autumn brings form and texture into focus, especially when hoar frost emphasizes every line and point. Plantings can be appreciated at many scales: drifts of differently textured plants, intricate frostings of grass seed heads, rosettes of foliage where every edge is lined with ice. Turkish sage (*Phlomis russeliana*, below right) is a rare example of an evergreen perennial, one of the more strongly defined shapes of the winter garden. An aster seed head (below left) is one of many perennials with strong enough stems to give several months of winter interest.

→ ↓ Winter grasses tend to be paler than perennial seed heads and are more likely to be softly textured, sometimes so diffuse that they look like they could evaporate altogether. Ironically, they tend to be physically stronger than the seed heads of flowering perennials, some of which collapse with the first autumn storms. Korean feather reed-grass (*Calamagrostis brachytricha*, right), for example, hovers above the semi-evergreen palm-branch sedge (*Carex muskingumensis*). Perennials, however, tend to be darker and have more defined shapes than grasses: a few robust ones like species of mullein (*Verbascum*, p.120) and button snakewort (*Liatris spicata*, p.121) stand as exclamation marks much better than many of their fellows.

→ (Overleaf, pp.122–3) The planting is organized around a mound (area at centre-top with seat), which enables visitors to get a view over the prairie – invaluable for ornamental vegetation that can be very tall in places, as well as offering a different perspective on the plants.

Visitors arriving at the 6,000-square metre (1.5 acre) garden that Olivier and Clara Filippi have been creating since 1985 are presented with something very unexpected. Mediterranean gardens have traditionally been dominated by a limited range of evergreen species, often clipped into formal shapes and arrangements and interspersed with water-demanding lawns and bedding plants. In contrast, there is little here that is lush green. The predominant colour is grey, in many shades: grey-silver, grey-blue, grey-green, grey-brown, all on low, hummocky plants that mostly rise to no higher than waist height. What could be monotonous is given a dramatic lift by a scattering of classic Mediterranean cypresses, the narrow shapes of which act as powerful counterpoints. A few other trees, notably pines, are here too, along with some taller shrubs, grasses and areas of open gravelly soil, but they seem rather incidental. Beyond is a bay that draws the eye, full of metal frames used for farming mussels.

The low waves of grey foliage shrubs speak powerfully of place, habitat and climate, for these are technically termed 'sub-shrubs': densely branched, twiggy plants with evergreen foliage, typical of regions with dry summer climates. The tendency for grey leaves (often dubbed 'silver' in plant nursery catalogues) is a characteristic particularly strong in the Mediterranean, and is mostly the result of leaves being coated in microscopic hairs that reflect light, shade the leaf and help reduce water loss. This sea of grey characterizes many Mediterranean habitats, places that the Filippis have explored in detail – from Morocco to Syria, and the peninsulas and islands in between. They understand the region's plant life and how it survives drought, fire and hungry goats. They have built up thousands of seed collections, creating one of the most impressive botanical gardens in the region, even though it is, strictly, only the private display and mother plant collection for their accompanying nursery, Pépinière Filippi.

This low, shrubby vegetation, so quintessentially Mediterranean, is by no means entirely natural, but often the result of deforestation so ancient that the recovery plants – lavender (*Lavandula* spp.), rock roses (*Cistus* spp.), rosemary (*Salvia rosmarinus*) and many other aromatic-leaved species – have become almost permanent. 'The Mediterranean is a totally man-made landscape', Olivier explains, 'and as such it's an immediate model for gardens, because it's artificial and beautiful. It's also extremely resilient through a long history of disturbances – whatever happens, from fire to erosion to overgrazing, it always comes back, cycle after cycle.'

Visually, Mediterranean floras offer great possibilities: there are many effective ground covers, the vegetation resists drought and usually has flowers in spring or early summer, and with its rounded cushions it makes for a soft and

Le Jardin Sec

pleasing look. While a few species have become very popular as garden plants or herbs (like the three just mentioned), there are many more worthy of inclusion in a climate-sensitive garden, and it has been the mission of the Filippis to explore these possibilities. 'There are at least 25,000 drought-tolerant species in the Mediterranean', says Olivier – one-tenth of the world's flora. 'How many of these thousands of plants are grown in cultivation? Maybe a few hundred.'

Le Jardin Sec ('The Dry Garden') shows how this plant diversity can be used in many different ways, particularly when it comes to thinking creatively about the thirsty beast that is responsible for so much water (mis)use, the lawn. There are areas here planted with very tight ground covers that offer the next best thing to grass; other parts that are similar mix planting with areas of gravel, the predominantly grey species offering a contrast to the stone with a rich variety of textures; this range of textures is a major bonus of the Mediterranean flora. These latter areas grade into steppe, the characteristic vegetation of regions with cold winters and hot, dry summers – plants here are lower, the look particularly sparse but with opportunities for colourful flowering bulbs in spring, and sometimes annuals. There are also practical advantages to this ascetic, gravelly look – it can make a good fire break, important in dry regions (see pp.40–5). The downside of many classic Mediterranean shrubs is that they can be highly flammable.

Taller planting typically revolves around low shrubs that form a closed evergreen canopy, so excluding there the possibility of bulb or annual planting. This canopy does a good job at preventing weed competition, which explains why these plants, including species of rock-rose, lavender and santolina, have long been popular with landscape and garden designers in non-Mediterranean climates. However, these species are very often short-lived; in some cases after only five years or so the shrub can begin to age, opening up and becoming (in the eyes of many) untidy. Their period of value can be prolonged by lightly pruning them, which effectively imitates the nibbling of goats or other animals that many of these plants experience in the wild. While the pruning at Le Jardin Sec is done simply to maintain the plants, it can be used creatively, too (see pp.54–7).

The low sub-shrub planting is interspersed with groups of taller, still drought-tolerant shrubs, a reflection of how, in nature, taller growing species and trees eventually take over. Here, trees such as almonds (*Prunus dulcis*) are regenerating naturally. Olivier expects that in time they will change the environment at ground level to be more like that below the pines, where a different range of species thrive, forming a much sparser canopy.

Mediterranean planting involves species that at first sight seem similar, but on further inspection reveal a wide range of colours, leaf shapes, textures, densities and, above all, different ways of reflecting the often harsh and unyielding light. Le Jardin Sec points the way to a sustainable future for the dry summer garden.

↑↓ The distinctive forms of the Italian cypress (*Cupressus sempervirens*) are a key part of this garden's aesthetic (also p.124), lifting the eye skywards and contrasting with the low, rounded form of other plants. Most of the tree cover is stone pine (*Pinus pinea*), which casts enough shade to alter the habitat beneath it. Grasses are few, although some, like golden oats (*Stipa gigantea*; below left), a western Mediterranean plant with evergreen foliage and airy panicles of flower and seed, make an impact. Spreading and mat-forming plants such as *Psephallus bellus* (below right and p.127 lower centre) are very important.

↑↓ Much of the thinking here about ground coverings as
a sustainable alternative to irrigated grass concerns
combinations of gravel with planting that to a greater
or lesser extent can be walked around. The garden has
a continual gradient; higher levels of vegetation have
visual impact, and the slope controls how we move across
it. The high number of low Mediterranean plants come
from a limited range of genera: rock rose (*Cistus*),
Turkish sage (*Phlomis russeliana*), lavender (*Lavandula*),
germander (*Teucrium*). Given often limited flowering
periods, foliage colour and texture is very important
in design terms.

↑↓ Of the huge range of plants here, euphorbias stand out,
especially early in the year. A wide-ranging and versatile
genus, they tend to be early-flowering, with bracts that last
for several months after the flowers have died. *Euphorbia
characias* (pp.128–9) is well known, and *E. rigida* (above and
p.131 top), with pinkish bracts, is attractive and, like
many in the genus, self-sows; *E. ceratocarpa* (p.131 below,
centre) is more typical, with yellow-green bracts.

↑↓ Dotting plants in gravel allows for foot traffic, but move away, and the planting appears to be continuous. Yellow-flowered Jerusalem sage (*Phlomis longifolia*) is in the foreground and white rock rose (*Cistus* x *cyprius* var. *ellipticus* 'Elma') at the rear (below). Many plants here are aromatic, which adds another sensory dimension.

MANHATTAN, NEW YORK CITY,
NEW YORK, USA

PUBLIC GARDEN

DESIGNERS: JAMES CORNER FIELD
OPERATIONS, DILLER SCOFIDIO + RENFRO,
AND PIET OUDOLF

With only the birds and the occasional jogger to disturb the peace, early morning is the best time to appreciate the High Line – to marvel at just how extraordinary it is to be surrounded by plants, high above the streets of New York City. Encircled by towering architecture that long ago became the iconic modern city (or urban jungle, depending on your view), to be surrounded also by small trees, shrubs, perennials and grasses is amazing.

The High Line is precisely that – a disused railway line that cuts through the city two storeys up. It is high enough to feel elevated, but its linearity soon takes over, and the urge is very strong to look along or up, rather than down. Looking up, one cannot avoid noticing the disjunction between a view of relatively wild plant life juxtaposed with the buildings of the city: from magnificent architecture to advertising hoardings to urban decay.

Focusing on what is actually growing on the High Line, we soon appreciate that there are two communities of plant life here: an open, meadow environment, and a sort of mini-woodland one. The first is planted with lots of ornamental grasses (including the native blue stem, *Schizachyrium scoparium*) and perennials, which in late summer and autumn can feel quite prairie-like. The second situation feels more enclosed, as the architecture closes in and casts some shade. Here small trees tend to dominate – birches (*Betula* spp.), dogwoods (*Cornus* spp.) and others of a similar scale – so there is vegetation at both the tree level and on the 'forest floor'. At some points the walkway becomes quite narrow, and at others it splits into multiple levels; taking the higher path gives us a chance to look down and appreciate the patterning of the ground-level plants that grow in the artificial woodland.

The story of the High Line is well known: an abandoned elevated freight railway that acquired its own distinctive urban flora and was adopted by a pressure group that wanted to save it from demolition. Once the idea for an urban park had evolved, and had secured the all-important political support, a competition was held to develop the line. It was won by landscape

architects James Corner Field Operations, who then brought Piet Oudolf on board for the planting design, along with Diller Scofidio + Renfro design studio. When the first stage of the 2.3-kilometre (1.4 mile) long project opened in 2009, it was instantly popular. Further stages opened in 2011 and 2014, each fuelling more interest, and the disused railway line is now one of the most popular attractions in the city; walking the High Line now means negotiating crowds of tourists. Despite the crush, it is remarkable how the attention of so many visitors is directed at the plants; indeed, one gets a feeling that this is the first time in their lives that many of these people have noticed the plant life before them.

Around 640 species are used in the planting, an incredible number compared

High Line

to a 'normal' landscaping project. The vast majority are perennials and grasses, with a smaller number of trees, shrubs and climbers, and some spring bulbs designed to wake the city up after the winter. The sheer diversity of the plant life is part of the appeal of the place. It is like going to a nature reserve and constantly coming across rarities, species you have never seen before or had only heard about. The alternation between open grassland areas and woodland – sun and shade – helps to create a kind of rhythm. Distinctive species appear again and again, helping to evoke a sense of place, but at the same time there is constant change, a feeling of never knowing what is around the corner.

For many urban visitors to the High Line, the planting must seem wild, whereas the naturalist would not be taken in – it is too tidy, too ordered. It is also dependent on irrigation. Nevertheless, Oudolf's planting is far closer to nature than the work of any conventional landscape architect or garden designer. There are the characteristic layers of natural vegetation: tree, shrub, taller perennial, ground cover perennial; the grass-dominated areas

have the proportions of natural meadow or prairie, with flowering species in the minority. But this is very much nature as interpreted by the artist, presented to an audience of city dwellers who are unfamiliar with anything truly wild. It is 'nature perfected', and as such it is perhaps the ideal kind of naturalistic planting for the city. Research has firmly established that people in urban areas are increasingly open to having naturalistic planting in the city but have a low tolerance of untidiness or wildness, which is often read as being a sign of neglect. Arguably, the High Line strikes a perfect balance.

There is a price to pay, however, since nature perfected takes a lot of maintenance. Private donations fund the management of the High Line, and there is no shortage of volunteer labour. Moreover, New York City, with its wealth and its highly educated population, is exceptional: funds can be raised, the best staff appointed, the most highly motivated volunteers sought. Achieving that level of maintenance elsewhere could be much more difficult.

This might not necessarily be a bad thing, however. Before the High Line was redeveloped, it had a reputation among the few adventurous nature-lovers who managed to get up onto it as an urban wilderness, with a unique flora composed of native species and garden escapes. Without any soil, it was a harsh environment and would dry out every summer, which limited the growth of aggressive weeds. According to Rick Darke, a well-known local commentator on landscape, 'If maintenance dropped off, the worst thing that would happen to the High Line is that it would go back to what it was like before, and that was actually an attractive and biodiverse landscape.'

The challenge, for local governments and citizen bodies around the world who are trying to develop their own versions of the High Line, or any similar planting-focused landscape spectacular, is to find a way to capture that sense of 'nature perfected' that Oudolf and his design partners have achieved in New York City. The High Line is a hugely successful and instructive model.

← ↑ Old railway tracks and sleepers are part of the conceit of the High Line — that it really is an old railway. In reality, its construction involved almost total renovation.

↓ The High Line is the ultimate example of nature groomed for city life (also pp.134–5). Its original inspiration was the wild flora of the abandoned railway line, and much of the planting does genuinely evoke this, particularly in the ebb and flow of its diverse range of species. It is, however, irrigated, and it is intensely managed. Shallow-rooted birches, well-adapted to stressful conditions, are ideal for this kind of urban planting situation.

↑   In early to mid-summer, much of the
    High Line planting comprises perennials,
    with the promise of flowers to come:
    yellow foxtail lilies (*Eremurus* spp.)
    poke up among the foliage, along with
    the white flowers of wild quinine
    (*Parthenium integrifolium*).

←↓ Being narrow and linear, the High Line
    is a dynamic and rather restless public
    space, one for walking; nevertheless,
    where space allows, some provision for
    relaxation has been created.

↑↓ Species of stag's horn sumach (*Rhus*) create an autumn splash.
These small trees with flexible growth habits and an ability
to regenerate after hard pruning are ideal for this confined
environment. Purple aster (*Symphyotrichum oblongifolium*),
one of the last flowers of the year, is one of many native
species. Korean feather reed-grass (*Calamagrostis brachytricha*,
below) is one of several grass species used in mass plantings.

← ↓ Whereas the open areas are planted with a dense ground layer, woodland areas accurately mimic natural environments by having a very low, relatively sparse vegetation, with a lower level of diversity. By autumn, herbaceous growth in the open areas will be at a peak, with some species showing good colour, such as the yellow-leaved Arkansas blue star (*Amsonia hubrichtii*, below), an almost perfect plant for this environment, as it slowly forms dense clumps that become very stable over time.

Ludwigshafen am Rhein is a working city, but one with a network of parks and green spaces, many dating back to the early twentieth century, when the city grew as an industrial centre. Its parks and other city-owned planted areas have been rejuvenated with innovative new planting, thanks largely to the city's Head Gardener and Perennial Specialist, Harald Sauer. The Hauptfriedhof (Main Cemetery) is particularly striking. Drifts of perennials and grasses move in and out of trees and shrubs, showing off striking colour combinations over an area of 2,000 square metres (0.5 acres). The feeling is reminiscent of central European parks but with livelier and more confident planting. It does not involve any of the Mixed Planting systems (see p.103), with their tightly controlled, distinct mixes, as there is too much variation here and not enough repetition; there is, nevertheless, more reiteration than in traditional perennial plantings. One gets the impression that Sauer has noted Mixed Planting but decided to do his own thing.

Visitors to the cemetery are greeted by plantings dominated by drifts of fountaingrass (Pennisetum spp.), an ideal species for this purpose, as its fluffy plumes have a very long season (mid-summer to late winter), and it is high enough to make an impact but not so tall as to obscure other components. The planting of herbaceous perennials and grasses is dubbed 'Flow of Life', a phrase that focuses attention on the character of the herbaceous planting as symbolizing resurrection and eternal life.

There is definitely a sense of continual creative development here. In 2014, five years after the initial plantings, the construction of a new administrative centre for municipal green space operations near the entrance to the cemetery necessitated the redevelopment of some existing plantings and the creation of new areas. Another new area was created in 2018, enclosed by buildings, to be used as a relaxation area for staff. The new areas address some of the concerns expressed about the Mixed Planting concept, namely that if it becomes too successful, the opportunities for creative site-specific

planting design may become limited. In addition, there has been increased concern over the balance between perennials and woody plants.

Much twentieth-century planting design worked with a backbone of shrubs, often dominating plantings to the point of excluding herbaceous perennials altogether. The naturalistic planting movement can be seen partly as a reaction to this, but its foregrounding of perennials by many of the pioneer designers arguably sent the pendulum too far in the other direction. The integration of perennials and woody plants in the Ludwigshafen Main Cemetery borders is a good example of the balance that an increasing number of designers are now seeking to achieve.

Woody plants, with their year-round structure, are invaluable for

Hauptfriedhof Ludwigshafen

defining spaces and directing the eye; the reluctance of most contemporary perennial designers to include many, or any, can be seen as a failure, creating unnecessarily bleak open spaces from mid-winter, when the perennials are usually cut down, to early summer, when there are just about enough taller ones to break up vistas again. At the Hauptfriedhof Ludwigshafen, shrubs are deftly used, as Sauer says, 'to define garden rooms or spaces'. A dramatic example is some loosely-clipped yew (Taxus baccata) arranged in a roughly spiral pattern from the administration building into the surrounding perennial beds.

Clipping box or other shrubs into formal shapes has deep historic roots in the Western garden tradition, and their use here is something of a bold statement, as such traditional materials are usually eschewed by naturalistic designers. Needless to say, loose, unpruned shrubs are used here more extensively than clipped examples. More innovative is Sauer's

practice of coppicing, an adaptation of a traditional technique long used by rural communities for the production of rods used in fences and construction. Many woody plants, if cut down to the ground annually or every few years, produce straight stems with larger-than-normal foliage, and have an overall shape more compact and tidier than if left to grow untended. It is a useful garden technique for managing the sometimes wayward growth of certain woody species.

The presence of woody plants creates areas that, by obstructing vision at eye level, have the effect of concealment. Consequently, there is a greater sense of intimacy and detail than in many naturalistic gardens. Tall, but often quite open-structured perennials also feature; Sauer describes them as 'salt in the soup'. Some are grasses, like the giant feather grass (Stipa gigantea); others are less familiar, such as species of Silphium – 3-metre (10 ft) high prairie perennials with yellow daisy flowers. Their semi-transparency is invaluable for breaking up space and 'veiling' what is behind them.

The courtyard area between the administrative buildings is home to plants that balance the permanent structure of small trees and the relatively long-season perennials and grasses such as feather reedgrass (Calamagrostis 'Overdam') with more dynamic plants – short-lived species that self-seed and thus change their positions. The paths are gravel, so the separation between walking route and growing space is fluid, the gravel being a fruitful substrate for these species to sow into. The fluffy Mexican feather grass (Stipa tenuissima), the blue-flowered meadow sage (Salvia pratensis) and the very statuesque Miss Wilmott's ghost (Eryngium giganteum) are among a number of plants that will ensure this area never stays the same.

Re-establishing a balance between woody plants and perennials is part of the planting zeitgeist. Research indicates that wildlife, birds in particular, benefit from shrubs and trees, and that perennial-only plantings have limited biodiversity. More rounded and diverse plantings will please many – and not just people.

↑ Much contemporary naturalistic planting is self-consciously aiming at what has been dubbed 'enhanced nature'. However, the planting in the Main Cemetery in Ludwigshafen is more artistic, in the way selected plants are juxtaposed on strictly aesthetic grounds. There may be a lull in flowering in midsummer, but the range of foliage shapes and textures still ensures a range of interest. The visual appeal of some species, such as the very tall false hemp (*Datisca cannabina*, centre left), is primarily for these qualities.

← Pure white loosestrife (*Lythrum virgatum* 'White Swirl') creates an elegant light flush of flower during mid-summer, when much else has either already flowered or hasn't yet started.

Grasses such as Mexican feather grass (*Stipa tenuissima*, right) and rough feather grass (*S. calamagrostis*) provide continuity, as they have a long season, often maintaining their looks well into the winter. Their pale colours add to tonal depth, as do the dark forms of the clipped shapes of yew (*Taxus baccata*; bottom right). Plant heights here are carefully orchestrated: the bulk of the planting can be seen over, but views are always slightly impeded by occasional taller species, which encourages exploration. A key rule of garden design is that not everything should be visible at once.

Hauptfriedhof Ludwigshafen

Natives vs. Exotics

A debate of fundamental importance, and one that has caused a certain amount of rancour, is over the extent to which regionally native plants should be prioritized in naturalistic planting. This is a complex and many-faceted discussion, but two main issues stand out: the importance of natives for biodiversity and the dangers of alien invasive species. ¶ Natives are generally understood to be those species that are found in a particular region because they spread there naturally; those that arrived later, usually as a result of human settlement or transference, are described as non-native, or, to use the American-English parlance, exotics. These may have been deliberately introduced or may have arrived by accident, as seeds embedded in crates of other products shipped from one country to another, for instance. The introduction of turf-forming European pasture grasses to all temperate regions of the globe, as feed for livestock, has had a huge and often negative impact on grasslands and the wildlife that live in them, and a further impact are the fellow travellers: other non-grass species that came with them. Some of the latter have gone on to become very common wildflowers and may be relatively benign in terms of any negative ecological impact – an example includes the wild carrot, Queen Anne's lace (*Daucus carota*), which is now widespread across North America. ¶ The 'web of life' – that whole complex of interactions that gives us animal and plant diversity – is dependent on its lowest levels: the millions of usually unseen invertebrates (mostly insects) that chew their way through plants, supporting the more prominent (and popular) birds and mammals. Many of these invertebrates are specialists, only eating particular plant species; replace the plants they can eat with plants they cannot, including introduced species that did not co-evolve with them, and the web of life and biodiversity can become seriously impoverished. A minority of introduced species can spread aggressively, in the worse cases eliminating entire ecosystems. So it is not surprising that non-native, 'exotic' plant species may be viewed with suspicion. ¶ Other reasons for wanting to use only native plants often revolve around a desire to celebrate local diversity and regional distinctiveness. The global reach of certain species in particular climate zones has undoubtedly created a predictable sameness about many urban environments. Stylized versions of local habitats or prominence for iconic local species can help add a distinct stamp on localities wanting to define themselves. That said, the local flora may not visually have much to offer. People in urban areas, in particular, want public plantings that they see as attractive, distinct and somehow 'sophisticated'. Those that are not appreciated rapidly lose support and therefore funding. There are good political reasons for such pragmatism. ¶ Then why not blend the locally native with familiar and visually exciting outsiders? This is the obvious solution to the problem for many in the horticulture and landscape professions. Indeed, some plantings that seek a natural look but are not particularly habitat-focused do just this. However, those that are more genuinely ecologically functioning almost inevitably concentrate exclusively on native plants. Nevertheless, some practitioners, among them James Hitchmough (see pp.104–9) in England, stand out for their determination to change this state of affairs and integrate natives and non-natives to create ecologically functioning 'artificial' or 'novel' ecosystems. Hitchmough argues that 'ecological rules apply, whether or not species are locally native'. There is no doubt that many developments in the future will seek to integrate natives and exotics. ¶ The extent to which native plants support biodiversity varies greatly from one place to another; northern and central European invertebrates, for example, tend to be nutritional generalists, not that fussy about the species they eat, and it is no surprise that several academic studies about this region have shown that there is little necessity to focus on native species in order to support high levels of biodiversity. Rather, these studies point towards the necessity of not importing an argument from one region, let alone one continent, to another. ¶ The invasiveness issue can also vary enormously from place to place, but it would be wise to assume that climate change may enable certain currently benign species to step out of line. It is difficult to predict which species may become problematic, but a good guess is that anything that seeds profusely or spreads sideways through suckers or runners could become so. The fact is, though, that many regions have experienced the introduction of vast numbers of plant species, and it is rare for more than a tiny minority to become difficult. ¶ A final word of warning on alien invasives: the language used to refer to them, especially in the popular press, is very similar to that used to describe immigrants by nationalist politicians. It behoves us all to be very careful how we discuss these issues.

Broad paths curve around through very tall perennials, many of them in flower and many above head height. By mid-summer there is a lot of colour, with butterflies part of the spectacle. The paths are angled so that it is never possible to see too far ahead, an effect that naturalistic planting, with its rejection of straight lines, is good at achieving, making us feel we are somewhere wilder than we really are. Trees mark the edges of this perennial garden, and there is a central pond with a gravel beach, but the focus is the exuberance of the planting.

The Children's Garden at Fort William Park was built by Mitchell & Associates landscape architects in an attempt to introduce children to nature, out of doors and away from their screens. The planting was carried out by local garden designer James McCain, who describes his work as 'bookended by Piet Oudolf and Larry Weaner' (see pp.20–7, 290–7); indeed, it is looser and less controlled than the former, and more precise and managed than the latter. Paths wind and weave, taking children into places where, for much of the summer and autumn, the plants are taller than they are – in some cases, taller than the adult visitors.

The 6,000-square metre (1.5 acre) garden uses predominantly North American native plants, most of which are species of open prairie habitats. A fine example of a type of landscape planting becoming popular in the US Midwest and northeast, it is not really a prairie, having been planted and not sown. The plants do not have the dense network of ecological relationships with their fellows as do prairie plantings created with seed mixes (see pp.258–63 and 290–7). On the other hand, the plants are exactly where the designer intended them to be. It could be called a 'cultivated prairie', with those attributes of the habitat that human users want. Insect consumers are well pleased too, for the diversity of species and nectar sources here are vast.

McCain is one of a younger generation of designers which was inspired by the work of Piet Oudolf, as well as by the American firm Oehme van Sweden Associates, whose approach to planting design caused something of a revolution in the 1970s. Planting had by this time, at least in the Midwest and on the East Coast, reached a nadir of boring, formulaic, almost sterile landscapes of endless mown grass and stiff blocks of evergreen shrubs. The partnership formed by Wolfgang Oehme and James van Sweden used large blocks of perennials and grasses to create dramatic, yet soft and romantic compositions. Crucially, they enabled and inspired a younger generation to work with perennials and native plants, and stimulated vast innovation within the nursery industry.

McCain grew up in the Midwest and remembers his family as avid gardeners; his mother grew some prairie natives in the 1970s, when this would have been relatively radical. 'She grew them with

Fort William Park

Children's Garden

cottage garden flowers, and planted very densely', he recalls. Another key influence has been *The American Woodland Garden* (2002) by American landscape designer Rick Darke, arguably one of the most influential books in the field over the last two decades. In it, Darke combines the analytic, ecological and aesthetic in a unique way of looking at the potential of woodland as a landscape element.

'I go for a tapestry effect in all my plantings, with a lot of repetition', says McCain. 'I put larger groups of plants at the entrance [to the Children's Garden], to make it easier for visitors to read, including *Agastache foeniculum* [anise hyssop], with its distinctive lavender spikes, and *Baptisia australis* [blue false indigo], a burly, almost shrub-like perennial. There is one area where you can see across a longer distance, so I repeated those plants there to tie it all together.

… In the central area I used more block plantings, for example *Echinacea purpurea* [purple coneflower], with its daisy-like flowers, and *Monarda fistulosa* [bee balm], a pink-mauve plant that is a very good pollinator, and I made a very large group of *Helianthus* 'Lemon Queen', the yellow flowers of which would be very visible from a distance.' Beyond this the garden gets somewhat wilder, 'so it is possible to feel a little lost among big grasses such as *Panicum virgatum* [switch grass] and *Sorghastrum nutans* [Indiangrass], and some tall asters'. Variation across the site is also generated by responses to microclimates created by gradient or other changes; for example, a common regional wildflower, white wood aster (*Eurybia divaricata*) was planted where trees have an impact on light levels.

McCain accepts that a weakness of the planting is the shortage of earlier flowering plants. 'It kicks off in June', he notes, adding that 'in clients' gardens I use a lot of Eurasian early-flowering species along with natives.' Europe has a rich meadow flora which, in contrast to the North American prairie flora, has largely finished flowering by late July. The plant palette in the Children's Garden is overwhelmingly native North American, and its appearance reflects the strong preponderance of late-flowering species for open, sunny situations. In the northeastern United States, the huge diversity of late-flowering species for open habitats reflects the climate and the central role of grasslands in the centre of the continent; additionally, these plants are easy, quick and cheap to propagate, and so have rapidly become commercially available. Spring-flowering species, however, are mostly woodlanders and very often slow-growing, difficult to propagate and not produced in large enough quantities for this kind of project.

Perennial plantings inspired by prairie grasslands are becoming part of public and private horticulture in the USA. More integration with non-natives may bridge seasonal gaps or fulfil particular aesthetic considerations, but given the range of species, there many reasons to rely on natives for the foundations.

↑ ↓ ← 'Classic' prairie plants tend to flower late, from July to September. Many are members of the daisy family – fast-growing, vigorous and often seeding strongly. Typically, these are plants of early succession environments, the ones that quickly grow back if land is cleared. In nature, they would be displaced by grasses over several years; good management and a reduction in the number of grasses is needed to keep this kind of display going long-term. The exception is where shade reduces grass vigour. In these areas (below, and p.149 top left), species such as white wood aster (*Eurybia divaricata*) can form long-lived colonies.

↑↓ Concentrated floral impact provides a good public spectacle, and biodiversity is well-served, as many of these are very good pollinator species. The tall plant with impressive seed heads (above right and p.148 top) is Carolina lupin (*Thermopsis villosa*), one of several earlier-flowering species with foliage and seed heads that ensure a longer season of interest. The paths that wend through the planting are broad, ensuring that during wet weather, when this kind of vegetation tends to flop over, visitors do not get wet. It also reduces the anxiety that some people feel on narrow paths in public places; as many prairie species are tall (often shoulder height or more), the relationship between plant size and path dimensions are crucial design decisions.

↓ → Canada goldenrod (*Solidago canadensis*) has a bad name for aggressive spreading, but there are many goldenrods that do not misbehave, and public projects such as this show what can be used. *S. rugosa* (below, centre), known as rough goldenrod, is a genteel clump-former that can be used in small gardens; grey goldenrod (*S. nemoralis*) also appears here. Purple coneflower (*Echinacea purpurea*; bottom) has become something of a poster boy for the native plant movement. It is, however, relatively short-lived and needs to be allowed to self-seed if it is to persist.

→ An aerial view makes plain that many of the plants here are growing as distinct clumps, which is typical of many horticultural situations, but not necessarily of the wild. For many visitors, this makes these plantings easier to read and appreciate.

Fort William Park

It is easy to think of the Hermannshof botanical gardens in Weinheim, in Germany's southern wine region, as a very nice public park, comprising 1.8 hectares (4.5 acres) on the edge of the centre of town, with lawns, borders and mature trees around a nineteenth-century villa. But even the most casual visitor will soon notice that there is a lot going on in these borders, and a gardener will find much to look at, from unfamiliar plants to striking plant combinations. There are colourful annual and perennial plantings at one end, but the style elsewhere is much more naturalistic, with different plant groupings in an assortment of habitats: various levels of shade, a moist area around a pond, and dry, stony areas.

These dry areas are some of the most colourful spaces here, at least in early summer, when the often wispy, grassy prospect is dominated by yellow or purple flowers. Some of these are modelled on the natural dry habitats of central Europe and tend to have a relatively short season, looking very dry from mid-summer onwards. Others are less naturalistic, focusing on ornamental plants that often have attractive seed heads or include species that flower later in the summer. One of these is the Yarrow and Sage Bed, where a yellow and blue-purple colour combination looks radiant in early to mid-summer. Several varieties and hybrids of Balkan clary (*Salvia nemorosa*), a common dry-situation wildflower with blossoms in various shades of purple, dominate. The spikes of this plant contrast with the flatter shapes of the yellow-flowered yarrow 'Cloth of Gold' (*Achillea filipendulina*), creating a powerful contrast. In summer, the garden's main interest lies in the perennials in open, sunny conditions; these become even more colourful as the autumn advances, with flowers in colours from yellow to rusty-orange. The predominance of these shades is partly a reflection of the number of daisy (*Asteraceae*) species, many of North American origin; they tend to be good for pollinators late in the season, which gives them biodiversity value. Winter interest is maintained through their seed heads and those of the many species of grasses.

Combination is key here. The German tradition in planting design is very distinct, and Schau- und Sichtungsgarten Hermannshof is a good place to appreciate it. Whereas much planting design history has been primarily concerned with putting plants together as individuals, the approach here has always been to think about plant communities. It is an approach that lends itself to the naturalistic, and to creative ways of looking at the eternal question of management. The words *Schau- und Sichtungsgarten* – literally, 'show and viewing garden' – imply that this is a place for trialling plants and ways of using them. In many countries, education was historically often part of the function of public parks, but here in Germany, with continual development still very much part of a sophisticated approach to

Schau- und Sichtungsgarten Hermannshof

planting design, this function of public planting remains an important one.

There has been a garden on this site since the eighteenth century, with designs created in the 1880s and 1920s for the Freudenberg family – local industrialists who still own it and continue to fund it in collaboration with the town council. In 1983 it was opened as a trial garden designed by Hans Luz, to show the principles of planting design that had been developed by Professor Richard Hansen, who created similar gardens in the more severe climate of Bavaria; the first director, Urs Walser, wanted to develop a stronger aesthetic. The planting was based on the concept of creating communities, mostly perennials, each of which would function as an ecosystem, naturalistic in appearance and with a long period of interest. A wide range of habitats, or 'biotopes' would be included, from pondside to stony and dry.

In the years since the appointment of Cassian Schmidt as director in 1998, the garden has become the jewel in the crown of Germany's very sophisticated approach to planting design. A lawn was replaced with prairie-style planting, divided into a series of micro-habitats that reflect the enormous diversity of prairie conditions. More recently, Schmidt has made an area of what he calls 'monsoon forest', inspired by habitats in southwest China, northern Japan and the Russian far east, where long, cold winters are followed by brief, relatively warm and wet summers. Plant growth is intense, and perennial species grow tall and expansive, with large leaves and, in some cases, a strong tendency to spread. 'There is an almost sub-tropical appearance', Schmidt says, with 'herbaceous aralias, Japanese anemones [*Anemone* x *hybrida*], hostas, different woodland plants, but all hardy'. These tend to be taller and bulkier than the other woodland or woodland edge plants. Flowering is often relatively late, in contrast to most shaded situations, where flowering is in spring or early summer. There is a ground layer of sedges and Japanese forest grass (*Hakonechloa macra*), which tolerates some shade; its arching stems with relatively broad leaf blades always look somehow combed and tidy, and it is much valued by garden designers. The concept of the Monsoon Border planting serves to inform us of these plants' origins and native climates, and to flag up that the familiar can be combined with the unfamiliar and given new life. The area also emphasizes the importance of long-season foliage, as opposed to a reliance on flowers.

There is a 'popular' side to Hermannshof, with colourful, high-maintenance plantings, including massed tulips in spring, some vibrant annual plantings and spectacular late-flowering borders. The bulk of the garden, however, is more naturalistic plantings that work ecologically, lasting for many years without major interventions and with reasonably good co-existence between the component species. The aesthetic is wilder, and the focus is on plant survival and co-existence rather than

visual characteristics. An exception is the small number of Mixed Plantings, which, because they involve, typically, only around fifteen species, can be designed much more precisely.

The Mixed Planting system has been a big idea in German horticulture since 2004 (see p.103). This is essentially a modular system designed to make it easier (and cheaper) for landscape architects and other large-scale specifiers to install high-quality perennial plantings. The Mixed Planting concept was launched with a perennial mix for dry, calcareous soils called 'Silversummer', based on the Yarrow and Sage Bed here. Hermannshof, along with several technical universities and other publicly-funded institutions have combined with an independent research circle that brings together academics with practitioners, to design around forty-five mixes, each tested for at least five years, with co-funding from the German Perennial Nursery Federation (BdS). The concept has been taken up by some commercial nurseries selling their own (much less vigorously tested) mixes. The colour theme and growth height of each mix is an important aspect of both their development and their marketing.

Walking around the different planting habitats at Hermannshof, it soon becomes clear that there are real differences in the look of the various plantings. The idea of the gradient or spectrum is a good way of understanding naturalistic planting. Perhaps the most obvious gradient here is between the most cultivated areas and the wildest ones: the bright, flowery plantings near the entrance as opposed to the grasses in the steppe area, the former needing far more maintenance than the latter. Dry-to-moist is another gradient, as is the gradient is between sun and shade – and with the legacy of nineteenth-century tree planting here, there is a lot of shade. Many shade plants have wide leaves, positioned horizontally so that they intercept the maximum amount of light. In open, light habitats, on the other hand, plants compete for space, grow quickly and are tightly packed. Once these habitats are past peak flowering, they can look very ragged and disordered. In shade, however, growth is slower, and plants are more separate from each other, many spreading at the base to form extensive patches. To the human eye, the results are simpler and more graphic, easier to read. While there has been some replanting in some of the areas of shade planting at Hermannshof, what we see is the result of many years' growth. The ecologically-minded gardener will be fascinated by the different ways in which the plants grow, in particular those that naturally form colonies or patches – and where they meet, who is winning? Others may be fascinated by the contrasting forms, textures and colours of different foliage types, the resemblance of the interlocking patches of plants to quilting or abstract art. Shade plants tend to be low-growing, with the taller ones standing out; the contrast between them and their lower companions make for a clear and graphic expression, especially if they too have attractive flowers, as with several lily (*Lilium*) species. Leaves are often simple in shape and quite broad. Plants with different shapes or proportions stand out: some grass-like sedges, for example, have tight clumps of linear leaves, while ferns, with their dense, finely-divided fronds, are markedly different.

Beneath the obvious beauty of Hermannshof, there is a serious sense of purpose. Schmidt uses the extensive range of plants here to develop simplified plant mixes, and he is, as well, Professor of Planting Design at nearby Geisenheim University. The seven staff in the garden log maintenance times and task details, so by the end of the year he can tell how many staff hours per square metre each one of the plantings has taken. Hermannshof is thus a rare example of scientific attention to detail applied to planting design, in this case one that succeeds in being both naturalistic and controlled.

Boehmeria japonica grows with several species of fairy bells (*Disporum*) and northern maidenhair fern (*Adiantum pedatum* 'Maryland', below). The taller *Chrysopogon gryllus* makes an impact alongside a wide range of flowering perennials (pp.156–7).

← Very slender feather grass (*Stipa capillata*, p.154 top), with long awns (bristles) attached to the seed, is an iconic species in steppe habitats. *Carex* 'Kyoto' (p.154 bottom) and white wood aster (*Eurybia divaricata*) thrive in late summer in the East Asia Glade, with red bistort (*Persicaria amplexicaulis*) varieties at the rear.

← ↑ Yellow yarrow (*Achillea filipendulina*) front
silver-white clary sage (*Salvia sclarea* var.
turkestanica, p.158); the deep crimson heads are
Macedonian scabious (*Knautia macedonica*). Above,
yellow dyer's chamomile (*Anthemis tinctoria*),
purple rose campion (*Lychnis coronaria*) and white
Oenothera lindheimeri border a path. Seed heads of
Allium amethystinum 'Forelock' and grass *Melica
transsylvanica* are dramatically highlighted (left).

→ In the East Asia Glade, *Hydrangea paniculata*
'Early Sensation' joins red bistort (*Persicaria
amplexicaulis* 'Dikke Floskes'), pink bistort
(*P.* 'Fine Pink') and *Anemone hupehensis* 'Alba'.
The grass *Hakonechloa macra* 'All Gold' is a ground-
covering matrix along the edges of the planting.

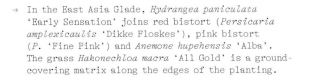

Spectacular flowering plantings are not what you might expect to see in an industrial environment, but during the summer months that is what the employees of ABB, an energy and automation technology company, see every day at the company's site in Mannheim, in Germany's Rhine valley. The buildings are modern steel and glass structures with a limited amount of space between them, the overall atmosphere functional and purposeful. A number of beds, clearly leftover spaces between buildings and roads or walkways, have been planted with startlingly bright and wild vegetation, and the contrast with the buildings could not be greater. Perennials flourish in the car park, too, but the largest area of planting is in front of a terrace outside the works canteen. A very ordinary industrial environment has been transformed by 2,000 square metres (0.5 acres) of plantings.

The planting was designed by Bettina Jaugstetter and illustrates a twist to the German Mixed Planting style (see p.103), which typically relies on formulas developed by research institutions and academics that are repeated throughout the space; this is an example of a site-specific planting formula. Inevitably, as more designers and horticulturists appreciate the example of randomized mixed plantings, there will be more places like this, where a plant mix will be designed to be unique to that site. The concept potentially offers a great many opportunities for the expression of artistic creativity by practitioners who have the plant knowledge to put successful combinations together.

Jaugstetter has been an early adopter of this method, working mostly for private garden clients. The commission from ABB, however, was for a series of planting modules 'that could be applied at their sites all over Germany … they wanted predictable maintenance.' The company wanted to project a

positive image of sustainable resource management and ecological awareness, as well as create a good working environment for its employees.

Jaugstetter has designed seven different planting mixes, each one typically comprising several species of structure plants, companion plants, two or three groundcover plants and some bulbs. Plants go in (mostly) out of 9-centimetre (3.5 in) pots, randomized at equal spacing, the method used for most German Mixed Planting systems. The bottom line here was that the plants had to be reliable and low maintenance, and combinations should look as good as possible for as long as possible; beyond this, Jaugstetter

ABB Factory

made selections based on visual criteria. Unusual for planting in industrial or commercial situations, where planting that differs little from one month to another is the norm, the company was happy to embrace seasonal change. The result was a change in the atmosphere at the facility, 'to feel like somewhere with a more residential character'.

The different plant combination modules were developed for various levels of visual impact; entrances had to have the strongest effect and be the most predictable, while other areas, such as car parking areas, streets, paths and temporarily empty areas could be what Jaugstetter describes as 'more dynamic and wilder'. To achieve consistency, certain 'lead plants' were used to create visual links between one area and another: feather reed grass (*Calamagrostis* x *acutiflora* 'Karl Foerster'), the vertical grass much loved by many designers; *Salvia nemorosa* 'Caradonna', a form of a tough, drought-tolerant relative of sage; and species

and cultivars of coneflowers (*Echinacea*), whose large daisy flowers have the advantage of being prominent against more diffuse and wispy elements and are produced over a long summer season. At a lower level, certain plants were repeated across several mixes to create continuity. Although the planting is essentially random, certain species with particularly distinctive characters have been planted at a regular intervals: the *Calamagrostis* cultivar just mentioned, red hot pokers (*Kniphofia uvaria*, with distinctive columnar spikes of orange flowers), the tussock-forming grass Atlas fescue (*Festuca mairei*) and the very upright Russian sage (*Perovskia abrotanoides* 'Blue Spire').

A minor but still important role is played by a number of short-lived plants that were included to create interest in the first two years; with their demise, longer-lived but slower-growing neighbours have expanded to take their places. Regarding the short-lived plants, Jaugstetter points out that 'these vagabonds are able to fill any gaps that develop because they seed, so they are a very important part of the self-regulated system – blanket flower [*Gaillardia aristata*], for example, in the red-themed mix'. Short-lived, self-seeding species play an important visual role in a great many naturalistic plantings, because they add a sense of spontaneity; most do not present other species with serious competition, although in some circumstances their seedlings will need 'editing' with the gardener's hoe.

Conventional planting design has focused a great deal on achieving striking colour combinations, often at the cost of combining plants with different cultural needs and therefore not necessarily stable together. Naturalistic design, on the other hand, has tended to focus so much on ecological compatibility and reducing maintenance

that sometimes these aesthetic considerations have been ignored. Not here,
however – partly because the number
of species in the modules is generally
lower than in the normal mixed planting
combinations, so Jaugstetter has been
able to develop a tighter control over
colour. One module is blue and pink,
another – used on the route to the
canteen – is yellow-orange, while the
view from the canteen terrace is red,
silver and white.

One advantage of the German
Mixed Planting system is that it is very
flexible: a core mix can be added to with

more maintenance-demanding plants
if there is funding for their management;
certain species can be added to provide
particular visual effects; or, alternatively,
species can be deducted if more challenging environmental conditions or
reduced management are expected.
Jaugstetter meets twice a year with the
company's maintenance team; she is
pleased that 'the same staff come every
year, so there is continuity. That's very
important.' Her visits enable her to do
some training, a large part of which
consists of 'seedling recognition, as
replacement of certain species through

continuous seeding is important, for
example with *Echinacea* species'.

The ABB planting is a wonderful
example of what can be achieved with
randomized planting systems in an
environment in which commercial and
functional considerations are paramount.
The system appears to offer both the
advantages of something modular,
which can be repeated, with all the cost
advantages of this, but also enough
flexibility to allow small changes to be
made according to circumstances. For
ABB staff, the impact on their working
lives can only be positive.

↑↓ The flowers of the yellow coneflower (*Echinacea paradoxa*) hover above other planting. Appropriate height is vital in situations like this, where space is tight. Echinacea foliage is relatively low, and yet its ability to project flowers above the leaf canopy is fully taken advantage of here. Scarlet sneezeweed (*Helenium* 'Rubinzwerg'), seen here with *Allium* 'Mount Everest', is an early summer-flowering plant with seed heads that remain attractive for the rest of the season. Grasses form a large part of the biomass here, ensuring a vegetation canopy at the appropriate level.

← ↑ ↓ Low planting ensures good visibility, but
it can also appear to be continuous, even
though it is composed of discontinuous
blocks. Effective use is made of grasses
such as moor grass (*Sesleria autumnalis*),
which fill space at a low level and act as
a foreground for slightly taller flowering
perennials; their ability to project flowers
above this level creates an attractive
meadowy appearance. The lavender purple
flowers of catmint (*Nepeta* x *faassenii*
'Walker's Low') is a feature here. Nepetas
are very useful for situations like this:
their low stature and slightly sprawling
habit makes them traditional favourites
for path-side locations.

ABB Factory

Drifts of flowering perennial combinations stretch out in surroundings defined by an enclosing wall of pine trees, beyond which are the hills of Hokkaido. Japan's vast northernmost island offers a sense of space and wildness often lacking in this densely populated country: wide agricultural landscapes, mountains, extensive forests. With a climate borrowed from eastern Siberia, the growing season is short and winter long; pleasant summer temperatures and the sheer abundance of space, however, mean that it is increasingly becoming a holiday destination. This is the background for a remarkable and visionary conception with, at its core, an important new garden designed by Dan Pearson. The Meadow Garden is the centrepiece of a landscape project that aims to open itself to visitors, the 97-hectare (240 acre) Tokachi Millennium Forest.

The owner of a local newspaper, Mitsushige Hayashi, bought 400 hectares (988 acres) of land here in 1992. The hillsides were severely deforested, and where there was forest, the ground was choked with *Sasa*, a dwarf-growing but aggressive broad-leaved bamboo species. Hayashi's aim was reforestation (part of making his business carbon neutral) and the restoration of natural ecosystems. He has been very successful in this, but he has had to work hard to entice visitors. Japan is a very urban country, and many people have very little experience of countryside or nature. Hayashi saw a garden as a halfway house, providing a stepping-stone between the familiar and the unfamiliar. A traditional Japanese garden, with its stylized representation of nature, would not be wild enough to serve as a transition. Something more naturalistic, expansive and spontaneous was needed. First he turned to Fumiaki Takano, a local landscape designer,

to plan the project; for more detail, he consulted British designer Dan Pearson.

Pearson was asked to create a space that would be colourful and ordered enough to be instantly recognized as a garden, albeit a Western-style one, but wild enough to get visitors used to the idea that they could go further and explore surroundings filled with landforms (also designed by Pearson), sculptures and installations, or even follow the paths into the forest.

Tokachi Millennium Forest

The Meadow Garden

The Meadow Garden, which covers 1.5 hectares (3.7 acres), is designed as the centrepiece of the Millennium Forest's welcome to visitors. Here, Pearson has developed his own technique for intermingling perennial varieties. Working on the wider landscape over a number of years, Pearson began to appreciate the wild plants in the surrounding woodland. 'I was able to see it at different seasons, with a whole succession of species through the summer.' This led to him becoming 'very interested in creating a layered planting, based on having one thing overtaking the previous, and the picture you were creating as being something that changed from week to

week.' This would, he thought, 'make a connection for the visiting public with the way things work in the wild. ... There is a lot of interest in Western gardens in Japan', he says, 'and Hokkaido, with its cooler climate, is an opportunity to grow perennials that do not flourish on the mainland ... Combining their native flora and garden plants in this naturalistic way should help people appreciate wild plants more.'

Wide paths stretch through the plantings in the meadow garden, encouraging exploration of eighteen different mixes. 'The paths', says Pearson, 'are designed to have the same mix on each side, to get a sense of walking through. ... Some mixes have an additional component added to get a sense of one panel segueing into another.' Each mix started with around six plant species and covers several tens of metres; more are being added as time goes on. Contrasts are highlighted: between flower colours, between flowers and leaves, and between different colours and forms of foliage. Each mix has a distinct character: one, dominated by low-growing tickseed (*Coreopsis verticillata*), with its yellow daisy flowers, and the grey foliage of false indigo (*Baptisia australis*), comes across as contrasting gold and silver, while another, with pink *Astilbe chinensis* var. *taquetii* 'Superba' and dark red forms of great masterwort (*Astrantia major*), reads quite differently, bright but harmonious. The transitions are intentionally seamless, with bolder shifts in colour or character separated by 'hedges' of tall feather reed-grass (*Calamagrostis* x *acutiflora* 'Karl Foerster').

Each mix includes 'emergents', which stand above the other species, such as baneberry (*Actaea* spp.), with their tall, spire-like flower heads, or giant scabious (*Cephalaria gigantea*), with its numerous

flower heads that dance well above the rest of the combination; 'space-fillers', plants for bulk and lower-level foliage; low-level 'procumbents'; and 'treats' – eye-catching splashes of unexpected colour or form such as peonies (*Paeonia* spp.), with their large, showy flowers.

Using his knowledge of how plants grow, Pearson worked out a series of percentages appropriate to the plant form – 'emergents would be a low percentage, space-fillers higher' – then designed a modular strip, the repetition of which would be used to fill the planting area for that mix. 'It is', he says, 'creating a formula that would be understandable in another language.'

Pearson describes the repeating combination module in each mix as being 'like a strand of DNA ... We have designed a system in which the combination within the mix is never repeated the same way twice, so that it is random ... The idea is that the mixes will develop their own balance and rhythms.' A computer programme is used to generate a pattern using random numbers, based on repeating the modules. The result is rather like woven *ikat* textiles, in which patterns build up naturally rather than as a result of conscious design.

Once established, plants in the mixes will begin to compete, just as they do in nature. 'I wanted something which would have its own life, be something which is a manipulated environment, rather than a controlled one ... there was an element of risk I wanted to take.' It is the responsibility of Head Gardener Midori Shintani to manage the risk. 'Midori has been absolutely crucial', says Pearson. 'It would not have worked without her ... She uses the plans as a template, and then makes adjustments. Inevitably, some species have not done so well, and others spread at their neighbours' expense.' It is Shintani who has to decide whether to replace failures or try new plants, and whether to weed out over-enthusiastic growth, while Pearson offers guidance and makes his own suggestions on annual visits to the garden.

Tokachi's Meadow Garden is a unique and very successful experiment in large-scale planting design that offers much of the softness of naturalistic planting. With the relative simplicity of its mixes, the design produces clearer contrasts and more depth of interest than many other nature-inspired styles.

→ Each of the individual mixes of plants created for the Meadow Garden has its own character. Mix L includes (top to bottom) *Nepeta transcaucasica* 'Blue Infinity', lamb's ear (*Stachys byzantina*) and bloody cranesbill (*Geranium sanguineum*). Elsewhere (pp.168–9) bands of feather reed-grass (*Calamagrostis* x *acutiflora* 'Karl Foerster'), recalling reeds or other wild grasses, are used between drifts of mixed perennials, especially to provide autumn and winter interest.

← ↓ Occasional clumps of *Rodgersia podophylla* bring distinct accents to the Mix A combination of plants, along with *Euphorbia griffithii* 'Fireglow' (left). White Bowman's root (*Gillenia trifoliata*) and blue false indigo (*Baptisia australis*) mark the border between two separate mixes (below). The purple foliage is that of *Rosa glauca*, a popular plant for mixing with perennials because of its foliage colour and appropriate size.

166

Each mix incorporates 'emergents' that rise higher than the surrounding species; here, for example, the flower heads of common valerian (*Valeriana officinalis*) hover above shorter planting. Over time, this species moves around within a planting, adding to the effect of spontaneity. A boardwalk arcs its way through the Meadow Garden, enabling the perennial mixes to be seen from a variety of different angles.

Among the last flowers of the early Hokkaido autumn, smooth violet prairie aster (*Symphyotrichum turbinellum*) lines the boardwalk, with the seed heads of *Astilbe chinensis* var. *tacquetii* 'Superba'.

(Overleaf) Sparkling in the mist, white Bowman's root (*Gillenia trifoliata*) mixes with purple *Salvia nemorosa* 'Caradonna'; the two species flower together here but might not in climates with a longer growing season. In the background is an ivory band of the locally native Kamtchatka goat's beard (*Aruncus dioicus* var. *kamtschaticus*).

Trentham is a vast, almost overwhelming country house landscape, which after a chequered history (the house was demolished in 1912, and a motor sport race track was cut through the formal Italian Garden in the 1970s) has been reborn as a privately run public park. Dominated by a lake that is nearly two kilometres (more than a mile) long, it is now a commercial 'visitor destination', but one accompanied by some of the most ambitious in scale and generous in spirit of any new planting design in Britain. The much-abused Italian Garden was restored and replanted by designer Tom Stuart-Smith in 2004, using perennials rather than the annuals that would originally have filled it, and a Piet Oudolf perennial garden was installed soon after. Pride of place, however, belongs to the perennial plantings by Nigel Dunnett (see also pp.224–31), who was commissioned here as a result of the work that he and James Hitchmough (pp.104–9) carried out for the 2012 Olympic Park in London.

The visitor is greeted by colourful swathes of meadow-style planting at the lakeside; indeed, all the new planting here is within sight of the lake, introduced along some 3 kilometres (1.9 miles) of paths within a 120-hectare (297 acre) landscape. Originally laid out by Lancelot 'Capability' Brown, the greatest English landscape designer of the eighteenth century, the surroundings are still recognizably a legacy of that period. Restoration of the woodland, which reaches down to the waterline around much of the lake, by the removal of commercial forestry planting and naturalized rhododendrons, has brought back enough to make any eighteenth-century landowner happy.

The new plantings by Nigel Dunnett are another layer of garden history superimposed on this older landscape.

Low-level and multicoloured, the perennials echo what the nineteenth-century Victorians did to many of these earlier landscapes, with the installation of exuberant displays of formal bedding. But whereas the rigidity of those highly intensive plantings must have been somewhat jarring against the deliberate pseudo-naturalism of the Brownian landscape, the modern perennial mixes are a complete fit (even with their flower colours), owing to their absence of straight lines or rigid divisions between groups of plants and the designer's conscious attempt to produce a stylized version of a natural environment.

Trentham Gardens

Lakeside and Woodland

The meadow areas feature a mix of relatively familiar colourful border perennials with various grasses. One successful area uses the native tufted hair grass (*Deschampsia cespitosa*), the soft, fawn-yellow flower and seed head tones of which act as a buffer between stronger colours. There is enough grass to make the onlooker think 'meadow', although an ecologist would know immediately that there is nothing like the density of grass matrix to make this a real meadow. A high proportion of the species used are relatively short-lived, and their self-sowing will be an important part of the survival and development of the planting.

Whereas the German Mixed Planting systems (see pp.103, 160–3) that lie behind this planting approach nearly always randomize, Dunnett uses a 3+1 system, whereby plants are grouped in threes, with a single individual placed nearby. The groups of three are, however, random. He argues that this gives a little more structure to the mix, while still keeping a very naturalistic look; it also enhances the chances of survival of slower-growing species and provides more opportunities for different competition outcomes.

There is a real vibrancy to these meadow areas, with some strong colours in the deep scarlet of Maltese cross (*Lychnis chalcedonica*), the golden yellow of yarrow 'Cloth of Gold' (*Achillea filipendulina*), and the purples of wild sage (*Salvia nemorosa*) varieties. In many cases this is enhanced by contrasting shapes, which for these three perennials are rounded heads of cross-shaped flowers, flattened umbels and clumps of narrow spikes, respectively.

On the other side of the lake, in an area called Burke's Wood, there are very extensive areas of woodland planting. The scale of these is particularly impressive, as the use of shade-tolerant perennials is almost never seen beyond areas of a few tens of square metres, fitting in among shrubs or between paths and woody plants, rather than in expanses of this scale. The very pale pink or creamy-white flowers of varieties of foam flower (*Tiarella* 'Spring Symphony') are scattered among yellow-green cushion spurge (*Euphorbia polychroma*), the bronze young foliage of several barrenwort (*Epimedium*) species, the silvery leaves of Siberian bugloss (*Brunnera macrophylla* 'Jack Frost') and, later, blue *Phlox divaricata*. Compared to the meadow areas, 'plants are distributed in more solid, bigger groups', says Dunnett. 'They are still randomized, but the intention is

to be more rhythmical.' This reflects the fact that woodland plants often naturally grow in distinct clumps, whereas in grass-dominated habitats such as meadows, they almost never do.

Dunnett has always been colour-conscious in his planting design, more perhaps than some others in this field. 'In May we have a mix of blue phloxes and white tiarellas, and then in late summer and early autumn asters in blue and white again', the asters being *Symphyotrichum cordifolium*, *Eurybia* x *herveyi* and *E. divaricata*. All these are North American woodland or woodland edge species, a reflection of the much greater diversity of that continent's woodland flora

compared to Europe's. Even though this is a relatively young planting, it is interesting and encouraging to see quite a lot of shoots of the sensitive fern (*Onoclea sensibilis*) scattered between other plants. This is a plant with a strong running habit, which is very useful for creating the sensation of this being a genuinely wild environment. Such plants have tended to be feared by traditional gardeners because they were seen as spreading aggressively, whereas the majority are engaged in a risk management strategy of sending growth into a range of possible future growing locations, rather than being set on world domination.

Some woodland plants have a reputation for being very slow to grow. Inevitably, on this scale, there are none of these here. 'We had to go with easy to propagate plants', says Dunnett. 'The plants were contract-grown, and what is interesting is to see that the nurseries are now offering these plants on their normal lists, so it's like we've started a trend.' He adds that 'it's good to use plants in public places with which people already have some familiarity'. Trentham, with its high visitor footfall, may well play the role that large-scale park projects have in Germany, in promoting naturalistic planting to a wider public – especially a non-gardening public – in Britain.

↑→ An exuberant mix of
grasses and perennials
runs alongside the lake
and up to the park's
nineteenth-century trees.
Historically, all this would
have been maintained as mown
grass. The scarlet (above)
is Maltese cross (*Lychnis
chalcedonica*), a useful
perennial for naturalistic
planting, as it regenerates
rapidly after being cut back
and often self-seeds. The
fact that it is not clump-
forming means that its
strong colour never becomes
too concentrated, and
instead can be distributed
widely to create splashes
of red. The crimson of
Macedonian scabious
(*Knautia macedonica*, right)
creates a similar impact,
with scattered dots of
intense colour.

Form and structure are as important as colour in the visual spectacle, although they often tend to be appreciated subconsciously. The umbels of the yellow yarrow (*Achillea filipendulina*, right) are highly effective when repeated across space. The purple-flowered *Verbena bonariensis* behind it is a stemy, insubstantial plant, which means it integrates well with others and has a see-through quality. Dark purple sage (*Salvia nemorosa*, below) is a robust, drought-tolerant perennial, with tight clumps of foliage that make it invaluable for lower-level plantings.

→ (Overleaf) Scarlet *Lychnis chalcedonica* and deep purple *Salvia nemorosa* with yellow *Achillea filipendulina* make for a striking summer colour combination in the lakeside planting. More subtle colour combinations appear on the edge of a woodland area: blue Siberian iris (*Iris sibirica*) with white sweet rocket (*Hesperis matronalis*) and pink common bistort (*Persicaria bistorta*).

Trentham Gardens

↑↓ Woodland flora is generally low-level, and the visual impact
    is often of a uniform layer of vegetation and clear sight
    lines through the trees. The white-flowered woodruff (*Asperula
    odorata*, above) is a modest creeping plant that flowers in
    early summer, while ferns (several species of *Dryopteris*,
    below) will flourish if soil is not too dried out by tree roots.

← ↑ ↓ Where there is more light, there is scope for more vigorous plants such as red bistort (*Persicaria bistorta* 'Superba', above), a common north European wildflower of meadows and woodland edges. Cultivars of several low-growing species of phlox (e.g. *Phlox stolonifera*) and foam flowers (*Tiarella*, below) grow here; like many woodland plants, they will form extensive clumps with time. A visual drawback of shade planting is that flowering is restricted to spring and early summer; hence the importance of varieties of *Brunnera* and lungwort (*Pulmonaria*, left), with their attractive silver foliage.

Perennials in city squares, on traffic islands and along roads. Wild-looking planting mixtures, too – some obviously colour-themed, others much more disparate, as if the contents of several suburban gardens had made a break for it and occupied the city centre. Most dramatic of all is Grey to Green, a 1.3-kilometre (0.8 mile) long former highway converted to pedestrian use, which integrates parts of Sheffield's city centre that were formerly isolated from one another by roaring traffic. From the beginning, perennial and shrub planting was designed to play a major role here.

The University of Sheffield has, since the mid-1990s, earned itself a reputation as the leading British centre for research into contemporary naturalistic planting design. James Hitchmough and Nigel Dunnett (see pp.104–9, 224–31) have led a research programme into various approaches to planting, including green roofs, living walls, annual mixes for colourful and cheap public plantings and, above all, long-term, low-maintenance, bio-diverse, perennial-based plantings. Having established a global reputation among horticulture and landscape professionals, the two professors' big break came in 2012, when they were chosen to design major areas of planting for the London Olympics. The legacy project that remained, the Queen Elizabeth Park, remains a test bed for the longevity of the plantings they devised.

It has taken some time for the university Landscape Department's work to be utilized in the city of Sheffield itself. The Grey to Green project, however, launched in 2014 and led by Zac Tudor, the city council's Principal Landscape Architect, is making up for lost time. The project is an integral part of the city's new vision for British urban horticulture and new thinking about city centres. 'If people do not come into the city centre for shopping any more', says Tudor, 'it has to find a new role. There has to be a reason to live, work or visit the centre. Bringing the garden into the city is also a way of reconnecting people with nature, and the health and well-being aspects are, of course, very important.' In addition, it is increasingly being recognized that there are major environmental benefits to urban planting, counteracting what is known as the 'urban heat island effect' and trapping dust and micro-plastics; vegetation is also crucial to a city that has frequently suffered flooding.

'We are not just about planting', explains Tudor. 'These designs are truly multi-functional, in that I try to make everyone in our landscape team look at all the functions. Most of our plantings are for SUDS – Sustainable Urban Drainage Systems. We see water as an asset in our

Grey to Green City Garden

urban spaces, and by trapping, cleaning and holding it until it can drain away more slowly, we can better manage high rainfall events.' Swales – shallow basins or channels with sloping sides – and other mechanisms for temporarily holding water runoff are an integral part of these systems, and planting is the best way to secure the soil in them, as well as giving them an both an aesthetic and an environmental function.

The substrate for the plantings is manufactured from quarry waste, with a small quantity of organic matter (mostly from the city's green waste). 'It's very similar to green roof mixes', says Tudor, 'which is where I started. And these planting sites are often quite shallow, with 450–600 millimetre [18–24 in] soil depths ... They have to be very free draining, holding water through porosity but able to release it quickly.' Such a substrate means that plants will get dry in summer, so there is a strong tendency to use drought-tolerant species, but

'they must be able to survive occasional flooding.' Turkish sage (*Phlomis russeliana*) is a good example of such a plant; its combination of robust foliage and seed heads giving it value long after the golden-yellow flowers have finished.

From mid-summer onwards, the Grey to Green plantings assume an atmosphere of controlled chaos, with plants, many of them familiar to gardeners, tumbling over the edges of the paving: cultivars of yarrow (*Achillea*), beardtongue (*Penstemon*) and knautia. The planting involves a wide range of perennial species put together on a relatively *ad hoc* basis compared to the tightly-controlled and well-defined mixes used in German Mixed Planting (see p.103), while there is nothing like the intensive maintenance involved in New York's High Line (see pp.132–9), perhaps the most famous of urban public garden schemes in the naturalistic style. Low fertility soil and low organic content help with the aesthetics of the plantings by stopping perennials getting too big and top-heavy, as well as greatly reducing weed growth. In addition, starting with a manufactured sterile soil mix means that there are no weed seeds or roots to begin with. 'We do some weed-pulling in summer', says Tudor, 'a visit every three to four weeks. The only other maintenance is once in late winter, when everything gets cut back and removed ... It's important that by using low-input maintenance techniques we are not creating a further burden for city budgets.'

The Grey to Green planting aims to achieve a canopy of vegetation for as much of the year as possible, which also helps reduce weed competition. 'Emergents' are an important part of the Sheffield planting philosophy – occasional plants that are markedly taller than the surrounding vegetation, such as species of Culver's root (*Veroniscastrum*), red hot pokers (*Kniphofia*), Siberian flag iris (*Iris sibirica*), and some seasonal bulbs, notably foxtail lilies (*Eremurus*). These are very useful for early summer,

maturing to rather majestic seed heads that often stand the winter. 'Some bulkier emergents, such as species of *Eupatorium* [gravel root], are useful for later in the year', Tudor adds. These 2-metre (10 ft) plus prairie plants are popular with butterflies and add a statuesque quality to plantings. A few species are used to create dramatic effects, such as the feather reed-grass (*Calamagrostis* x *acutiflora* 'Karl Foerster') running the entire length of one section, breaking up the spaces, 'a kind of grassy wall, creating a sinuous flow along the road'. Planting is intermingled – there are no monocultural blocks so beloved by conventional landscape architects. 'We do loose, open clusters and drifts of three and five to create impact and strong accents, with large areas of the beds planted randomly in high densities – twelve plants per square metre [3 sq. ft] from 9-centimetre [3.5 in] pots. This allows the subtle environmental changes in the urban soils to influence the final appearance of the plantings', Tudor explains.

The planting mixes used in the Grey to Green project have brought together the functional and aesthetic, matching species to specific environmental ground conditions: dry, semi-wet and wet habitats that change throughout the seasons. Later phases are adding further complexities of design, with species also grouped according to height and colour combinations. Public reception has been very positive: 'The only complaints have come from some ecologists who complain that there aren't enough native species', says Tudor. Anecdotally, it does appear that there is an enormous amount of insect life buzzing around the plants, especially in late summer.

The Grey to Green project will, almost inevitably, be the topic of a student PhD at the University of Sheffield before too long. The university is also the home of the BUGS projects, run by the Department of Animal and Plant Sciences in 2002 and 2007. These aimed at quantifying the wildlife benefit

of domestic gardens and looked at differences in how much invertebrate life was supported by native and non-native plant species. Their conclusions – primarily that diversity is far more important than whether or not a plant is native or not – have been a major support for the Landscape Department's promotion of diverse urban planting.

Sheffield's wild-style urban planting is well placed to continue, and to inspire other cities. The city council, staffed by many university landscape graduates, also collaborates with The Green Estate, an innovative community-interest company that is involved in managing green space as well as developing seed mixes based on the Landscape Department's research. This triangle of interested parties is all the stronger for their focus on developing manage-ment techniques alongside new planting strategies. It all makes for an increasingly nature-friendly and colourful city.

← ↑ ↓ The exuberant city-centre display of plants is composed, necessarily, of species available cheaply in large quantities; in many cases these are familiar to Sheffield residents as garden plants, a factor that is important in gaining public acceptance for radical new measures such as this. These plants tend to be vigorous, and tolerant of a wide range of conditions – both advantages for low-maintenance situations. Native species such as the hemp agrimony (*Eupatorium cannabinum*, left) are included; to passers-by familiar with the local landscape, these will remind them of the countryside. Showy plants are important too, such as the pink coneflower (*Echinacea pallida*, above), red *Penstemon* 'Garnet' (below left) and dark pink rose campion (*Lychnis coronaria*, below right).

↑↓ Feather reed grass (*Calamagrostis* x *acutiflora* 'Karl Foerster'), a hybrid first grown by the influential German plant breeder of that name, is a useful plant for urban locations, as it is strong and vertical, making it a valuable screening plant; when grouped, it can be used for a variety of visual effects. Having a presence from June until it is cut back (generally by February), it can almost serve as a hedge.

← Black-eyed Susan (*Rudbeckia fulgida*) has long been popular with urban designers, as it is relatively short (60 cm/ 24 in) compared to most late-flowering yellow daisies.

Grey to Green City Garden

Self-Seeding

There was a time when any plant that seeded itself around the garden or spread by runners and popped up in places the gardener could not predict was seen as undesirable. Conventional horticulture until the late nineteenth century was very controlling, in that it emphasized the importance of keeping all plants to their gardener-allotted places. A more relaxed attitude came in during the early twentieth century, often linked to a greater appreciation of wild plants and natural habitats. This period in Britain also saw a growing idealization of the gardens of country people, with the birth of the 'cottage garden' movement. As it matured, this style rapidly left behind any notion of emulating the usually very functional gardens of the rural poor, but it did become a way of allowing the development of a more relaxed style of gardening. The movement peaked in the 1960s with the writings of Margery Fish, who promoted a planting style that encouraged people to let plants move around of their own accord a bit more, making the gardener less of a director and more of a manager and editor, sometimes allowing the plants to rule, sometimes holding the reins of the seeding and spreading instincts of those plants. ¶ Genuinely ecological planting not only welcomes plants reproducing themselves, it positively demands it – and in some cases actually needs it. Certain species simply look wonderful scattered artlessly through a border or park planting. No designer could place them as perfectly as nature could. The air of spontaneity and 'naturalness' so created is greatly valued by naturalistic garden designers, especially when it is engendered by tall, thin plants that take up little space, such as foxgloves (*Digitalis* spp.) and mulleins (*Verbascum* spp.), or by short-lived ones that perform briefly and then disappear, such as the yellow-green perfoliate alexanders (*Smyrnium perfoliatum*) or the blue forget-me-not (*Myosotis sylvatica*). The tall plants generally stand well after flowering and can often look their best in late autumn or early winter, with mist swirling around their seed heads; the short-lived ones are usually early summer flowering and look best *en masse*. The apparently random distribution of self-seeding plants can look especially attractive when counterposed with such formal garden features as topiary, hedges in straight lines or neatly mown lawns. ¶ The ability to self-seed is closely linked to plants being short-lived, for obvious reasons, and there are many highly regarded and much-desired species (those just mentioned, for example) that have to self-seed if they are to survive; self-seeding is essential for the continuance of certain visual effects as well. The proportion of short-lived species, usually annuals, tends to rise in drier environments, because surviving as a seed is easier than surviving as a plant. Consequently, self-reproducing species may play a particularly important role in dry habitats. Those who work with plantings in dry climates, such as the Bassons (see pp.96–101) or Alejandro O'Neill (see pp.234–41), do encourage self-seeding but tend to proceed cautiously. The level at which plants self-seed is dependent on a great many environmental factors, including soil type and climate, as well as there being enough space between existing plants. There is, therefore, great unpredictability. This is regarded by many as part of the joy of this style of planting, unplanned change from one year to the next being seen by many as desirable. The unpredictability can be problematic, however: too little, and the plant loses its visual impact; too much, and it can become a weed, sometimes a very bad one – hence the caution when working with less familiar plants. ¶ Genetic variation is another positive aspect of self-sowing in the eyes of those who champion it. Many garden plants have a narrow genetic base, such that all the individuals of a cultivar, or even species, may be identical. Seed-grown populations that are actively reproducing themselves, on the other hand, often comprise individuals that look slightly different, with flowers that are paler or darker, or which start flowering at a different time. Such variation is not only visually attractive, it also indicates a certain level of genetic health, as the variation will probably also indicate different levels of resistance to disease and to various environmental stresses. ¶ The 'potential weed' issue becomes a bigger problem when the self-seeders concerned are larger, longer-lived or difficult to control. There are certain plant species that can look magnificent but are regarded with great caution, to be used only in situations where they are unlikely to become a problem. One such is the teasel (*Dipsacus fullonum*), which has the most distinctive of seed heads but self-seeds aggressively. Well-established permanent planting that reduces areas of bare soil available for seed germination seems to be the best way to prevent this. ¶ Sometimes a mixed blessing, but offering many exciting possibilities for adding a natural spark, self-sowing is an integral part of nearly all naturalistic planting styles.

'Sense of place' is one of those frequently used but rather abused terms, often bandied about but rarely defined. For the garden at Dyffryn Fernant (Fernant Valley), however, it is central. Christina Shand, the garden's creator, talks about it as a key concept, and it is very clear what she means. Standing on a mount at one end of the property, it is possible to get a view over the whole site and beyond, over the surrounding landscape to a rocky hill on the horizon. This provides an axis for the garden – not for its physical or legal limits, but for its occupation of visual space. The hill, Garn Fawr, is a strong reminder of where we are – in west Wales – but with its rockiness and bracken-covered slopes, it could be one of many places in the west of the British Isles.

The garden is richly varied in the way it creates a series of very different spaces, ranging from the relatively conventional to the almost unmanaged. The 'conventional' horticulture here is actually pretty adventurous, both in the range of species and in the creative shoehorning of plants into micro-habitats. There is a real sense of Shand and her husband, David Allum, playing with the borderlines between the cultivated and the wild. It is not always clear what is garden and what is 'wild', and one way in which the elusive sense of place is manifested is in the way the garden is tied to the landscape through the presence of local wild flora, seeping, creeping, seeding and rhizoming its way in. This is especially true in the bog garden and areas such as the meadow, which are basically wild nature anyway, just defined as 'garden' by legal writ. That they are garden is affirmed only by the presence of certain plants that manifestly are not part of the native flora: the giant rhubarb (*Gunnera manicata*) and some tree ferns (*Dicksonia antarctica*) planted in a grove. Some purists might find these Southern Hemisphere exotics an affront, but they express well the fluidity of the garden's boundaries and of our notions of garden-ness and wildness. The blending of nature

and design blurs entirely the size of the property – in fact, it is 2.4 hectares (6 acres), of which around 1.2 hectares (3 acres) is actively cultivated.

It is always interesting and fun to speculate on what might happen to a particular garden if it were to be abandoned. Here, there is the Waun Fach (Small Marsh) to provide an instructive example of such speculation – a meadow of damp soil and rough grass that is never cut or maintained, edged by the low, scrubby willow so common beside streamlines or damp ground along the Atlantic fringes of Britain. Despite its rough texture, there are plenty of wildflowers, the off-white umbels of wild angelica (*Angelica*

Dyffryn Fernant

sylvestris) being particularly prominent. This and other species every now and again infiltrate the garden, where they are allowed to remain (within limits).

The key site for a blending of the wild and the gardened is the bog garden. Naturalistic enough not to feel out of place, but very definitely to be read as 'garden', there is further ambiguity here, where the exuberance of things that grow in wet places make it feel wilder: various Himalayan primulas (e.g. *Primula florindae*), the native purple loosestrife (*Lythrum salicaria*), and horsetail (*Equisetum arvense*), that most unbeatable of weeds, which Shand admits she has given up trying to control. 'I have a relationship with it', she says, probably tongue in cheek. The primulas (cowslip) and loosestrife seed around, so much of what we see is the result of natural processes of plant spread. There are also a few cannas here – tropical and colourful and probably, in the eyes of some, quite inappropriate; they are taken in for the winter, their presence

a sign of a confidence in spanning the whole spectrum of horticulture, from the most natural to the most artificial.

The bog garden feels liminal, on the edge, as if in one blink nature could take over. Shand talks about having to rationalize the area at some point, as she and her husband get older; this may be one of the first areas to be let go. Given the lush growing conditions, some of the garden plants – not just the native species – need frequent limiting to prevent them overwhelming their fellows. One, a variegated form of the common (and very vigorous) wild reed (*Phragmites australis* 'Variegatus') is in danger of escaping from the bog garden. 'I would not want it spreading into the marsh', says Shand.

At the centre of the bog garden is a 3-metre (10 ft) high stainless-steel obelisk. 'We saw one at Chelsea', recalls Shand, 'and it gave us the idea to get one made here in Wales. We would not be without it, or would move it. Its position is perfect.' The obelisk solves a problem that is perhaps at the core of how we perceive much naturalistic planting: often, because of its relative formlessness, such planting can be seen as vague and ill-defined. Indeed, when photographing it and so rendering three dimensions down to two, much of our ability to judge space and distance is lost. Having a point of focus, of structure and clear form, makes all the difference to our ability to perceive and interpret what is around it. The obelisk here is the perfect focal point, physically and visually. That it is at the core of the part of the garden that brings together most perfectly the wild and the cultivated seems entirely appropriate.

There is an extraordinary amount of freewheeling to-ing and fro-ing between imaginative, plant-focused gardening and the welcoming in of the wild here. The precise balance is dependent on one couple's preferences and decisions, but as a model of what can be achieved by those sensitive to their environment and its flora, it is a very useful one.

← ↓ → This is planting that segues into the landscape, and boundaries on the ground become almost imperceptible in most of the views out. Naturalistic planting can appear somewhat formless *en masse*, which is why the occasional point of focus is very useful – a stainless-steel obelisk forms an anchor for our perception, alongside native wildflowers such as marsh mallow (*Althaea officinalis*). Moisture-loving plants have a tendency towards big, lush leaves, which also help provide structure and visual reference points. The huge leaves of giant rhubarb (*Gunnera manicata*, bottom) make a big impact, but here it does not dominate, either physically or visually.

The first thought on seeing Catherine Janson's garden is that here is someone who has taken the ideas of the New Perennial Movement very seriously indeed. In late spring the soil is completely invisible beneath a dense canopy of vegetation, the dominant impression being that of fresh, vigorous leaves, full of promise for the year. By late September it is a mass of stems and seed heads, amid which the last flowers of the year shine out. This is clearly the garden of someone with the confidence to use plants densely and let them get on with it. It is also relatively small, only 800 square metres (0.2 acre), so any problems with weeds or failing plants can be quickly seen and dealt with.

The garden is surrounded on three sides by a half-timbered barn and other farm buildings that Janson's husband, Charlie, has converted into their home, and a greenhouse he rescued from the ruined kitchen garden of nearby Hay-on-Wye Castle; the fourth side looks out over trees, farmland and a distant vista of the Black Mountains in Wales. The profusion of perennials seems entirely appropriate to the setting. In particular, the texture of everything here is very fine – the most graphic and exotic-looking plant is actually a native, the white-flowered wild angelica (*Angelica sylvestris*), which Janson, a professional garden designer, is allowing to self-seed; its broad, divided leaves make a strong contrast with the more finely textured foliage around it. Close juxtapositions of plants are a big part of the appeal here, and bring home to us how differently plants can appear when grown at this more natural density. The flowers of columbine (*Aquilegia* spp.), for example, become visually detached from the rest of the plant, their foliage merging with that of the other species around them; this can sometimes make flowers more, rather than less, prominent, as our eyes try to make sense of what they see.

Conventional planting design has tended to separate plants. This is the opposite of what happens in nature, and is a practice that inevitably condemns some species to be labelled messy or formless. This planting style, however, enables those that tend to wend their way through other plants, like species of cranesbill (*Geranium*), masterwort (*Astrantia*) and Macedonian scabious (*Knautia macedonica*), to show off their flowers with a more satisfying background, one composed of not just their leaves and stems but of other species as well.

Stansbatch Barn

Colours are relatively muted, which is very much a reflection of the range of wild species of northern and central European plants from which these are selected. The *Knautia* has the strongest colour – a vivid cerise-crimson – its comparative rarity helping to highlight the subtle transitions of pink to blue to white of everything else. The colour range is perfect for the grey skies of northern Europe, where the soft light enables every fine distinction of tint and tone to be appreciated.

The garden clearly has an important role to play in Janson's work. 'The more plants you can grow the better, because then you know what to use in clients' gardens. Unless you are growing all the things you use, you don't know what they'll do', she explains. The density of the planting was initially driven by the simple desire to grow as much as possible, but it has turned out to have its own virtues. 'It has lots of advantages: wildlife like it, you don't lose soil moisture, there's no

staking, there's less room for weeds. I like the meadow feel and finding out which plants shouldn't be crowded. Good form can be lost, though, in the mêlée, like the grass *Stipa gigantea* [golden oats], sun lovers that would need to be on the edge, and bearded irises [*Iris germanica*], which need to be on their own.'

For anyone who appreciates the visual diversity of plants, this is a fascinating place. The close proximity of species more normally grown at greater distance from each other can make us look at them in very different ways. Early in the year, when foliage dominates and well before there is any untidiness from tired leaves or flopping seed heads, the impression is that of an Alpine valley bottom, where perennials wax lush and luxuriant in the continual flow of mineral-rich water that flows from the mountain slopes.

Conventional garden practice tends to hold fast to the idea that plants need space – either because if crowded they cannot be appreciated, or because they will somehow conflict with each other and only thugs will survive. In nature, of course, plants grow at densities several orders of magnitude greater than in designed plantings. The planting here is one of very few that really begin to get anywhere near the density of natural plant communities. That some of the species self-seed is one reason why the plants have built up the way they have, as naturally regenerating plants will insert themselves into gaps in the existing canopy. Although there are species that need occasional 'editing', the meshing together of the component plants is one factor in assuring its relative stability, as the thicker the canopy gets, the more any aggressive species are checked by the growth of others, including the germination of some more vigorously self-seeding components.

Self-seeding plants, by reproducing themselves spontaneously, choose places

where not even the most nature-focused designer would have put them. They are a vital part of the naturalistic aesthetic in many gardens. Several species illustrate this well here. One in particular, *Anthriscus sylvestris* 'Ravenswing', a form of cow parsley that grows in hedgerows and along country lanes, is a dark-leaved form of a very common British wildflower that many would be horrified to admit into their gardens. But here its delicate white flower heads float above the planting, while the stems and foliage are very light and narrow; combined with the plants dying back by early July, these characteristics mean that it does little to compete with other plants. By having it here, Janson is not just including an

attractive plant but also creating a strong link to the British countryside in the sub-conscious of anyone who sees it.

Seeing how plants grow in nature has helped Janson develop her high-density planting style. 'I travelled a lot when I was younger, and although I did not know then what I was going to do, I must have been thinking ... My old diaries are full of bits of plants, stuck all the way through ... I remember cloud forest in Cameroon, Himalayan mountainsides, the lushness of Kerala.' Some years ago she joined a trip to Kyrgyzstan, where mountain meadows have an extraordinarily diverse perennial flora. 'Understanding how meadows grow, you can layer in so much more. You can have bulbs in spring,

then things like aquilegias [columbine], which don't take up any room at all. You can cram it all in, far more than the traditional four or five plants per square metre. I think bulbs work fine in this denser type of planting – at least the taller species.'

Surrounded by a rural landscape, Janson sees her 'grasses and self-seeding plants as making the transition to the landscape easier', but then she laughs. 'They're also so tall that you can hardly see the view!' The garden here might alarm some with its slightly unruly profusion by the end of the season, but it points the way towards a new gardening style that genuinely brings an enhanced experience of nature to the back door.

← ↑↓ Herbaceous planting in early summer has a fresh sense
of lush promise. Much of the visual interest here
is from narrow plants – forms of columbine (*Aquilegia
vulgaris*), cow parsley (*Anthriscus sylvestris*) and
foxglove (*Digitalis purpurea*). Many of these are
short-lived and self-sowing, continually regenerating
themselves in the gaps available between other plants –
which means they do not impinge much on the space
of later-flowering species, such as asters and species
of joe pye weed (*Eupatorium*), bistort (*Persicaria*)
and burnet (*Sanguisorba*). Management might include
pulling out stems after flowering, to give visual space
to later developing plants and to reduce seeding.

→ (Overleaf) The planting around the central lawn may seem
conventional, but all these borders can be seen from paths
around the outside, too. The opportunity to see plants
from many different viewpoints, meaning that planting has
to work 'in the round' visually, is a distinctive feature
of naturalistic planting.

GRANGES-SUR-VOLOGNE,
ALSACE, FRANCE

PRIVATE GARDEN
OPEN TO THE PUBLIC

DESIGNERS:
MONIQUE AND THIERRY DRONET

'People are quite often moved to tears when they get here', says Monique Dronet about the visitors who make the long trip up to the garden she and her husband, Thierry, created in northeastern France. The journey increases the sense of anticipation, and there is undeniably something special about this place.

Le Jardin de Berchigranges is perched 650 metres (2,130 ft) up in the Vosges Mountains; the temperature can drop to -15° C (5° F) in winter, and it can rain as much as 3,000 millimetres (118 in) a year. The growing season is short but lush: mosses, for example, need little encouragement to cover ground in the areas of old spruce plantation that border the garden. Surrounded by stark, steep hills and deep, dark forests, the garden spreads generously down from the cottage-style house. Perhaps it is the contrast with the surroundings, or the feeling of coming to an oasis after a long drive, or simply the sheer perfection of this place that makes a very powerful emotional impression on visitors.

A walk through the 3-hectare (7.4 acre) garden offers a range of experiences that start from a relatively conventional lawn-plus-border formula but then take the visitor through to the boldly experimental: miniature ravines constructed of logs of rot-resistant false acacia (*Robinia pseudoacacia*, an invasive species locally), sprouting ferns and other shade-lovers, a labyrinthine series of hornbeam hedges (*Carpinus betulus*) best described as being like a castle, but which Thierry Dronet calls the 'pinball garden', as 'visitors are ejected into another world ... We want to have something to be the end of one part of the garden and the start of another'. Beyond, the garden gets wilder, with an extensive meadow that sprouts an extremely wide and vigorous range of garden perennials.

'The garden started when we met', explains Monique, a rather bald phrase behind which is a most extraordinary and passionate love story from the garden world. Monique was running a nursery at the time, and transferred it to Thierry's property, but eventually they reduced their plant growing and opened the garden as a business instead.

The top end of the garden approaches many people's idea of the perfect garden space. The lawns are immaculate – indeed, far too immaculate for most practioners in the naturalistic planting movement. The planting of the perennial borders is a great deal more

Le Jardin de Berchigranges

dense than is normal, and those borders very often have edges that are kept regularly trimmed, an unusual practice but one that does result in a very tidy edge. It all feels very controlled, until you look into the borders and see just how much is going on there – a lot of plants, a lot of different species and a lot of jostling for space. To use plants in this way, there has to be a confidence that a few will not take over and overwhelm the rest. The result here is that the borders have a lush, full look, with none of the gaps that often disfigure perennial plantings. They achieve the miracle of appearing both very naturalistic and very managed.

When questioned about the seeming contradiction of the flawless lawns with the rest of the garden, Monique replies, 'This is France, without the lawn French people do not understand. It is contrast, for us landscaping is contrast, it is the basis of our idea of design. Without a lawn it is impossible to present a wild

garden ... We are purists in the garden, we observe plants in the wild, but this is not the wild, this is a garden, and the garden is a search for the aesthetic. This is why we make this combination.'

The lawns and the densely-planted borders offer the more conventionally-minded visitor a vision of a different way of developing a traditional and familiar garden feature, but the meadow lower down is much closer to the Dronets' hearts. The 5,000-square metre (1.2 acre) area of rough grass was ploughed up in 2012 and planted with perennials, the grass re-establishing itself through natural regeneration, with more perennials planted every year. As noted with Piet Oudolf's meadow at the Hauser & Wirth gallery garden in southwest England (see pp.20–7), the difficulties of creating a balance between perennials and grasses are considerable, but here Monique notes that 'after ten years we have a good balance. The meadow is self-regulating, and some species are self-sowing.' These are mostly European natives, including the spontaneous arrival and spread of several orchids, but also lupins, whose colour and shape are a dramatic addition. There is a natural progression from a drier top of the garden to a moister lower area, with the latter dominated by some quite rank vegetation, such as broad-leaved ragwort (*Senecio fluviatilis*), a tall yellow daisy rarely given garden space. The Dronets battle against some problem weeds, such as bindweed (*Convolvulus*), but the balance between perennials and grasses seems fair. The short growing season must surely help to limit grass growth, and yellow rattle (*Rhinanthus minor*), a semi-parasitic annual that selectively reduces grass vigour in an increasing number of meadow plantings, has also been introduced.

Early in the year there are many daffodil varieties (*Narcissus* spp.), followed by lupins, and then in July to

September the meadow is dominated by varieties of phlox, bee balm (*Monarda* spp.), aster and kalimeris, most of these being North American prairie species. There is also much Culver's root (*Veronicastrum virginicum*), a prairie plant whose flower heads, which take the form of a bunch of spires, create a very strong effect when repeated, as here; indeed, the randomized repetition of narrow uprights makes for one of the strongest impacts in the toolbox of naturalistic planting special effects. The meadow is viewed from a path that sweeps around in a circle, allowing for its complex array of plants to be appreciated from many different viewpoints, as well as against a range of backdrops, including the couple's cottage when looking up, and against the distant hills when looking down.

This very successful perennial meadow is simply one of many experiments at Le Jardin de Berchigranges. The place has a special and perhaps rather challenging climate, which in many ways may have made some aspects of what the Dronets do easier, but there are few other gardens where one feels there is so much to learn. 'Everything is a risk, but gardening is all about risk', says Monique. 'We research and research and research; for us research is creation.' We can all gain from their experience in this garden.

↑ Le Jardin de Berchigranges plays with visual and technical innovation at many different levels, using hydrangeas in woodland, for example (left) and the Moss Garden (right), both projects taking advantage of the fact that this is an extremely wet area.

↓ Areas of stony soil are often more welcoming to self-seeding and therefore naturalizing, as with a Japanese lily (*Lilium speciosum*) and the elegant, narrow spires of rusty foxglove (*Digitalis ferruginea*, also p.199 lower right).

↑ The planting is overwhelmingly naturalistic
and, in the case of the Bohemian Meadow (also
pp.202–3), very successful at creating a genuinely
dynamic integration of non-native garden plants
(mostly North American prairie species) with
native pasture grasses and wildflowers.

Le Jardin de Berchigranges

↓ → The creative tension between the wild and the cultivated lies at the heart of some of the best naturalistic gardens. Here, immaculate lawns (also p.199 bottom left) and disciplined clipping can be within metres of plants like the pink rosebay willowherb (*Chamaenerion angustifolium*), an aggressive spreader that many would eliminate as soon as possible. Willow gentian (*Gentiana asclepiadea*, p.201), a slow-to-establish plant of alpine woods, flourishes in the cool, wet summers here.

→ (Overleaf) Another plant that often needs patience, Culver's root (*Veronicastrum virginicum*) has begun to spread in the Bohemian Meadow.

Le Jardin de Berchigranges

There are so few gardens that really embrace the coast. The normal reaction of gardeners who find themselves anywhere near the sea is to plant a big windbreak and carry on behind it as if the water was not there, because the sea, or more accurately, the winds that sweep over it, are very damaging to a great many of the plants we conventionally grow. There is also the notion, deep within many of us, that the garden should be somewhere restful and relaxing, and that a strong wind is conducive to neither emotion. Jackie and Will Michelmore faced both these issues in 2002, when they moved into their new home on the Exe estuary in southwest England. The view is not over open sea, but their garden has a long southwesterly fetch for the wind, so they get everything an Atlantic gale can throw at them. The coming and going of the tide dominates – the view is either a stretch of water or a wide expanse of mud flats.

The Lookout's 0.8-hectare (2 acre) garden stretches some 250 metres (820 ft) along the eastern shore of the estuary and has a roughly tadpole shape, its lower end a large sunken lawn, above which rises a slope with a swimming pool and the weathered grey clapboard house. Beyond this is a small wildflower meadow and the long tail of the garden, which becomes increasingly wild until it is eventually little more than a shelter belt adjacent to the slope of a sea wall.

While they were making the garden, the Michelmores faced a number of contradictory demands. It had to have a windbreak of trees and shrubs tough enough to divert the wind over the house, but not so full that it stopped them looking out. They wanted a wide range of plants but, realistically, could only grow those that survived. They also wanted a feeling of wildness – but in a situation where the wildness of natural forces would sometimes be overwhelming, they wanted a garden that also felt under control.

The planted windbreak atop the sea wall is relatively light, enough to filter the wind but 'with plenty of windows to give framed views out over the estuary', says Jackie. 'The change of weather and the tides are a big feature, and there is a balance between enjoying the view and coping with the wind.' Part of the screen is blackthorn (*Prunus spinosa*), which because of its vicious thorns and suckering habit, is pretty much the most unpopular shrub in the British Isles. It is, however, very wind-resistant, and here it has been shaped so that it forms a sculptural lower level below a higher layer of sea buckthorn (*Hippophae rhamnoides*). The shaped blackthorn plants look not dissimilar to the intensely-clipped

The Lookout

shrubs seen in some traditional Japanese gardens, but the impact of control is counterbalanced by the very wild and grassy layer of herbaceous planting that fronts most of the windbreak and weaves its way through a series of narrow beds further into the garden. The planting, in turn, is held in check visually by means of a very crisp edge between the plants and a well-trimmed lawn. These several levels of closely juxtaposed wildness and order create a powerful impression. Few other gardens attempt to achieve such a balance between extremes.

Jackie works as a garden designer, but her plant knowledge has been pushed to the limits here, as the salt-laden winds drastically reduce the range of plants that thrive. 'We've trialled a lot', she says, 'and settled on those that perform, so we have about ten key plants.' A crucial issue is that 'the summer storms are far more damaging than winter ones, which do much less harm to dormant deciduous plants.' Jackie explains that 'I like things that weave, that look as if they have put themselves there … there is a lot of self-seeding. I take out what I don't want, and

self-seeding achieves its own matrix.' So, a limited range of robust plants is repeated in the borders around the house and for a short stretch at the base of the wind-break. The repetition of a few species – one of the key points of much of the new naturalistic planting design – has therefore been more or less dictated by the environment here. The effect of this repetition creates a calm sense of unity.

The planted borders are relatively narrow and tightly defined by their crisp edges alongside the mown grass, which minimizes much of the untidiness that can accompany naturalistic planting at certain times of year, especially in a situation where wind turbulence can wreak havoc. The wildness is repeated on a much larger scale but with a simpler and softer texture in an area of wildflower meadow that marks the end of the more conventional end of the garden. Grasses play a key role, simply because they are especially wind-tolerant. The tussock shape, rare among British native species but very common elsewhere, and generally indicative of stressful and exposed environments, is repeated through three frequently appearing species of varying sizes. Among the most interesting in design terms is golden oats (*Stipa gigantea*), an Iberian species with relatively low evergreen tussocks and tall, wide-ranging but very airy and see-through seed heads; it grows to a height of around 1.8 metres (6 ft). The resulting straw-coloured haze at around eye level makes for an attractively ethereal visual element.

Below the windbreak and towards the narrower tail end of the garden, the garden segues into a series of paths mown through native shrubs and patches of steep wildflower meadow – not nature, not a garden, but a mesh of minimal control overhanging the meeting point of sky, sea and land. To borrow a word from the arts world, this is a truly 'edgy' place – a fitting final point for a garden that achieves such a successful and disciplined transition between worlds.

↓→ Blackthorn (*Prunus spinosa*) makes a dense
windbreak but is an aggressively spreading
plant. Keeping it in check has been turned
into an art form, with windows cut into the
line of trees to frame views, and smaller
plants of it sculpted into shapes. Its trunks
and branches are rarely seen, but here the
pruning out of lower growth makes the most of
them. A low bank in front is densely planted
with grasses and perennials; it is rare to see
this kind of planting on a small scale.

↑ ← The bank facing the sea is planted with a wild meadow mix, featuring robust native species such as hogweed (*Heracleum sphondylium*). The path is part of an extensive walkway along the top of the bank. Grasses tend to be very windproof, so are used here a lot. Golden oats (*Stipa gigantea*, left and p.204) has scale but also an ephemeral, see-through quality.

↓ The main garden area is around the house itself, on the seaward side. The bank above the beach was rebuilt with rock and infill (foreground, pp.208–9); it now supports a garden rich in wildflowers with a windbreak line of trees at its top, behind which is the wildflower meadow.

The Lookout

↓ Sheltering behind the windbreak, ox-eye daisy (*Leucanthemum vulgare*) dominates the wildflower meadow during early to mid-summer. Paths are clearly defined, emphasizing the contrast between mown grass and wilder areas.

→ Planting of borders is tight, with a focus on grasses that ensure the seasonal continuity vital in small spaces. Windproof shrubs are used around the house, with paths protected from the worst of the wind by blackthorn and other wind-tolerant trees. Their low stature and the intimate feeling of the paths evokes tracks through clifftop scrub often encountered on the coastal footpaths of southern England.

The Lookout

At the heart of the Royal Horticultural Society's garden at Wisley, south-west of London, is Oakwood, a 1.8-hectare (4.5 acre) area of mature oaks and varied planting – shady and quite wet, with a network of drainage ditches as well as paths. Wisley, as it is known, is a very well-managed garden, as one might expect from one of the world's leading horticultural bodies. Step off the main path into Oakwood, however, and it all looks very different – much wilder, and to some visitors slightly out of control, at least in comparison with everything else here. Mature oaks cast shade, beneath which there is a sparse canopy of ornamental shrubs (rhododendrons, camellias etc.) and a thick ground cover of herbaceous plants. Some species have clearly been let off the leash to form extensive patches, such as the ground cover plant periwinkle (*Vinca minor*). Most, however, grow cheek by jowl with their neighbours, spreading into each other in a way that closely resembles how plants grow in the wild. To cap it all, there are a lot of British native species here, such as bluebells (*Hyacinthoides non-scripta*) and wood anemone (*Anemone nemorosa*) – plants typical of the woodland habitats many visitors would be used to seeing in the countryside.

These areas where the ground is covered in a rich tapestry of foliage stand out, but the extent to which they are the result of competition or co-existence can be difficult to judge, and much can be speculated about the relative strengths of the different species. Indeed, this is one of the best places to discuss with students the ecological relationships plants establish among themselves, and to appreciate how garden plants can behave like their wild ancestors.

Oakwood is not just a good example of a particular kind of nature-culture hybrid; it is actually one of the oldest there is, having been established in the 1880s as part of an experimental garden run by George Fergusson Wilson (1822–1902). A successful career as an industrial chemist allowed him the time and resources to indulge his passion for gardening, in particular for informal plant trials in a variety of habitats. Wilson's management of the area was developed partly under the influence of the Irish gardener and writer William Robinson (1838–1935), whose book *The Wild Garden*, published in 1870, proposed a model of gardening very different to the stiff formality and

Oakwood at RHS Garden Wisley

love of exotica characteristic of the Victorian era. From the beginning, the area now known as Oakwood was deliberately allowed to be wild, in the hope and expectation that many of the garden plants introduced into it would naturalize.

People took notice of what Wilson, a prominent horticulturist of his time, was doing, and visitors who wrote about the garden stressed his management philosophy. J. Cornhill reported in an article in *Garden* magazine of 25 May 1895: 'Therein the spade, fork and hoe are almost unknown, the cultural system apparently consisting in creating suitable conditions, placing the plants there, and allowing them to grow as they would in their native haunts, the attention given consisting merely in pulling out weeds and keeping rampant growing things within due bounds.'

This is more or less how Oakwood is managed today. The staff keep an eye on strongly competitive species, choosing to limit their growth on occasions or, sometimes, relocate slower-growing choice species in their path. Certain weeds, such as ground elder, are very problematic but tend to be managed on a cyclical basis. Much of the time ground elder simply infiltrates the desired vegetation, looking much like it does in its natural surroundings (woods in central Europe), but it is regarded as undesirable, so after a number of years an area affected by it will be entirely dug up and the site thoroughly cleaned, as are any plants that are to be replaced there. The result is, rather like the parks at Amstelveen (see p.8), a patchwork of areas of different ages, where the species mix and the level of mixing in with native species varies from one patch to another. There is, nevertheless, a huge level of plant diversity, far more than in more recently created naturalistic plantings elsewhere.

As is generally the case with shaded habitats, most flowering is early, starting at the end of winter with bulbs and some early perennials and flowering shrubs. Certain native species such as the bluebell (*Hyacinthoides non-scripta*) and wood anemone (*Anemone nemorosa*) infiltrate in many places, but like many spring-performing species they die back by early summer. Late spring sees some spectacular flowering by *Smyrnium perfoliatum*, an annual with yellow-green flowers – a colour complemented perfectly by the pale mauve of perennial honesty (*Lunaria rediviva*). According to the staff, this combination is one of the most popular features at Oakwood, but it is a beauty that needs managing; both species self-seed, and the former, an annual, can seed prolifically and has to be restricted, lest it smother slower-growing plants.

High summer at Oakwood tends to be very green, with the rich range of colour, shape and textural variations in foliage the main source of interest, brought out best by the shade. The soil here is damp, so a number of luxuriant moisture-lovers play an important role, including royal fern (*Osmunda regalis*), which tends to line the ditches, and the expansive leaves of species of *Rodgersia* and ragwort (*Ligularia*). The latter, which bloom with mid- to late summer flowering yellow daisies, are among the 'rampant growing things' that have to be managed to avoid them becoming dominant.

Wilson's experimental garden of the 1880s continues to thrive because of management, but much less than would be needed in full sun. Shade helps, as it limits the growth of those native species, notably grasses, which combine strong rates of spread with seeding. The limitation placed on these strong competitors enables 'fairer' competition for a wider range of plants. A nice touch is that certain areas are briefly dominated by colourful East Asian-origin primrose (*Primula* spp.); these seed profusely and, like many relatively short-lived 'weeds', their seed lasts for long periods buried in the soil. Attempts at redeveloping areas here can be joined by hundreds of their seedlings – an example of how the long history and sensitive management of this area has resulted in it developing its own distinct ecological dynamic.

Oakwood is not only an interesting, engaging and attractive space in its own right, but its long history of embracing ecological process makes for a strong contrast to the rest of the garden, which is maintained to a very high but overwhelmingly conventional horticultural standard. That it sits at the heart of a very managed public garden emphasizes the quiet statement that is also made by the contrast between the topiary and the wildflowers of Great Dixter (see pp.282–9): that the creative tension between the wild and the tame can help us appreciate both better.

← Surrey is famous for its rhododendrons but in Oakwood they are quite modestly spaced, and their bright flowers are a relatively small part of the planting.

↓ Much of the fascination of Oakwood is in the tapestry of ground-cover plants; these are in a state of constant ebb and flow between different species, tidal movements driven partly by natural processes and partly by occasional staff interventions. In the foreground, species of lungwort (*Pulmonaria*), bleeding heart (*Dicentra*) and Arum are being slowly overwhelmed by barrenwort (*Epimedium*), behind which the ostrich fern (*Matteuccia struthiopteris*) is gradually advancing.

↑↘ Oakwood's ecological dynamism incorporates a number
of short-lived species whose presence may be quite
fugitive, such as dame's violet (*Hesperis matronalis*,
above) and various brightly-coloured Himalayan species
of *Primula* (bottom right). Primulas tend to rejuvenate
whenever gardening operations disturb the ground
and bring buried seed to the surface; over time, the
species have hybridized to produce a range of colours.

→ (Overleaf) Almost inevitably there are problems with some
wild species becoming too dominant, such as ground elder
(*Aegopodium vulgare*) – an attractive enough plant *en masse*,
but one that management here aims at controlling.

Oakwood at RHS Garden Wisley

Oakwood at RHS Garden Wisley

Deep in the woods of rural New Jersey hides a prairie garden. Begun in 2006, it is in some ways a secret and private place, even paradoxical – for this is a prairie in the woods. In spring, it may only be a glade in the forest, with perennials and grasses at ankle height, but by mid-summer this woodland glade is a distinct garden habitat in its own right; by summer's end, much of it is shoulder or even head height, producing at once the feeling of prairie but surrounded by a wall of trees, mostly red maples (*Acer rubrum*) and American beech (*Fagus grandifolia*).

There are just enough reminders of the human presence and the artist's eye to make us aware that this is a garden: the occasional low-impact piece of sculpture, gravel paths, low walls made of the local rock, argillite – dark, hard and austere – and a few clipped evergreens, which on the one hand stand out as possibly inconsistent, but on the other add a subtle counterpoint. If they were not here, we could be too easily taken in that this really is all nature's doing.

That this is a prairie-inspired garden comes as a surprise after driving through the woods. Yet if it was a natural woodland glade of this size (6,000 square metres / 1.5 acres), there could well be sun-loving prairie plants here. Besides, as designer James Golden points out, 'the soil is heavy, wet clay, saturated much of the year; you have to have plants that suit the conditions'. Those that thrive grow lush on the moisture and high level of fertility. 'Most are highly competitive, even aggressive', Golden notes, 'and I try to match them so they keep each other in control. Then I stand aside and intervene only when necessary.' Everything is very big and luxurious, and there is clearly a lot of self-seeding and natural spreading going on, but nothing seems to take over at anything else's expense. Fore-stalling what some might say, he explains that 'I think of mess as a positive term. My gardening process is a series of inter-ventions to control mess, refine line and legibility, sculpt mass from mess.'

Like many other gardeners in the United States (see pp.146–51, 242–9), Golden was greatly inspired by the work of land-scape architects Wolfgang Oehme and James van Sweden, who from the late 1970s made a major impact on the East Coast. They used masses of perennials and grasses to sweep around public buildings and swirl through parks and along roadways, breaking with what had become a very sterile set of conventions around the way public space was designed. They promoted their work as sustainable, 'bold and romantic', but also determinedly 'New American'. Strongly graphic and relying heavily on large monocultural masses of planting, other designers and, crucially,

Federal Twist

private gardeners such as Golden, took the elements of the new style and developed something more complex and softer, more genuinely naturalistic.

By the time Oehme and van Sweden were well-established, the native plant movement had become a force to be reckoned with in the US garden and landscape world, and the growing of native plants had become almost an article of faith for many. Golden clearly draws inspiration from both movements, but he is no 'nativist'. 'I can't find the visual richness and expressiveness I want with native plants alone', he says. Nevertheless, it is very much the big natives that seem to set the pace here: species of tall, yellow-flowered *Silphium*, the dull pink butterfly magnets of several *Eupatorium* species and grasses like switch grass (*Panicum virgatum*). The exception might be the various Asian-origin silver grass (*Miscanthus*) cultivars, which are, by the end of the year at least, visually dominant. Many gardeners, at this time and in this place, might have gone with the *zeitgeist* and used only natives. That Golden so

successfully integrates native and non-native makes his achievement here important – firmly stating that this is a garden, a human and cultural space, not a re-creation of nature or habitat restoration. His determination to combine natives and non-natives may, in fact, make him especially forward-looking, as the sheer popularity of many 'traditional' garden plants and the tenacity with which many grow in their new home will inevitably keep many garden and landscape people coming back to them.

I admit to a deeply personal interest in this garden. Its creator once found a 'wish book' in a bookstore, called *Designing with Plants*, which I wrote with Piet Oudolf in 1999. Golden, a semi-retired marketing expert, told me he was 'powerfully moved by the book: its photographic details of plant shape, texture, colour, structure, and the rampant, almost tactile beauty of the Oudolf garden photos ... The big plantings recalled an Alice in Wonderland world ... and the appreciation for all stages of a plant's life, even death in winter, hit my bullseye.'

For somewhere that feels so hidden away, this is a very public garden. This is because of Golden's blog, 'View from Federal Twist' (which refers to the name of the road). The subtitle is 'Ramblings of a 'New American' Gardener', which is an apt description, for the blog offers a view not only out into the garden (there is some stunning photography, the kind of intimate, day-by-day photography that only a garden owner can do), but also the thinking aloud of one of the most reflective of gardeners. It records his very emotional reactions to the sounds, feelings and atmospheres of his experience of the garden. He quotes poetry and essays and explores philosophical concepts in a seemingly endless attempt to understand what he has made, and does so in an engaging and lyrical voice that pulls you in to his inner world. In making it digitally public, this is, very quietly, a truly twenty-first-century garden.

↑↓ With the surrounding woods there is the feeling of being in a green bowl, and occasional focal points are important for orientation and anchoring vision. Here, they are surprises, like the formal pool, or are very subtle, such as the dark foliage of the dwarf Japanese maple (*Acer palmatum* var. *dissectum* (Atropurpureum Group). From the porch, orange leopard plant (*Ligularia* dentata) is prominent; by blocking the view so emphatically, the vegetation seems to be saying, 'come out into the garden to see what there is'.

→↓↘ Paths here are distinctly 'immersive', plunging into vegetation that is often at head height during the summer. Seed heads of varieties of Chinese silver grass (*Miscanthus sinensis*, right) will maintain this height through the winter. Among the perennials that flourish in the clay soil here, the large leaves and yellow flowers of self-seeding *Inula racemosa* (centre left and bottom) are notable.

↘ Plants with bold foliage contrast to the more nondescript forms of many native prairie species. The dark forms of *Thuja occidentalis* 'Smaradg' (centre right) make a surprise focal point.

→ (Overleaf) Paths are relatively narrow; nothing wider is needed in a private garden, and their scale vis-à-vis the planting emphasizes the immersive quality of exploring and the sense of anticipation.

The Barbican, in central London, is well known as an arts centre and as a supreme example of Brutalist architecture – concrete, grey in tooth and claw, uncompromising and unforgiving. Most of this 16-hectare (39.5 acre) estate is given over to housing, in the form of privately-owned apartments. The original landscaping (the estate was built between 1965 and 1976) featured some water features with marginal planting – a clear quotation from the Brazilian designer Roberto Burle Marx's work within the modernist architectural icon of Brasilia – as well as some of the grass-and-shrubbery typical of most urban planting of the time.

Since 2015, however, things have been different. The dull, stressed shrubs have been removed and replaced by – for want of a better word – meadows: diverse plantings of grasses and perennials over 1,600 square metres (0.4 acre). There is a lot of grey foliage – to be expected, perhaps, as the soil depth here is limited – and there is no irrigation, so drought-tolerant plants, which often have foliage made grey or silver in appearance owing to coatings of microscopic protective hairs, tend to predominate. This is, in effect, green roof planting, with a soil depth of around 35 centimetres (14 in).

The Barbican plantings have become one of the best-known works by Professor Nigel Dunnett, whose academic career in the Landscape Department at the University of Sheffield has taken a more practically orientated turn. Dunnett focused on summer drought as the main issue in selecting plants, but as with so many ecologically orientated designers, he thought first of an appropriate reference habitat – in this case, the steppe grasslands of eastern Europe and Central Asia. Three plant combinations were developed: one for full sun, one for areas where deeper soil allowed for some shrubs to be mixed in with the perennials, and one for more enclosed areas with somewhat deeper soil, where small trees and shrubs were combined with woodland edge perennials.

Spring and early summer is colourful, with purples and pinks to the fore; there is a bulb layer of species tulips for April and May, while the bulk of the perennial flowering happens in May and June. In summer, the planting takes on the sere look to be expected of dry habitats, but is given life by the rich textures of a wide

Barbican Estate

range of foliage shapes, and by many species with good seed heads for the post-flowering period. Dry habitat perennials tend to be sparse in size and shape, and a lot of their texture is quite fine: small leaves, grasses with very fine leaves, dense branching patterns; so the planting here has a lot of detail, which might be lacking in a more resource-rich environment.

The nature of the planting is visually complex, partly because of the fine textures but also because there is much interweaving of the different plant species and a large number of species per square metre. This complexity is, arguably, particularly important for places like this, where much of the viewing is from foot traffic that is relatively close to the planting and, it being a residential community, very frequent. It also feels alive in winter, as several of the grass species are evergreen. Indeed, the sense of life in the winter was something that local residents particularly asked for in the public consultation that preceded the new planting.

Since the entire area of the planting is overlooked on all sides by the residents, a community consultation exercise was vital. Many wanted something that gave them more colour, others a sense of seasonal change (always lacking with the evergreen shrubs that were here before), others wanted more possibilities for wildlife. There was concern over the removal of some trees (which, realistically, were too drought-stressed to survive) and the impact this would have on birds. 'The planting needed to look good, continuously good, every day of the year', says Dunnett, 'but had to do so with minimal effort.' Shallow-rooted birches (*Betula* spp.) and other small tree species such as varieties of dogwood (*Cornus*) and serviceberry (*Amelanchier*) were used in the woodland areas, but the main resource for wildlife was intended to be the diversity of the planting.

Having been inspired by steppe, a crucial role in this garden belongs to species from that habitat, including Turkish sage (*Phlomis russeliana*), a plant from the eastern Mediterranean region that is evergreen in Britain and which has particularly strong and distinctive seed heads for winter structure. Its chunky good looks are the perfect contrast to such grasses as sea thrift (*Armeria maritima*) – a small, cushion-forming species familiar to any who walk the rocky coast paths of northern or western Europe – and forms of Balkan clary (*Salvia nemorosa*), whose vibrant purple flowers adorn dry meadows across Eurasia (and, indeed, the central reservation of the highways around Vienna). Other species from elsewhere include plants valuable for later flowering interest among the increasingly dry surrounding vegetation: yellow and orange *Crocosmia* varieties from the Drakensberg Mountains in eastern South Africa, red hot poker (*Kniphofia*) varieties, also from South Africa and with a similar colour range, and purple *Verbena bonariensis*.

There is a paradox about including some of these species, which illustrates more generally something quite crucial about the Sheffield University approach to planting. Kniphofias are popular in dry habitat plantings in Britain as they look 'deserty', with their dramatic orange flower spikes above rosettes of leaves. They are, however, by no means desert plants; in their native South Africa they are often found in moist places. 'I used them in an early trial', said Dunnett of this choice, 'and they did very well, so we have used them on other green roof situations.' *Verbena bonariensis*, another paradox, is an annual of moist places in Argentina. It has become a fixture in many British gardens, however, as it is semi-transparent, flowers for months and is much loved by butterflies.

The Barbican is in some ways a harsh environment, as it becomes very hot and dry in the summer without any irrigation. 'The hot, dry summer of 2018 was not great, but it got through it', says Dunnett. On the other hand, the situation has its advantages: being enclosed and in the middle of a city, there is almost no weed seed blowing in, which greatly reduces one of the main maintenance tasks. There is, however, a high level of self-seeding of the plants in the planting – and not just the components that seed in most gardens, like evening primroses (*Oenothera* spp.), but the more long-lived ones, too. It is this self-seeding, this natural regeneration, that makes the Barbican planting feel so alive and suggests that it has the capacity to be a completely ecological planting.

Over the winter of 2019/2020 there were some changes to the planting. 'You can't leave things that long [seven years] before doing some work', says Dunnett. 'It had become too grassy, I think.' Intriguingly, this has not been perceived negatively by residents: 'There has been no negativity at all from the public', Dunnett reports. 'A lot of people like the tussocks [of the grass *Sesleria nitida*], but I think there needs to be more room for flowering plants.' This public acceptance shows, perhaps, how attitudes are changing to wild-type vegetation in high-density living environments, and may be the crowning accolade for what is proving to be a singularly successful example of how unpromising situations can be good growing places.

↑ The concrete-dominated environment of London's Barbican has conditions similar to those found in steppe habitats. In early summer, *Allium* 'Globemaster' and 'Purple Sensation' (also pp.228–9) are a colourful feature.

↓ The planting around pools takes advantage of a slightly deeper layer of substrate to include varieties of cherry (*Prunus*), birch (*Betula*) and serviceberry (*Amelanchier*) trees, and a rich ground layer of vegetation; in flower are white New Zealand satin flower (*Libertia grandiflora*) and pale green *Euphorbia characias* subsp. *wulfenii*.

→ (Overleaf) Grasses evoke the dominant plant
for steppe environments. The pale green flowered
Euphorbia characias subsp. *wulfenii* is tolerant
of summer drought and some shade, and is more or
less evergreen.

↑ → In areas shaded by the
buildings, and where soil depth
allows, trees with a woodland
edge planting mix are used.
In June, grass-like snow rush
(*Luzula nivea*) is in flower
alongside the distinct leaves
of *Anemone* x *hybrida*, which
will flower from August to
October (above). Deep pink
Manescau storksbill (*Erodium
manescavi*, right and p.226
top right) is a short-lived
perennial that self-seeds
and so maintains its presence.

There is mid-summer colour from red hot poker (*Kniphofia* 'Tawny King') and *Crocosmia* 'Emberglow', alongside seed heads of moor grass (*Sesleria nitida*) and silky-spike melic grass (*Melica ciliate*).

← In autumn, colour is provided by varieties of prairie aster (*Symphyotrichum* 'Little Carlow' and *Aster ageratoides* 'Asran') in blue-purple shades. Grasses are either clumping (e.g. blue oat grass, *Helicotrichon sempervirens*) or form relatively tidy mats (e.g. *Sesleria nitida*) and are mostly low, which minimizes maintenance.

↓ A few taller grasses, notably varieties of *Miscanthus sinensis* (see also p.225) are included for their winter seed heads.

The Dry Garden

The use of irrigation to overcome any shortages of one of the most crucial inputs to the successful growth of ornamental plants is widespread. However, regional water shortages exacerbated by climate change are surely going to restrict the future growth of this arguably extremely wasteful practice. Gardeners and landscape designers are already paying more attention to the natural vegetation of dry climate zones, with a view to importing something of their aesthetic as well as their resilient wild plant species. In the world's temperate zone there are, very broadly speaking, two dry climates, each with climatically defined vegetation types that act as models and sources of plant material for gardens far removed from their original habitats. One is the so-called Mediterranean climate (here represented by gardens in southern France (see pp.124–31, 234–41), in which cool, moist winter and spring seasons are followed by hot, dry summers and autumns; the other is a steppe climate, defined by cold winters and hot summers, with low annual rainfall (see pp.58–65). The former has an air of romance about it, and garden-makers have long used many of its plants in parks and gardens in very different (usually much wetter) climates. The hummocky shapes, silver-grey colours and rich aromas of lavender, rosemary and sage have made these very popular plants, and as they thrive in a dry climate, most garden visitors do not need much persuading that an irrigation-free garden can be attractive. The steppe flora is more ascetic and less immediately lovable. It has far fewer shrubs, and of those, few are attractive, but it does produce a great many perennials, grasses and bulbs; tulips, for example, come originally from the harsh steppe landscapes of Central Asia. All of these plants, from both steppe and Mediterranean habitats, look much their best in spring, which can be extraordinarily, if briefly, beautiful. ¶ Seasonal disparity is something that those who genuinely wish to have a sustainable, irrigation-free garden have to learn to live with. The main barrier to the successful development of dry gardens is not horticultural, as there are tens of thousands of species that flourish in these climates and will do very well in wetter ones. Rather, the difficulty is cultural and psychological – summer is a time for relaxing and holidays, and these are activities that for many people are inseparable from green grass and colourful flowers. The solution is probably to have small zones of high-irrigation planting, with more extensive dry areas that are less visually prominent. ¶ Many advances have been made in developing this garden style, mostly in California and the American Southwest (see pp.36–9, 46–53) where a Mediterranean climate merges into steppe and desert zones. Progress is helped by the fact that the bottom line on seasonal disparity is not so clear cut. Summer may have a reduced colour palette and stressed-looking plants (which are not actually unhealthy but are simply dormant in that season), but winter gardens can look a great deal better than those in a cooler and wetter climate. An enormous array of evergreen foliage is one of the joys of the drier climate zone garden – with great variation in colour, texture and form, there is a lot to choose from. Some of these evergreens have always been highly rated by dry climate cultures for their sculptural properties, such as the box and myrtle of the Mediterranean zone; others are less amenable to shaping but have qualities that a more contemporary sensibility is able to appreciate. Among the latter are the charismatic madrones (*Arbutus*) and manzanitas (*Arctostaphylos*) of the American west, with their eccentric branching, cinnamon-toned bark and grey leaves. ¶ The use of succulents in seasonally dry areas has, not surprisingly, long been popular. However, there are no succulent species adapted for areas with sub-zero winters, and in warmer climates there is the danger of creating an alien look by using non-native species. These are often very visually prominent and frequently appear again and again across the world in similar climates, creating a global, lowest-common-denominator, clichéd landscape. ¶ Apart from the individual psychology involved in accepting the sere dry look, the main barrier to progress in dry climate gardening is perhaps that of plant management. Many of the most attractive species are relatively short-lived and need regeneration from seed; this affects Australian flora to an inordinate degree (see pp.40–5) and has surely done much to limit horticultural use of that continent's otherwise highly attractive flora. To a lesser but still significant extent, the same is true of the ornamental flora of the Mediterranean region. Learning new pruning techniques, engaging in successive replanting, and handling the natural processes of vegetation change all have a part to play in the creation of attractive dry gardens. ¶ Sustainable, inviting and arguably beautiful – dry gardens are an increasingly fast-moving area of garden and landscape making.

'Many people don't know that the flora is much richer in Mediterranean climate regions than in cool temperate climates', says Alejandro O'Neill. It is this awareness of the diversity of the region's flora and the resilience of much of it to climatic extremes that is driving naturalistic planting design in southern Europe, as well as in similar dry summer climates around the world. O'Neill often works with the Bassons (pp.96–101) and uses plants supplied by Olivier Filippi's nursery (pp.124–31). His approach is subtly different, however, showing that despite a philosophy in common, the range of the plant palette and the ability of the plants within that palette to cope with the climate in different ways means that there is much scope for creative innovation. This small (1,200 square metres / 0.3 acre) garden in Cap d'Antibes, which includes the base of a historic water tank, illustrates the potential for developing a drought-tolerant garden with a light, airy and intimate planting style perhaps more typical of northern European cottage gardens.

Two regional ecosystems serve as an inspiration: the low, scrubby garrigue and the taller Mediterranean woodland. Both include species that are frequently kept in check by animal grazing, exposure to wind or occasional fires; such acts of disturbance, far from being destructive, usually enhance plant diversity by limiting the growth of species that would otherwise dominate. The implications of this for gardeners and landscape managers is that maintenance techniques are very important for the success of plantings.

In the garden, frequent trimming helps to maintain the plants in a condition that means they are read as tidy garden elements, but it also helps lengthen the lifespan of frequently short-lived species. The idea of 'goat pruning', as O'Neill refers to it, should perhaps make us look at clipping as an activity more in tune with nature here than it might be in other environments. Frequent light clipping encourages increased basal growth, which helps plants to survive drought better. 'Wind pruning' aims at imitating the shapes plants develop in exposed coastal environments. Others may need what is popularly known as the 'Chelsea chop', a hard prune, almost to the base, at around the time of London's Chelsea Flower Show in May, or the selective pruning out of older branches and stems.

Small native trees or shrubs such as snowy mespilus (*Amelanchier ovalis*), tree spurge (*Euphorbia dendroides*) and Judas tree (*Cercis siliquastrum*) play an important role in this garden, any shade being valued by plants and humans alike. There is a higher proportion of herbaceous plants here than in many Mediterranean gardens, giving it a looser, slightly more ragged feel. Despite O'Neill's focus on pruning, sub-shrubs do not play a visually dominant role, although he reckons they make up to 60 per cent of the planting. Different parts of the garden are planted

Cap d'Antibes Garden

with different combinations of plants, but certain species run through the whole to create continuity. There is a feeling that the design here is driven by the desire to show off the particular aesthetic qualities of certain plant species. This may be a reflection of the greater diversity of plant form and texture in this climate zone than in cool temperate gardens as well as the fact that a Mediterranean climate limits the soggy end-of-season collapse which is a danger further north.

Among the crucial continuity plants are horned spurge (*Euphorbia ceratocarpa*) – an upright, green-leaved species, and rock lettuce (*Petromarula pinnata*), which emerges 'looking like salad rocket' in spring, with spikes of blue flowers in early summer. Both of these species self-seed, ensuring that the plants will potentially reach all parts of the garden. O'Neill stresses how he likes to use emergent plants (see pp.104–9) and grasses, neither of which have been part of even recent naturalistic Mediterranean garden looks. He particularly likes *Cephalaria ambrosioides*: 'super emergent, up to three metres [10 ft], it really stands out', with a light, airy character that contributes height without bulk. The well-known and very drought-tolerant shrub French tamarisk (*Tamarix gallica*) is also here, but pruned to the base occasionally to produce long shoots that also have an emergent character. Another popular shrub, tree germander or shrubby germander (*Teucrium fruticans*), is also judicially pruned in order 'to make it more feathery'.

Different in character to these rather wispy plants is rock samphire (*Crithmum maritimum*), a coastal species for much of Europe. O'Neill describes how he is 'absolutely in love with it. It looks like summer never happened, with its lush green leaves ... I use it as a matrix with other plants and in blocks. When you have branched asphodel (*Asphodelus microcarpus*) emerging from clumps of it, with tall spikes of white creamy flowers, it's quite a unique combination.' Thorny burnet (*Sarcopoterium spinosum*), a compact, spiny shrub, he likes for its 'cloud-like shape, interesting through the seasons, as it's leafy in winter but is a leafless ball of spines in summer; a great combination with perennials with flower spikes or narrow flower heads'.

For early spring there are bulbs, primarily crocuses and some *Allium* species for later, such as *A. sphaerocephalon*, whose small, dark purple heads make a big impact when scattered through other planting, but whose ultra-light foliage makes it usefully insignificant. There are annuals, too, though in this relatively young garden they have not yet established their place; their eventual presence will be dependent on self-sowing.

The emerging model for dry summer climate gardens tends to stress the role of generally rounded forms of sub-shrubs such as lavender and cistus, but this garden illustrates the huge potential for using the rich flora of these zones to create more varied planting combinations, with seasonal dynamism in form and texture and a delightful lightness of touch.

↑ Within a framework of mostly pines and olives, the garden features complex plantings in a series of intimate spaces, rather than the low hummocks of more open Mediterranean gardens (e.g. pp.124–31).

↓ Light Mediterranean woodland plants include the silver stems of tree purslane (*Atriplex halimus*) and seed heads of *Lomelosia minoana* (below and pp.238–9). Zoysia grass with silver-leaved yarrow (*Achillea coarctata*; p.234) provides a lawn alternative.

← ↑ One of the effects here is the gradient
between neatly rounded and much looser
growth habits, partly the result of
different maintenance regimes, e.g.
the rounded forms of wild thyme (*Thymus
capitatus*) and the open habit of sage
(*Salvia* 'Allen Chickering', pp.238–9).
Some annual clipping is inevitable, but
modern practice is creative and selective,
geared towards developing the most
appropriate forms for each plant species.

↓ The relationship of the trees with the
vegetation echoes that of natural stone
pine (*Pinus pinea*) woodland: the clean
trunks and high-level canopy of the trees
maximize ground-level vegetation.

← Eroded chunks of limestone add a sculptural touch but are also a reminder of a fundamental fact of southern European ecology: the flora that has developed on shallow limestone soils are among the richest on the continent. Gardens on this apparently unrewarding substrate can, in fact, be extremely diverse and attractive.

↓ The nature of the planting here should be contrasted with that at Le Jardin Sec (pp.124–31). The clump forms in both are here complemented with looser forms, and seed heads play a role from late summer through winter; in this more confined space, the comparison is perhaps with traditional English borders. The yellow-green flowers are *Euphorbia ceratocarpa*, along with fennel (*Foeniculum vulgare*).

An elongated pool of dark intensity stretches into the distance, with a gentle rise to a woodland bank on one side and a higher slope on the other, this one in open sunshine. A boardwalk invites visitors to walk alongside the water and on towards the end of the pool. So begins the Native Plant Garden at the New York Botanical Garden. A sophisticated approach to design and construction, with cutting-edge sustainable technology for water circulation and a very carefully orchestrated plant collection, make this something of a *tour-de-force*, with a naturalistic planting of extraordinary richness. The garden aims to display a representative range of species and habitats from the northeast United States and adjacent areas of Canada, and does so in a way that also conveys the context of the plants growing much as they would do in nature – hence our considering it one of the most genuinely 'ecological' gardens discussed in this book.

Wandering through the garden, it is easy to lose any sense of being in a designed landscape, as the eye is constantly drawn into dense plant combinations that look amazingly undesigned. There are few of the distracting labels one generally finds in botanical gardens, and although the whole place is clearly designed to show off different habitats, each one segues effortlessly into the next. Once at the end of the pool, starting the gentle climb up the slope, it becomes even more difficult to believe that this dense mass of plants is anything other than untrammelled nature. 'It is definitely a garden, though', asserts Michael Hagen, who is responsible for managing the area. 'It does require maintenance, above all. The space would ultimately turn into deciduous woodland if we did nothing.' The wildflowers are all native, but they are not necessarily growing together in the combinations they would be in the wild. Hagen defines the approach as 'working towards creating artificial ecosystems

of plants that play well together and look aesthetically pleasing'.

Opened in 2013, the Native Plant Garden was designed by American landscape designers Oehme van Sweden Associates. The company was the most appropriate, indeed perhaps the only one, that could have taken on this project. And yet, as they worked on the design, the firm's approach to planting in its previous work became history, as its signature style of monocultural blocks was displaced by more naturalistic work produced by other practices. Wolfgang Oehme (1930–2011) was completely uninterested in native plants, which by

New York Botanical Garden

Native Plant Garden

2000 were becoming the focus of a very strong movement, and James van Sweden (1935–2013) considered naturalistic planting messy. It was a younger partner in the practice, Sheila Brady, who led the Botanical Garden project, working closely with the institution's experts to assess how many and what habitats could be included in the 1.4-hectare (3.5 acre) site. The garden staff then had to work out the species that could be used for each habitat. There is woodland, a woodland glade, a wet meadow, a mesic meadow (one with average soil moisture), and a rocky ridge; and, of course, all the transitions between the two. A range of special collections had to be shoehorned in: bog plants, spring ephemerals (early spring wildflowers), ferns.

Managing the Native Plant Garden is radically different from many naturalistic gardens, where plants are tended to individually, and different again from ecosystem planting such as meadows and prairies, where there is almost no attention paid to individual plants, and everything gets the same treatment. 'Editing' is probably the best word to describe it. 'It was very densely planted to begin with', says Hagen, 'and we are monitoring how the meadow is spontaneously regenerating – which species are growing, making sure that no one species takes over. We do a lot of targeted interventions. There have been some interesting spontaneous accessions, species that just arrive, and deciding what is allowed to stay is part of the management process. ... Everything is always a bit of a mystery, for example *Silene virginica*, red catchfly [a spectacular scarlet flower], disappeared for a few years and then re-appeared.'

Something similar could be said about another strong, short-lived, scarlet species, the cardinal flower (*Lobelia cardinalis*), which also comes and goes. Because of strong colour or form, species like this can play an important role in how the planting looks, but pragmatic decisions have to be made, based on how plants perform in what are very competitive conditions. Hagen mentions, as an example, that 'several *Liatris* species [Kansas gayfeather] were included for design reasons, but there isn't the depth of soil for them to effectively compete with other species, so rather than waste time and effort re-introducing it, we'd rather work with other species that create good effects at a similar time, like *Euphorbia corollata* [flowering spurge]. I know what Sheila Brady was wanting, so if something doesn't work, we'll find something else that will create a similar effect.'

While changes are constant in such an ecologically dynamic environment, and while there is an expectation that

as a botanical garden, new species are added from time to time, staying loyal to the design concept is important. The concept in this situation is one that emphasizes distinct plant combinations in particular places, which is important both for the interpretive role of the garden – showing how certain plant combinations occupy certain habitats – and to enhance visual interest. Hagen explains: 'For a few years we were trying to make the original planting plan work, but after a while it became apparent that with the sheer amount of plant material we poured in, we were

not going to get a 100 per cent success rate. We had to become more flexible, and in any case, we do not want to keep it static – we are curious as to see how it evolves.' In some cases, management decisions are clearly leading to improved visual effects, as with tufted hair grass (*Deschampsia cespitosa*) being allowed to spread, 'so it links areas together'. In particular, changing conditions such as increasing tree growth can mean that plants may move into better light by both vegetative spread and seeding. The context for decision-making is that 'we want to keep the overall design,

so that, for example, we would not change the north-south alignments of perennial masses.'

The Native Plant Garden is a fascinating project for the way in which a designer from a company with a planting design strategy that has always emphasized strong graphic effects has risen to the challenge of working in a very different way. What Brady has created is more akin to starting a design process rather than ending one, which skilful and sensitive handling is continually refining – maintenance as design, and design that never ends.

← (Previous) Alongside a large pool in the Native Plant Garden, the scarlet of cardinal flowers (*Lobelia cardinalis*) is prominent in early autumn; at the far end is false chamomile (*Boltonia asteroides*), and the blue in the foreground is blue mist flower (*Conoclinium coelestinum*).

↑↓ An area of woodland edge habitat runs along the lower side and is dominated at this time by the dull pink of joe pye weed (*Eutrochium maculatum*) and ashy sunflower (*Helianthus mollis*, above left). Insectivorous pitcher plants (*Sarracenia flava* and *S. leucophylla*, above right) attract attention in a wetland area adjacent to the pool. There are grasses too, with little blue stem (*Schizachyrium scoparium*, below) prominent around the rocks.

→ (Overleaf) White flowering *Euphorbia corollata* makes a splash in late summer amid species of goldenrod (mostly *Euthamia graminifolia* and *Solidago nemoralis*).

Innisfree has a romantic name and a slightly mysterious reputation. Despite its accessibility (it is not far from New York City and not hard to find), it does not promote itself commercially – there is no gift shop or café – and it remains remarkably unvisited. Even many landscape architects and horticultural academics have never been there.

Those who do make the journey soon realize they have reached somewhere special. Created between 1929 and 1960 by Walter and Marion Beck in collaboration with landscape architect Lester Collins, the 75-hectare (185 acre) garden is now managed by a charitable trust. It occupies a bowl around a 16-hectare (40 acre) lake, the sort of landscape that designers of eighteenth- or nineteenth-century landscape gardens created to suggest otherworldliness. The higher slopes are wooded, the nearer surroundings largely mown, but not too precisely. As Curator Kate Kerin describes it, 'the garden emerges from the woods', although she could also have described it as emerging from the lake.

A walk around reveals a series of plantings, trees, some carefully positioned stones and the very occasional clipped tree. The latter stand out as quite deliberate – emphasized by their rarity, they express far stronger feelings of intention than clipped woody plants normally do. The tradition of mown grass is deeply ingrained in American garden culture, but here it highlights those areas that are not mowed: wetland areas around the lake, where lush waterside plants are given their head, or steep banks that are clearly less managed. The property also includes much natural habitat, which tends to merge almost imperceptibly with the designed elements, many of which are so relaxed that some viewers would read them as wild.

Walter Beck's main inspiration was the eighth-century garden of Wang Wei, a Chinese poet-painter-politician. We only know of Wang's garden through scroll paintings, and in some ways it is more concept than reality – a set of ideas that has echoed through Chinese garden history. Innisfree's sense of flow from one subtly demarcated area to another

feels very much in the East Asian garden tradition. Lester Collins spoke of 'cup gardens', by which he meant self-contained garden areas that had their own distinct feel; they could be much smaller than the 'rooms' created by Arts and Crafts garden-makers, even as small as one rock. The Chinese garden tradition emphasizes small and intimate areas conceived as vignettes of something larger, an effect usually achieved through hard elements such as rock; here at Innisfree, it is planting that does this.

Innisfree's dialogue with its surroundings is perhaps why the place is so celebrated by landscape *cognoscenti*, but the planting is also very special, much of it a blend of American natives and introduced garden plants that is almost unique in an American garden.

Innisfree

This is partly the result of cuts in the maintenance budget, resulting in areas like the East Rock Garden being 'let go'.

The garden feels at the same time like an empty landscape (the house was demolished in the 1960s) full of meaning – to which there are few clues. Deliberate clipping, for example, of six ornamental pear trees near the lake seems to indicate something – but what? And the rocks, carefully placed but much more sparsely than in classic Chinese gardens. Each one feels like a work of sculpture, and perhaps fulfils the same function as abstract sculpture in some contemporary gardens.

The planting is low-key, much of it shrubs and perennials planted over decades – what we see today are the survivors of an early experiment in ecological management. Much of this planting is along the lakeside, but some of the most interesting is in the East Rock Garden, on the partially shaded slopes to the east of the lake. This area of thin, rocky soil includes a blend of garden and native perennials in a dense, novel ecosystem. There are garden plants, mostly, but not entirely woodland species: bugbane

(*Actaea* spp.), masterwort (*Astrantia* spp.) and barrenwort (*Epimedium* spp.), natives such as the local wood aster (*Eurybia divaricata*), and ferns. They are all growing in intermingled clumps, in some cases in juxtapositions that just should not be there, if the garden books are to be believed. For example, there is a supposedly sun-loving whorled tickseed (*Coreopsis verticillata*) mingled up with the well-known shade plant lily of the valley (*Convallaria majalis*). It's a horticultural free-for-all, apparently the result of decades of planting to make a conventional rock garden, along with benign neglect. 'After Lester Collins had to reduce the garden staff from twenty to five, in areas that were intensively managed, the natives have moved in', says Kerin. Collins saw this process positively, as a new form of management, making him a very forward-looking figure.

The wet areas very near the lake look wild too, but given the exuberance of many waterside plants, there is more management here. The grass stops suddenly and is replaced by a thick shoreline of vegetation. Waterside plants tend to be monocultural, as one species often establishes itself at the expense of all others. Here, though, there seems to be a healthy balance, the native sensitive fern (*Onoclea sensibilis*) being particularly good at infiltrating the growth of other plants and contributing its unique frond shapes to the general green mêlée.

Kerin describes how the garden undergoes 'different levels of maintenance, so different plant communities develop. Various levels of cutting, for example, certain plants edited out in some areas but not in others. If everything were managed to the same degree, it would all look the same.' Although the resulting vegetation is one of the most successful native/non-native mixes in a public garden in the United States, it is, Kerin says, 'about aesthetics and not about ecological restoration'. Reduced funding for maintenance has ensured that wild plants have remained and garden plants allowed to spread and mingle as much as they are able – a lesson that perhaps, sometimes, not doing can be as important as doing.

→ Reductions in maintenance have resulted in
ecological processes taking over in places,
producing interesting plant combinations.
Mown grass, carefully sited trees and
deliberately shaped water bodies (right and
p.253 upper right) contrast with more natural
water-to-land gradations, where native
species such as the sensitive fern (*Onoclea
sensibilis*) dominate (p.250, foreground).

← ↑↓ Evoking a traditional Chinese moon gate, rockwork (left) is partially covered in Virginia creeper (*Parthenocissus quinquefolia*) and climbing hydrangea (*Hydrangea petiolaris*). A bank of only occasionally mown grass (above) is one of several steep slopes that incorporate grass and naturalized perennials, here a white foxglove (*Digitalis purpurea*). Marshy areas (below) are minimally maintained, often dominated by native plants but with some garden species, such as these pink primulas (forms of *Primula japonica*).

→ (Overleaf) Shaded rocky areas include a blend of non-native species planted over many years, alongside natives that have spread from the surrounding woods. Here, *Primula japonica* (of Himalayan origin) flowers alongside native ferns and Virginia creeper (*Parthenocissus quinquefolia*). At the upper right is blue false indigo (*Baptisia australis*), a native species but almost certainly planted, as woodland is not its normal habitat.

← The garden at Innisfree segues imperceptibly into the surrounding woods, with ferns often blurring the boundaries.

↓ Features and plants surviving from the garden around the now-demolished house, such as the stone archway, stone-edged borders (p.257 bottom left) and the Chinese tree peony (p.257 bottom right) create a feeling of enigmatic nostalgia.

↑↓ Much of Innisfree is currently mown, though one can imagine
it as occasionally cut meadow. The many wet areas are
managed more sustainably, with periodic trimming, allowing
a mix of native and garden plants to thrive together. Rocky
areas (below) are managed only to remove tree seedlings and
limit the growth of aggressive spreaders.

Innisfree

In full summer flower, the prairie at Tom Stuart-Smith's garden north of London is an impressive sight, and to someone unused to the American original, it could almost be described as surreal. It looks like a wildflower meadow, but on a huge scale, with some plants exceeding 2 metres (6.5 ft) in height; there is almost a feeling of having blundered into an Alice in Wonderland world. Many of the component species look vaguely familiar, but not at this density: it is all very lush and, for much of the summer, very colourful. Broad paths wend their way through its 2,000 square metres (0.5 acre) and introduce the visitor to an impressive range of species, which occur in a variety of combinations and concentrations.

Creating a North American prairie in a British or, indeed, any European garden may seem an act of perversity. Why create a completely alien habitat out of context, one that occurs naturally in a markedly different climate? There is, however, a precedent in that many 'prairie' perennials have been grown extensively in northwest European gardens since the early 1800s; they were an essential part of the grand herbaceous borders that were a feature of public parks and the gardens of the British upper classes in the late nineteenth and early twentieth centuries. Growing these plants in a naturalistic 'prairie' is, arguably, just a different way of using the same material. With a growing interest in naturalistic and sustainable planting at the end of the twentieth century, European horticulturists realized that fertile North American soils have an immensely rich flora, and one that tends to flower in late summer or autumn, when most European species have long since finished. The attractions were obvious, and from a biodiversity perspective, the late flowers are a boon for pollinating bees and butterflies.

For Tom Stuart-Smith, 'prairie seems to be an interesting way of creating a diverse, colourful expanse of planting which does not require too much aftercare. I'm interested in how gardens can be an intensification of landscape patterns, in how they can have different plots, different management regimes, thinking of the landscape as being a kind of quilt. I have always been interested in the idea of low-intensity gardening.' Having developed areas of prairie for clients in collaboration with James Hitchmough (see pp.104–9), Stuart-Smith describes how 'I wanted experience in managing prairie myself.' He designed the initial seed list with two different mixes, one for an area of sandier soil and one for soils with higher clay content, although he has added various other species seeds to it since.

The Barn

Prairie Garden

A prairie is like a wildflower meadow on a large scale, with a matrix of grasses and a diverse minority element of flowering species. Prairies are almost invariably created from seed mixes, which means they are relatively cheap to make and ensures that the plant distribution is largely down to natural rather than designed factors. James Hitchmough and other European practitioners tend to leave out the grasses, partly because they do not always flourish predictably at more northerly latitudes; instead, they find they get good results by sowing a mix of flowering species. The outcome is a plant community far denser than any border, dense enough to keep out weeds for years. Says Stuart-Smith, 'I like the idea of mixing the familiar with the strange – a meadow, with meadow typology, but where all the components, the species themselves, are completely unfamiliar.'

'I have used prairie in large areas where a client does not want to cultivate intensively, but where something has to be done. I've done six or seven so far, for the more adventurous clients, those who enjoy being immersed in something different and unusual – interestingly, often the ones who know less about gardening.' Viewing prairie from the right perspective is important: 'If you see it from too far away, the forms and colours mush into each other ... You need to be close' – hence the importance of the paths inviting the visitor in.

The high points of prairie plantings tend to be summer and autumn, but with a good many seed heads to provide interest later on. In fact, the creators of prairies in northern Europe get a bonus denied to the Americans. The play onto dying foliage, grass stems and seed heads of the characteristic warm sunlight of late afternoon at latitudes higher than any natural North American prairie brings out an astonishing richness of tone – grass seed heads can glow with backlighting, and every subtle shade of russet is enhanced.

Normal management practice sees prairie plants cut down in late winter, to re-emerge in spring. The earlier part of the year may seem empty, though there are, in fact, plenty of smaller plant species that can flower now and become semi-dormant in the shade of the dominant elements later. Stuart-Smith describes planting a number of early-growing European species to improve interest at this time, and mentions his pleasure at the success of German pink (*Dianthus carthusianorum*) just before the American species get into their stride. It would also be possible to use bulbs such as daffodils (*Narcissus* spp.) and wild hyacinth (*Camassia* spp.) in prairies.

Thus, prairie planting seems to have arrived as a low-maintenance formula for European gardens. Perhaps it is the twenty-first century's response to the labour-intensive herbaceous borders of the early twentieth century. Many of the plants are the same, but the methodology and ethics behind them are very different – truly a 'novel ecosystem'.

←↑↓ Prairies can be extraordinarily rich environments visually, as well as being very biodiverse, which this garden illustrates. The grass component normal in European prairie-style plantings is largely missing, so the range of flowering forms is accentuated. The distinctive leaves of *Silphium* species are invaluable for their contrast with the fine textures of most of the species present here (left). This is prairie dock (*S. terebinthinaceum*), alongside the thimbles of another very architectural species, rattlesnake-master (*Eryngium yuccifolium*, also above, below and pp.262–3). Yellow predominates during the high point of prairie flowering (late summer to early autumn), with contrast from aster species such as the dark pink of Michaelmas daisy (*Symphyotrichum novae-angliae*).

→ (Overleaf) The tall stems and flowers of prairie burdock (*Silphium terebinthinaceum*) punctuate the network of paths through the prairie planting – vital for encouraging viewers to wander and appreciate the plants.

A Seasonal Approach

One of the reasons for the success of naturalistic planting has been the chance it offers, particularly in urban situations, to appreciate the seasons. Traditional bedding has also done this effectively, with its serried ranks of tulips in spring, marigolds in summer and pansies in winter. From the 1970s onwards, however, this expensive and high-maintenance style has been gradually replaced by banks of shrubs, many of them evergreen; these look more or less the same all year round, and have been perceived by many as dull and lifeless. In contrast, naturalistic planting of almost any type celebrates the seasons in ways far more vibrantly and sustainably than either of these. ¶ The whole movement towards naturalistic planting has been greatly dominated by the use of herbaceous perennials – indeed, the term 'New Perennial' gardening has been used as an alternative name. This domination of the field by one category of plant has been somewhat unfortunate, however; it has limited the appeal of naturalistic planting, reduced its usefulness to wildlife and checked its ability to provide interest across the seasons. Spring interest, in particular, is created overwhelmingly by trees, shrubs and bulbs, with a minority input from perennials. Flowering trees and shrubs are a big part of the joy of spring for many people, but their integration with other plants can be problematic, as they shade the ground beneath them; pruning may be needed to make space for smaller species. ¶ Fortunately, much can be done to distribute bulbs and some smaller spring-flowering perennials among the summer-flowering ones. Spring- and summer-growing perennials and bulbs complement each other in the sense that they extract moisture and nutrients from the soil at different times of year – this means that a great many smaller bulbs, such as crocuses, snowdrops (*Galanthus* spp.) and dwarf daffodils (*Narcissus* spp.), can be scattered around and create impact over many years. Bulbs, in particular, are very easy to 'retrofit' by shoehorning them in among clumps of established perennials. An early example of this was Chicago's Lurie Garden, when Dutch bulb specialist Jacqueline van der Kloet added an additional layer to Piet Oudolf's previously established perennial planting in 2006. Oudolf himself now often prepares a bulb plan in addition to his main perennial planting plan (see pp.20–7). ¶ Spring interest is distributed through space in a different way to that of summer, as flowering trees and shrubs tend to be head height or higher, whereas bulbs and early perennials tend to be lower than knee height. However, since most perennials and grasses are either just emerging or still dormant, they can easily visually dominate the ground layer in summer, and since they are easy to distribute in a way that appears random, a 'naturalistic' effect is readily obtained. ¶ At the other end of the year, the entire contemporary planting movement has made a very clear break with the past, which has had a major impact. Traditionally, the somewhat limited perennial plantings used in parks and gardens would be cut down in autumn, leaving bare ground during the winter. Largely led by Piet Oudolf (see pp.266–73), who essentially took the idea from a Dutch colleague, Henk Gerritsen, modern naturalistic planting makes a great point of leaving everything standing. Ornamental grasses and some perennials can look very fine just at that time, late autumn and early winter, which was traditionally regarded as the nadir of the garden year. Oudolf is a good photographer of his own work, particularly at this time, and his pictures, used to illustrate his own books or magazine articles, introduced the idea of low autumn light or, better still, hoar frost on seed heads. A brief fashion followed in which professional garden photographers followed suit. Oudolf had made his point, however – effectively redefining beauty in the garden or landscape planting at this time of year, with his emphasis on 'plants that look good when they are dead'. Seed heads are a major part of this, and Oudolf sets great store on those species whose seed heads are particularly distinctive or long-lasting. Grasses, in particular, are physically strong and tend to be storm-proof. At northern latitudes there is an additional bonus as the warm wavelengths of light in the late afternoon have an especially strong impact, bringing out immense subtleties of tone in the rather narrow yellow-to-brown spectrum of dead herbaceous material. ¶ The end-of-season look has proved enormously successful, as can be appreciated at the Hauser & Wirth Gallery (see pp.20–7) and at Lianne's Siergrassen (see pp.116–23). It can be applied at many different scales with plants that are long-lived and low maintenance, including, in many cases, those that are good species for biodiversity, providing seed for birds, winter shelter for insect larvae, etc. The spectrum of russet shades can seem almost infinite, and the shapes of grasses and late perennials are easy to appreciate in deteriorating weather conditions – all factors that an increasing number of garden and landscape designers are appreciating for a range of situations.

For those familiar with the work of the well-known Dutch garden designer Piet Oudolf, the area behind the old farmhouse where he lives with his wife, Anja, is a surprise: it seems much wilder than his normal plantings. However naturalistic the gardening public thinks those to be, they are actually very much within a conventional tradition of distinct plant clumps – or at least, where there are mixes, the identity of the individual plants is clear (see also pp.20–7, 132–9). Oudolf's 0.5-hectare (1.25 acre) garden in the tiny village of Hummelo, in the province of Gelderland in The Netherlands, is a meadow, where garden perennials and grasses grow in tight profusion, with several species often seeming to occupy the same space. A matrix of native grass species make up most of the biomass, with a minority of wildflowers and what appear to be garden perennials. One heretical thought that might cross one's mind is that this was once an area of the garden over which its owner lost control. On the contrary, it is a rare example of two contemporary garden features – a wildflower meadow and a perennial border – that seem to have merged, seamlessly.

The Oudolf garden lies beneath the big sky of the flat, intensely agricultural Dutch landscape. The area between the road and the house is a densely-packed perennial garden, but away from the road this very unusual meadow takes over. On its far side is an austere brick building that houses Oudolf's office and guest accommodation. As a garden, and a space in which to see a wide range of plants, it stands out in an agricultural landscape rendered bright green by well-fertilized grass. At the edge of the garden, a once conventional hedge has been clipped into irregular waves, quite unlike a normal country hedge but nothing like as even or regular as a garden hedge.

In 2011, Piet and Anja closed their on-site nursery, which Anja initially ran to supply plants for the design business, then to sell to the increasing numbers of visitors who came to see the garden. They then had to find a use for the 500 square metres (5400 sq. ft) of levelled ground. 'I want something simple to look after as we get older', said Oudolf. The idea, he explained, was to plant out perennials and grasses, such as the ornamental feather reed grass (*Calamagrostis* x *acutiflora* 'Karl Foerster'), and sow a wildflower meadow mix (mostly grasses, with a few wild perennials) between them. One might worry that within three years the grasses would take over, but this has not happened. For the first few years at least, the garden perennials, wildflowers and grasses all co-existed happily.

Oudolf reports, however, that over time, 'the big species have done well, although the lower levels have lost diversity. Some short-lived species and wildflowers are disappearing, but the yarrow [*Achillea millefolium*] and bedstraws [*Galium* spp.] have done well.' By 'big species' he means the late-flowering

Hummelo

Perennial Meadow

North American plants such as asters, joe pye weed (*Eupatorium* spp.) and ironweeds (*Vernonia* spp.) that stand somewhat taller than the grass. Indeed, their height and bulk rescues the meadow in a late summer and early autumn spectacle. Ordinarily, meadow grass looks lush and attractive until around the end of June, when, quite rapidly, it begins to look very untidy. An ordinary wildflower meadow of European native species would have been cut by that time. Here, however, the height of the later-flowering plants keeps it looking good, and in any case the grass does not get too long or coarse.

These late-flowering, mostly North American species are more usually seen in borders, and have been familiar cultivated plants since the nineteenth century. Their number has been increased recently by growers, Oudolf included, introducing more of them to Europe to use in perennial plantings. But they have rarely been used like this – usually they appear in heavily managed borders where the placement of individual plants is precise and where there is no question of anything other than selected garden plants growing among them. They are also great magnets for butterflies, and given that the north European flora is quite poor in later-flowering plants, they are a boon for pollinators. Each clump seems to hold its own, and some are even beginning to seed.

There are some weeds, Oudolf confesses, but not many, and they are easily dealt with. 'Tree seedlings have to be pulled out, but otherwise there is no maintenance apart from cutting back in late winter', he says. There is horsetail (*Equisetum arvense*), a notorious weed very common on damp Dutch soils, but it can only grow so high, and here it is kept in check by the taller growth around it.

This kind of healthy balance has eluded many who have sought to create perennial meadows, most notably the Irish/British garden writer William Robinson, author of *The Wild Garden* (1870). Robinson's romantic idea of a meadow of wild and cultivated plants in happy profusion never really took off. We now know that where there is a high level of mineral nutrients, grasses will dominate and generally suppress wildflowers and flowering perennials. Oudolf's success is probably due to soil chemistry. There is, apparently, a lot of rubble beneath the sandy soil at Hummelo. Soil poor in nutrients, especially phosphorus, reduces grass growth, allowing other plants to thrive.

This intriguing experiment in wild-style planting, late in the career of one of our most successful garden designers, has shown one way forward for low-maintenance and very biodiverse long-season planting. There are bulbs in spring and early summer (*Camassia* spp. making a great show of blue in May and June), and most of the Dutch native wildflowers bloom around midsummer; autumn segues into winter with strong seed head shapes standing proud of the grass. The goal of balancing a relatively wild vegetation like meadow grasses and garden perennials has been a long-held dream, and this inspiring example shows that, with the right conditions, it can be achieved.

An enticing view of Piet Oudolf's innovative
and very successful perennial meadow,
where — surprisingly rarely among naturalist
designers — garden perennials and wild
plants are combined.

This is the season to appreciate tall perennials as they move into their dormant winter phase, including the small globe thistle (*Echinops ritro*, p.266), tall joe pye weed (*Eupatorium maculatum*, below and p.271 top), tall tickseed (*Coreopsis tripteris*; pp.272–3 right) and purple New York ironweed (*Vernonia noveboracensis*).

→ ↘ Grasses, including species and varieties of
Achnatherum and *Stipa*, come into their best
season in the autumn, and most will stand
the winter well. The dark, narrow fingers of
Culver's root (*Veronicastrum virginicum*) seed
heads (below right) combine particularly well
with grasses.

→ (Overleaf) The edges of the meadow segue
towards older plantings around the buildings
of the former farm. The latter are in partial
shade, where grasses do not flourish,
although many of the flowering perennials
here can also be found in sun.

The ground beneath the trees is studded with wildflowers: the intense blue of Virginian bluebells (*Mertensia virginica*), yellow woods-poppy (*Stylophorum diphyllum*), drifts of lavender prairie phlox (*Phlox pilosa*) and fluffy white foam flower (*Tiarella cordifolia*). Some visitors might mistake it for a 'natural' woodland, in as much as any such might be found along the eastern seaboard of the United States. This is Bell's Woodland at Chanticleer, one of a new generation of garden areas where the aim is to use overwhelmingly native plants. In this way it is the nearest to nature of any of the spaces discussed in this book, the design input being limited to tweaking plant combinations to maximize visual impact.

Chanticleer is an exceptional public garden. Originally laid out by Adolph Rosengarten, Jr. (1905–90), a member of a family that made its fortune in the pharmaceutical business, it has made the transition from private to public garden along an unusual route. Having decided in 1976 to create a foundation to support a public garden, Rosengarten purchased several neighbouring properties, sought advice from landscape architects and, in 1983, hired Chris Woods, a young English gardener whose creative and idio-syncratic approach led to a unique model of garden management. Since then, high-powered garden staff have been given a great deal of autonomy in how they develop the parts of the garden with which they are entrusted.

Bell's Woodland (1.6 hectare / 4 acres) was the last part of the garden to be developed, from 2004 onwards, in a project that involved a private residence and major excavations for the installation of local services. It has been managed by Przemek Walczak since its inception. Walczak's goal is 100 per cent natives, reflecting what has become a major strand in US garden-making, and one very appropriate for east coast woodland, which is very rich in woodland wildflower flora. The first few years saw battles with the invasive alien species that all too often dominate disturbed ground in the region, such as English ivy (*Hedera helix*) and an Asian spindle bush (*Euonymus alatus*). The soil was in poor shape, but the tree flora was good, a typical local mix of tulip poplar (*Liriodendron tulipifera*), American beech (*Fagus grandifolia*), white, red and pin oak (*Quercus alba, Q. rubra, Q. palustris*), hickory (*Carya spp.*) and sycamore (*Platanus occidentalis*).

'The plants that dominated were weedy, early succession species', explains Walczak, 'whereas I was interested in the late succession ones.' The ground flora of mature North American woodland is a special one, composed of slow growing and slow to reproduce species that for the most part have intimate connections

Chanticleer

Bell's Woodland

with mycorrhizal fungi. 'So we wanted a fungal-dominated, humus-rich upper soil layer', he says, 'but construction activity had wrecked that layer. We have tried to rebuild that organic layer of the soil – a slow, ongoing process.' Part of the rebuilding work has been to ensure that all woody material that falls down from the trees 'only gets re-arranged to tidy it up, keeping it in contact with the soil so that it breaks down and feeds the fungi. I even started to incorporate woody material into the soil.' Walczak goes on to quote a recent biodiversity study that looked at terrestrial beetles and found that there were many more in Bell's Woodland than in another wooded area of Chanticleer, where there is more clearing of dead wood.

Essentially, this is garden-making as ecological restoration. The plants introduced should seed so that they form healthy reproducing populations, and this is what they are – slowly – doing. 'The sedges [*Carex* spp.] are doing well, and some of the rambunctious spring ephemerals like *Stylophorum* [woods-poppy]', reports Walczak, 'although rates of naturalizing vary.' Among native plant growers, opinions vary as to how important it is to grow plants from local, as opposed to regional, origin. Walczak is pragmatic: 'Anything east of the Mississippi is OK; we're trying to do some local ecotypes.' Another area of debate is the role of horticultural cultivars, as opposed to 'unimproved' species. 'In general', Walczak says, 'I am trying to stick to straight species. Many perform better, and cultivars can be less vigorous, less adaptable. There is so much potential with native plants that have not made it into the commercial nursery industry. I'm trying to experiment.'

The distribution of the plants across the forest floor, itself dominated by the dead leaves of the previous autumn (in which a lot of insects overwinter), is a very natural one. Some species, such as the phlox, naturally form drifts, a function of their spreading ground-level stems, whereas others, like the bluebells, seed to form more discrete clumps; some shrubs, such as azaleas, have also seeded. A number of *Dryopteris* wood ferns add another dimension, their foliage contributing height and a cool elegance during the summer months, when there is little in flower; as in nearly all woodland environments, flowering is overwhelmingly a spring affair.

'The garden is just getting to the point where people might begin to mistake it for a natural environment', says Walczak, while stressing that complete naturalism is not the goal, for this is still a garden. 'We have vignettes where there is a bit more impact, so there might be more of a showy species, and we think about how to add in species for succession in flower for longer.' As already noted, the regional woodland flora is an immensely rich one, and so the making of an environment which is both the re-creation of a genuine ecology and which gives a great deal of aesthetic pleasure is not only possible but makes eminent sense.

↑ Redbud (*Cercis canadensis*), a small tree that grows naturally beneath the canopy of taller dominant species, flowers in spring. On the ground, species of wake robin (*Trillium*), *Phlox* and *Camassia* are in flower. A bridge has been built in the form of a giant tree trunk, designed by Przemek Walczak, the gardener responsible for this area.

↓ Through much of the summer, the garden features the cool green growth of ferns and other forest floor plants, as in any native woodland. Among the ferns are Christmas fern (*Polystichum acrostichoides*), familiar to anyone who walks in the woods of eastern North America, and several species of wood fern (*Dryopteris*).

←↑↓ *Geranium maculatum*, a plant of woodland edge habitats, flowers *en masse* (above). *Phlox stolonifera* 'Sherwood Purple' (left) blooms with white foam flower (*Tiarella cordifolia*) along a path at the base of a willow fence. The distinctive foliage of Canadian wild ginger (*Asarum canadense*, below) illustrates the importance of shade-loving foliage plants during the summer, when there are relatively few flowers.

A traditional cottage with a thatched roof sits in the middle of a dense forest; another structure, a sort of pavilion, stands nearby, open on all sides and also with a thatched roof, this one covered in lush vegetation. It all looks like something out of a fairy tale. Yukiyo Izumi, a retired antiques dealer, lives here alone. The property, 5.6 hectares (13.8 acres) of woodland with a stream running through the middle of it, is named Tashiro-no-Mori (Tashiro's Forest) after Izumi-san's great-grandfather, who settled near here in 1897. This is Hokkaido, Japan's northern island, which was only effectively colonized in the late nineteenth century, with settlers coming from the main island, Honshu, to fell the forest and to farm.

As Izumi-san explains, 'I always felt that I had been promised this land.' He loves wildflowers, and felt that in his retirement this would be the perfect place to appreciate them. With a stream and undulating land to create lots of micro-habitats, and good tree cover, this should have been the ideal place. The island does have a very rich ground flora, but as in much of Hokkaido, the ground was overrun with a low-growing but intensely invasive bamboo – *Sasa nipponica*, which suppresses almost all other vegetation. The growth of sasa, a native species, has been linked to the widespread deforestation the island suffered during the twentieth century. At higher altitudes it is benefiting from climate change and having a very negative effect on many plant communities.

Here, however, there is hardly any sasa to be seen. Instead, in spring, there are drifts of wildflowers such as pink Japanese wood poppy (*Glaucidium palmatum*), a distant poppy relative, along with several species of wake robin (*Trillium*), flaccid anemone (*Anemone flaccida*), Asian fawnlily (*Erythronium japonicum*) and *Corydalis ambigua*. 'They were growing feebly among the sasa. It was a miracle that there was any', reports Izumi-san, for the bamboo shut out light and competed for moisture and nutrients. 'I started just with one hectare [2.5 acres]', he recalls, 'and quickly noticed that had a huge impact, so I gradually increased the area I cut. Now, thirty years later, there are woodland plants everywhere.'

Izumi-san also began to collect seed from the species he wanted to spread and to transplant others. He has noticed how very few of the seeds he sowed grew and matured to flower, in some cases taking many years; nevertheless, the number was much higher than would have happened naturally. One

Tashiro-no-Mori (Tashiro's Forest)

particular woodland plant, *Diphylleia grayi*, has taken the best part of twenty-five years to become established, 'but now it is seeding itself, and there are young plants everywhere'. Lily of the valley (*Convallaria majalis*) and an orchid (*Calanthe tricarinata*) are also flourishing.

Where more light penetrates to the forest floor, other species begin to appear. Hokkaido has an extraordinarily vigorous and rather graphic flora, including *Fallopia sachalinensis*, a giant version of the infamously invasive plant known as Japanese knotweed, and very large wild angelica (*Angelica ursina*). These can smother smaller plants, so Izumi-san is ready to remove them, 'but only if they threaten co-existence. I like to maintain a good balance from an aesthetic point of view.' He is finding that strong-growing species have relationships between themselves – reduce one, and another one can take its place. 'I cannot predict what will happen. I am learning all the time.'

Wetter places, such as along the stream, are dominated by wild plants with very large leaves typical of these habitats, such as giant Japanese butterbur, or bog rhubarb (*Petasites japonicus* subsp. *giganteus*), which was introduced for garden use to Britain and to the US in the early twentieth century and is now regarded as an invasive alien. Drier places, such as under some oak trees, have another flora, including day lilies (*Hemerocallis middendorffii* var. *esculenta*) and blood-red iris (*Iris sanguinea*). The strong foliage impact of many of these species is important visually in the summer, when there is very little in flower beyond some wild hydrangeas.

Izumi-san has introduced very few plants, mostly low-growing ones such as some species of cowslip (*Primula*) on the thatched roof of the pavilion. In Japan's rainy summers, the growth of plants on the roofs of country buildings has traditionally been accepted. Here, it is an opportunity to allow a few more species than might be found here naturally.

'Most gardening is about adding plants', says Izumi-san, 'but here it is addition by subtraction, taking away the more dominant plants to allow less vigorous ones to survive, and reviving plant communities through subtraction.' This is profoundly different from most garden or landscape planting. In many ways, what is happening here is habitat restoration rather than garden-making, but the techniques used are gardening ones – even if the end result is closer to a pre-deforestation Hokkaido forest floor than any kind of designed garden. This project stands at the meeting point of two traditionally separate disciplines. The product is an extraordinarily rich ecology and a lushly beautiful place.

↓ Kingcup (*Caltha palustris* var. *barthei*), a moisture-loving plant, flourishes along a stream in a situation too waterlogged for other spring-flowering species.

↓ → Japanese wood poppy (*Glaucidium palmatum*, bottom) flowers in huge quantities in spring, while *Primula jesoana* (bottom and right) has also spread, dominating large areas of the woodland floor.

Tashiro-no-Mori (Tashiro's Forest)

The garden at Great Dixter is one of the most legendary on the famously garden-mad island of Great Britain. Its exuberant planting lies at the core of that fame – it offers what so many expect of an English country garden: plenty of flowers, lots of colour, high hedges, topiary, spaces divided into intimate 'rooms', all around an exquisite medieval half-timbered house. Largely associated with Christopher Lloyd (1921–2006), whose writing introduced a great many people to a deeper understanding of gardening as a craft and an art, it occupies a unique place in global horticulture.

An integral part of the Dixter landscape are the areas of rough grass around the gardens. One large area (about 0.4 hectare / 1 acre) to the southeast of the house is historically meadow (cut every summer for hay), while others, such as the Front Meadow, have in the past been cut as lawn but are now also managed as wildflower meadows. In contrast to the many plantings in gardens that now get labelled as 'meadow', this is the real thing – and given the status of Great Dixter among the world's gardens, they should perhaps be treated as the 'ur-meadow' of the naturalistic planting movement.

Dixter's meadows are the genuine article in that they are cut for hay (or grass, which is then composted) in high summer, the traditional time for such an operation, and again in late autumn. Over the years, the removal of the cuttings has driven down the fertility of the soil, so it now supports an incredible range of plant species that are freed from the competition of stronger-growing ones, which tend to monopolize more productive environments. The meadows have become wildflower meadows *par excellence*, and they form a counterpoint to the various other gardens around the house, both directly – in that some are home to yew (*Taxus baccata*) topiary forms and purple-leaved smoke trees (*Cotinus coggygria*) that

arise out of the meadows' grassy haze in the ultimate expression of horticultural creative tension – and as something wild and local, in contrast to the exuberance and exoticism of the garden.

A wide range of wildflower species bloom in the Dixter meadows from spring until mid-summer, with four species of orchid – early purples (*Orchis mascula*), green winged (*O. morio*), bifoil (*Listera ovata*) and spotted (*Dactylorhiza fuchsii*) – the jewels in the crown, for these rather capricious plants are generally seen as the ultimate accolade for the British

Great Dixter House and Garden

Meadows

ecological gardener. A biodiversity survey conducted in 2017–18 confirmed that the garden's grassland, and indeed the entire Great Dixter estate, supports very high levels of biodiversity in terms of insects and other invertebrates, fungi and flowering plants. The meadow areas are a speckled glory of wildflowers and delicate grasses from May to July, but like nearly all European meadows they are not very colourful before this, and certainly not afterwards. The white ox-eye daisy (*Leucanthemum vulgare*) is prominent, as is yellow bird's foot trefoil (*Lotus corniculatus*) and yellow rattle (*Rhinanthus minor*); the latter plays an important role as a semi-parasite, weakening the grass and therefore improving the competitive chances of non-grass species (see also pp.196–203).

Some meadow habitats, at least those in central Europe, have rich displays of bulbs in spring. This has been successfully imitated in many British gardens with daffodils, and it would seem that Great Dixter was one of the pioneers of this practice, as Lloyd's mother, Daisy Lloyd (1880–1972) would have been influenced by Gertrude Jekyll (1843–1932) and William Robinson (1838–1935), two pioneers of this remarkably easy and generally successful way of bringing spring interest to rough grassland; indeed, many old daffodil cultivars survive here. Lloyd's mother is known to have grown a wild daffodil (*Narcissus pseudonarcissus*) and snake's head fritillaries (*Fritillaria meleagris*) from seed and planted them out here; both are still flourishing. Lloyd continued the practice enthusiastically, as has Fergus Garrett, who was Lloyd's last Head Gardener when he was alive and who continues in the role today. Garrett also continues to develop the garden as a centre for innovation and education, as well as sheer horticultural pleasure. Among the long list of bulbs he has planted out here, mostly successfully, species of wild hyacinth (*Camassia*) have been particularly good.

Bulbs offer a convenient way of creating a very effective spectacle in grassland in spring, as they present concentrated dots of colour; they are able to grow at low temperatures, and their flowers and leaves are projected above the new grass for long enough to feed the bulb for next year's performance before being smothered by the sward (which is liable to overpower much other plant life in climates with a long growing season). Flowering perennials, which start their growth later, have to face stiff grass competition in meadows, and tend to perform much less well. As already noted, wildflowers in the Dixter meadows flourish because generations of cutting for hay has brought down the soil

fertility, enabling grasses and wildflowers to compete more equally.

Lloyd, ever the experimenter, started planting perennials into the grass in the 1980s. As Fergus Garrett notes, 'He tried a whole lot of stuff, a lot of American natives. When everyone was talking about this in the 1990s, Christo had had ten to fifteen years of experimenting in there.' Most of the perennials have survived, but almost none has spread, and Garrett reports that almost no plants from the garden borders have seeded into the grass areas. This has been the experience of a great many of us who experimented with this from the 1990s onwards; only in special circumstances does inserting perennials into north

European grassland actually work (see pp.266–73).

The Great Dixter meadows are very much a 'natural' feature, then, in inverted commas – because they are the result of traditional hay cutting, and therefore anthropogenic. As the majority of Europe's meadows have been converted to pasture, arable land, or are managed for silage production with a high nutrient regime, a vast amount of very valuable habitat has been lost as the result of expanding human populations and their arguably unsustainable diet. Part of the value of the meadows at Great Dixter is simply that – they are intrinsically valuable for biodiversity in the way that much garden habitat, even

much naturalistic planting, is not. They also have an inherent beauty that draws people to them and is probably at the root of the widespread misunderstanding of what a meadow is.

Meadows are a seasonal and cyclical phenomenon, reaching a peak of flowering glory usually in June, then being cut and frequently being just green for the rest of the year. This limits their visual value, but the fact that there are empty expanses of short grass during the traditionally holiday period of August allows them to be used for events, games, or just sitting about and relaxing. No other garden or landscape feature is able to combine visual appeal, wildlife value and human functionality so elegantly.

→ The common spotted orchid (*Dactylorhiza fuchsii*, right and p. 283) is always a 'seal of approval' on anyone's attempts to make a meadow. Fickle, only predictable in their strong disapproval of fertilized soil, organic or otherwise, when they do well they can multiply in their hundreds.

←↓ Adding interest to early summer is the blue of common camassia (*Camassia quamash*), a prairie bulb easy to naturalize in grass (left). Roses and flowering meadows make for a wonderfully romantic early summer spectacle. Drifts of wildflowers (below) come and go in the meadow grass, often at different concentrations every year, especially for short-lived components such as the white ox-eye daisy (*Leucanthemum vulgare*).

→ The contrast between topiary and flower-rich grassland (also pp.288–9) is one of the most potent, partly because the clipping of the topiary makes the long grass of the meadow clearly intentional.

←↓ Dark pink *Gladiolus byzantinus* is spattered across an area of meadow grass. These, like the camassias (p.284, middle left), are non-native plants that thrive in rough grass and make a striking impression, increasing slowly over the years. Alongside them, in an area of meadow adjacent to the long border (below), is pale yellow rattle (*Rhinanthus minor*), a key species in the creation of many successful meadows. A semi-parasite, it saps the energy of the grasses, providing an opportunity for other plants to grow and thereby producing a more biodiverse and visually attractive sward. It has become common practice to introduce it by seeding when creating wildflower meadows or later in the process.

Great Dixter House and Garden

One of the great movements in garden and landscape planting in the twenty-first century has been the huge interest in growing native plants in North America, and this 6,000-square metre (1.5 acre) New England garden illustrates how far this movement has come. It was created by landscape designer Larry Weaner, currently the leading proponent of ecological planting and design, and founder of the educational programme series *New Directions in the American Landscape*. For many years it was possible to buy prairie seed mixes, but any variation was largely geared to different soil types. Weaner, in addition, has created tailor-made seed mixes for particular visual effects – in effect adding design to ecology. 'I'm putting plants together which are right for the habitat and which work together – that comes first', he explains. 'Then that list would be winnowed and maybe some species added in order to meet various aesthetic and practical considerations.' He contrasts this with conventional garden-making, which 'works the other way round – the aesthetic considerations come first, and plants are picked for that aesthetic.'

Here, grasses and prairie wildflowers sweep down to a lake, with broad paths of mown grass inviting us to explore and discover. There is a wide and colourful range of late-flowering perennials, most of them aster family members familiar to us as late season border plants. Earlier in the year (late May and early June) there will have been other species, such as the bright, greeny-yellow wild parsley (*Zizia aurea*), the pink-white flower spikes of *Penstemon digitalis* and, a little later, false indigo (*Baptisia australis*). Many of us would recognize the latter as a recently fashionable border plant, with its indigo-blue flower spikes and bushy clumps of grey leaves.

This dreamily romantic prairie grassland is big enough to feel as if it could be a natural part of the landscape and to complement the surrounding forest and the lake. It surrounds the house, but by being continuous and dominant, broken only by paths, the sense of its being a habitat and developing ecosystem is emphasized – an effect very different to that of having even a large prairie or meadow area as part of a garden with extensive mown grass. It is one of a growing number of gardens that Weaner and other practitioners are making outside the traditional prairie states of the American Midwest. Sown from seed, this could be taken for a real wild grassland, for the plant density is pretty much the same as would be found naturally. 'The basic plant mix is

Prairie Garden

of New England natives', Weaner says, 'but some from the wider northeast region or the Midwest might be brought in for particular effects.' The flora is sufficiently diverse for a range of different appearances to be developed. For example, 'The planting along the drive needed to be low, because there were stone walls there the client did not want to lose sight of', so shorter-growing species were selected. 'They wanted to have a grassy feel to the area around the house, so we picked flowering species that had narrow grassy foliage, like *Liatris spicata* [button snakewort] and *Pycnanthemum tenuifolium* [narrowleaf mountainmint]. These were set among the short-growing grasses like little blue stem [*Schizachyrium scoparium*].'

Created in 2013, this grass and wildflower combination was sown by Weaner as part of a design by local landscape architect Jamie Purinton, who specializes in making sustainable projects that fit sympathetically into New England

landscapes and ecosystems. Over time it will change, as the 60:40 ratio of grass-to-wildflower is more typical of young habitats, with the proportion of grasses increasing over time; much the same would be true of European meadow habitats. Weaner expects change to be slow, however, as he has largely kept out the tallest grasses. 'Not everyone wants an eight-foot high meadow', he says, and there are 'species like *Panicum virgatum* [switch grass] which are very competitive, so we use them in isolated clumps; they're keystone plants for the community, and I do not want to exclude them entirely.'

There is an obvious parallel with the New York Botanical Garden (see pp.242–9), as both use only locally native plants but in novel (not naturally-occurring) combinations. Whereas quite intensive management can be used in the botanical garden (removing individual plants, for example), this garden is mostly managed extensively, so that maintenance operations do not focus on individual plants but on the entire vegetation. Weaner is, however, resistant to the word 'maintenance', as he says that all processes carried out in a naturalistic garden impact on the species mix, 'so design is an ongoing process'. Likewise, he is somewhat famous for a minimalist approach rather than root and branch garden-making. 'Existing native flora can be encouraged and invasive aliens discouraged', he says, for example by mowing areas containing the latter and leaving the former to spread and seed. Short-lived but colourful and pollinator-friendly wildflowers can be encouraged by occasional disturbance to ensure that they re-seed. Understanding how wild plants operate enables the gardener to gradually shift the balance in their favour. It is an approach that minimises risks and builds on the strengths of existing plant communities. In some ways there is a strong link to the

processes of management that took place at Innisfree (see pp.250–7), but with a clearer understanding of the method and the desired result.

The gardener's control is partial in these spaces; little actual time may be needed for management compared to a more conventional planting, but far more knowledge of the plant species and their lifecycles is required. Recognition of the importance of development over time – the 'self-proliferating landscape' as Weaner calls it – challenges the traditional separation of design and management, and as such is perhaps the ultimate example of a successful resolution of the dichotomy between nature and culture. However, successful development depends on a skill and knowledge set quite different to that of the traditional gardener or horticultural professional, while the gardener's concern for aesthetics is never far from the concerns of the conventional ecologist either. This kind of work indicates the need for a professional training that brings together horticulture and ecology. Only with an understanding derived from both disciplines can landscapes both truly ecological and truly aesthetic be developed for the future.

Looking into that future, others may want to take the process of creating aesthetic ecosystems a stage further, with the introduction of non-native species, as James Hitchmough (see pp.104–9) has always proposed. With what are known as 'novel ecosystems' (plant communities composed of both natives and aliens) proliferating all over the world, traditional concepts of ecology are changing. The future of garden-making may well be plant communities created and managed to deliver combined outcomes – reflecting a balance of what contributes to biodiversity, planetary health and human pleasure.

↑ Yellow-flowered black-eyed Susans (*Rudbeckia hirta*; see also p.293 top) create a splash in a relatively young area of the planting. Short-lived, they inevitably get displaced by longer-lived but less dramatic species, a pattern frequently observed in meadow and prairie plantings.

↓ The purple New England aster (*Symphyotrichum novae-angliae*; see also p.293 bottom) is one of the most reliable end-of-year plants for many open habitats, and has long been cultivated as a conventional border plant.

→ This density can only really be developed by
seeding (rather than planting). It does mean that
future maintenance, such as mowing or burning,
has to work all at once, with no individual
attention given to plants. Over time, the balance
between the different species will change,
which means ongoing development – it is rarely
possible to 'turn the clock back' except by
starting again. This particularly applies to
situations where shorter-lived plants are a major
part of the planting, such as with black-eyed
Susans (*Rudbeckia hirta*).

↑↓ Late summer is dominated by complementary yellow and blue
   flowers (below). They are the colours pollinating insects
   respond to most at this time of year, with decreasing light
   levels. Broad paths offer wider views than the more immersive
   style often used in prairie plantings (e.g. p.261). Big blue
   stem (*Andropogon gerardii*) and Indian grass (*Sorghastrum
   nutans*, above) are key prairie species.

←↓→ Joe pye weed (*Eupatorium maculatum*, left and below) flourishes along the lakeshore, a damp situation where it would be found naturally. A statuesque plant, it is also a valuable butterfly and late-season pollinator plant; it has a long history as a border plant in Europe. Mist flower (*Conoclinium coelestinum*; bottom left) is a related species usually found in woodland edge habitats; it appears here with purple New England aster (*Symphyotrichum novae-angliae*) and Indian grass (*Sorghastrum nutans*). A variety of joe pye weed and goldenrod (*Solidago* spp.) overlook the lakeside (see pp.296–7).

This directory lists some of the plants that have become a key part of naturalistic gardening. All are widely available from nurseries (at least in central and northern Europe and North America). In many cases, the plant shown is one of many species or cultivars of a group – all (or many) of which may be useful for this kind of planting design.

The overwhelming majority of the plants here are perennials (i.e. not trees and shrubs, though there is a growing realization that woody plants should be taken more seriously as design elements). They are suitable for cooler temperate climates, reflecting the origins and interests of those who have promoted this style of planting to date. As gardeners and designers in other regions become interested in naturalistic perennial planting, the species available will grow enormously. In many ways, then, this represents a snapshot of the current state of naturalistic planting design. In addition to temperate species, there is a minority of specialist dry climate plants here, but they are all easily grown in many other climate zones.

Low < 0.3 m (12 in) / Short 0.3–0.8 m (12–32 in) / Medium 0.8–1.4 m (32–55 in) /
Tall 1.4–2.0 m (55–78 in) / Very tall > 2.0 m (> 78 in)

Directory of Key Plants

Achillea filipendulina

A medium-height drought-tolerant perennial with summer flowers held well above clumps of divided aromatic foliage. Known as cloth of gold, it is the parent of many *Achillea* hybrids in warm colours, all of which need sun and well-drained soil.

Sun
Hardy to USDA zone 3

Allium flavum

One of many garlic relatives, this flowers in early summer and has thin, often insignificant foliage. This low variety (and many others) often seed strongly, which can sometimes get out of hand. A good plant for green roofs or other thin, dry soil situations.

Sun
Hardy to USDA zone 4

Andropogon gerardii

The dominant grass of the tallgrass prairie. Clump-forming with an upright habit and distinctive late summer flowers and seed heads. Tall to very tall. Suitable for a wide range of well-drained soils.

Sun
Hardy to USDA zone 3

Anemone x *hybrida*

Many varieties with pink or white flowers in late summer and autumn above clumps of bold divided foliage. A slow to establish medium to tall perennial, but robust and long-lived, potentially out-competing smaller plants, with a strong, clump-forming habit.

Sun/light shade
Hardy to USDA zone 4

Aquilegia vulgaris

A medium-height, early-flowering cottage garden plant; the species is violet-blue, but many pink, dark purple or white forms also occur. Short-lived but nearly always self-seeds, often resulting in a rich selection of colours. Attractive foliage, narrow shape and not competitive.

Sun/light shade
Hardy to USDA zone 3

Armeria maritima

Low-growing evergreen perennial eventually forming wide, dense mats. Very tough, thriving on dry walls, banks and in coastal locations with high levels of sun, wind and salt exposure.

Sun
Hardy to USDA zone 4

Asclepias tuberosa

Asclepias species are food sources for monarch butterflies in the Americas. This one is a medium to tall, clump-forming variety with upright growth that thrives on drier, well-drained soils.

Sun
Hardy to USDA zone 4

Astrantia major var. 'Rosea'

A popular border plant with off-white, pink or dusky red flowers. Medium height and clump-forming, with upright flower spikes but a flexible growth habit, allowing it to interweave among other plants. Any reasonable soil, but dislikes heat or drought.

Sun/light shade
Hardy to USDA zone 4

Ballota acetabulosa

A short, woolly-textured, grey-leaved, evergreen, Mediterranean sub-shrub for full sun and dry soil. Attractively dense foliage makes up for minimal flower interest. Fast-growing but short-lived and often used as a filler before other longer-lived plants establish.

Sun
Hardy to USDA zone 8

Baptisia bracteata

A tall, robust perennial with an almost shrub-like presence, with branching stems and attractive foliage; all *Baptisia* species have striking seed pods. This one has spikes of pale yellow pea flowers in early to mid-summer. Slow to establish but long-lived on fertile soils.

Sun
Hardy to USDA zone 3

Betonica officinalis

A short, mid-summer-flowering perennial with several colour forms, including pink and white. Forms a tight, non-spreading clump. Happy on most soils.

Sun/light shade
Hardy to USDA zone 4

Centranthus ruber

A short, spring-flowering perennial, relatively short-lived but readily self-seeding in dry places, including walls and banks of rubble. It has an uncompetitive and woody nature.

Sun
Hardy to USDA zone 5

Ceratostigma plumbaginoides

One of several similar low to short shrubs, although most growers treat this as herbaceous; it has a spreading habit. Late summer flowering and good red autumn leaf colour.

Sun
Hardy to USDA zone 5

Cistus x canescens f. albus

A medium-height evergreen shrub, one of many of a group of highly decorative if usually short-lived Mediterranean climate species, with flowers in pinks, yellows and white. Ideal for hot, dry banks and poor soils.

Sun
Hardy to USDA zones 7–8

Deschampsia cespitosa

A medium-height grass that forms dense, semi-evergreen tussocks above which hover airy heads of tiny flowers (and later seeds) from mid-summer to mid-winter. A good plant to mix with a wide range of perennials, even to form a matrix. Good on poor soils, damper ones preferred.

Sun/light shade
Hardy to USDA zone 3

Dianthus carthusianorum

With its narrow, insubstantial foliage, this a short- to medium-height perennial that should be grown among others, where its intensely pink flowers will bloom in mid-summer. Good on dry, calcareous soils. Can self-seed.

Sun
Hardy to USDA zone 3

Doellingeria umbellata

A very tall perennial with white flowers in late summer, followed by shiny white seed heads. It has a running habit, which means it tends to emerge among other plants. Full sun and fertile soil.

Sun
Hardy to USDA zone 3

Dryopteris filix-mas

One of many attractive ferns of the genus Dryopteris, long-lived and generally forming narrow clumps. Medium height. Classically plants of shade, preferably damp, this one is semi-evergreen and is tolerant of drier soils and some sun.

Shade/light sun
Hardy to USDA zone 3

Echinacea pallida

Echinaceas have become very popular perennials for their long season of summer flowers and good seed heads in autumn. All are medium-height plants for full sun and fertile soils. This is the more long-lived of the two in this directory.

Sun
Hardy to USDA zone 3

Echinacea purpurea 'Alba'

Often short-lived, these medium-height perennials grow best without being crowded by neighbours. Many hybrids have been produced, but they are never as reliable as the species. Will self-seed in some gardens. Good for pollinators.

Sun
Hardy to USDA zone 3

Echinops ritro

Tall perennial with
thistle-like foliage and
spherical flower heads
in mid- to late summer,
followed by a short season
of rather fine seed heads.
Not spreading, and some
related species can self-
seed strongly. Full sun,
and tolerant of dry and
poor soils.

Sun
Hardy to USDA zone 2

Eryngium giganteum

A tall biennial that often
self-seeds, occasionally
to a problematic degree.
Flowering in early to
mid-summer, its seed
heads stand well into the
winter. Needs full sun,
thrives on poor and
dry soils.

Sun
Hardy to USDA zone 4

Eryngium yuccifolium

A tall perennial with off-
white flower heads that
make a strong impact from
afar; can be short-lived
but often self-seeds.
Full sun, most soils.

Sun
Hardy to USDA zone 4

*Eupatorium
cannabinum*

A tall perennial grown
largely because it is
one of the few northern
European natives that
flowers in late summer;
a very good pollinator
plant. Damper sites
are preferred.

Sun/light shade
Hardy to USDA zone 4

Eupatorium maculatum
'Atropurpureum'

One of a group of tall
to very tall late summer-
flowering prairie peren-
nials, known as joe pye
weed. Despite their height
they stand well, and are
good winter silhouette
plants. Very good butter-
fly plants. Full sun and
damper soils.

Sun
Hardy to USDA zone 4

*Eupatorium
perfoliatum*

A medium to tall
perennial, mid- to late
summer flowering, with
attractive greyish
foliage. Moister soils
are preferred.

Sun/light shade
Hardy to USDA zone 4

Euphorbia characias

A medium-height perennial
with an annual growth
pattern that results in
it being functionally
evergreen. A long season
of late winter to spring
flowering. Short-lived
but often self-seeds.
Tolerant of dry soils.

Sun/light shade
Hardy to USDA zone 7

Euphorbia cyparissias
'Fen's Ruby'

A short perennial with
a strongly running habit
and unusual, very fine
foliage; a superb gap-
filler. Early summer
flowering. This variety
has red-tinged young
leaves. Full sun, tolerant
of dry calcareous soils.

Sun
Hardy to USDA zone 4

Euphorbia myrsinites

A low perennial with a sprawling habit, silvery leaves and yellow, early spring flowers with long-lasting bracts. Can self-seed. Full sun, tolerant of dry soils, good for trailing over rocks.

Sun
Hardy to USDA zone 5

Euphorbia rigida

A short evergreen perennial with spring flowers, the bracts of which stay attractive for months afterwards. Upright stems but eventually developing a spreading habit. Self-seeds. Tolerant of dry and poor soils.

Sun
Hardy to USDA zone 7

Eurybia divaricata

A medium-height perennial with late summer flowers, forming extensive dense clumps over time. An effective ground cover. Thrives in most soils.

Sun/light shade
Hardy to USDA zone 3

Foeniculum vulgare 'Purpureum'

A tall perennial with, in this form, very dark foliage. Small yellow flowers. Forms an attractive 'negative space' in planting but can be short-lived and self-seed prolifically. Tolerant of dry soils.

Sun
Hardy to USDA zone 6

Galium odoratum

A low woodland perennial with small white flowers in spring and a running habit that is useful for filling in gaps between other plants; in dry summers it becomes dormant.

Shade
Hardy to USDA zone 4

Geranium phaeum

A medium-height perennial that forms low, spreading clumps of lush foliage, often attractively marked, flowering in early summer. Thrives in most soils; a good plant for naturalizing in rough grass.

Sun/light shade
Hardy to USDA zone 5

Geranium psilostemon

Flowering in early to mid-summer, this strongly coloured perennial always attracts attention; a big grower, although it does not spread especially fast. Will naturalize in rough grass.

Sun/light shade
Hardy to USDA zone 5

Geranium x *oxonianum*

Flowering in early summer and again in early autumn, this is a vigorous perennial available in many shades of pink; highly effective for weed suppression and good in rough grass. Grows well in most soils.

Sun/light shade
Hardy to USDA zone 4

Hakonechloa macra

A short-growing grass with broad, arching stems clothed in very elegantly arranged leaves, one of the few suitable for light shade. Slowly forms clumps that make a good contrast to broad foliage shapes.

Light shade
Hardy to USDA zone 3

Helianthus spp.

Tall-growing perennial flowering in late summer, with flowers of a paler yellow than is the norm for the innumerable late daisies. Slowly forms clumps. A very reliable and predictable grower for sun and fertile soil.

Sun
Hardy to USDA zone 4

Hylotelephium spectabile

One of a group of very similar short perennial species and hybrids with succulent leaves and late summer flowers, adored by butterflies and forming strong winter seed heads. Slowly clump-forming. Good on dry soils.

Sun
Hardy to USDA zone 3

Inula hookeri

Elegant flower heads on a medium-height perennial in late summer. Attractive foliage. Clump forming. Thrives on moist soils.

Sun
Hardy to USDA zone 4

Iris sibirica

Blue-violet flowers in early summer adorn a medium-height perennial that forms steadily expanding clumps of narrow, linear leaves; has long-lasting seed heads. A tough and resilient plant for sun on most soils, but damper ground preferred.

Sun
Hardy to USDA zone 3

Knautia macedonica

Striking deep red flowers spatter this short-lived perennial for much of the summer. Short in height but producing long, lax stems, so best allowed to sprawl over other plants. Often self-seeds. Good on drier soils.

Sun
Hardy to USDA zone 5

Lavandula angustifolia

Lavenders are a very useful group of short- to medium-height evergreen shrubs for sunny, dry places. Most flower in early summer. Pungently scented foliage. With a useful lifespan of five to ten years, this is one of the hardiest species.

Sun
Hardy to USDA zone 5

Liatris spicata

Pink flowers on elegant narrow spikes make this common summer-flowering prairie perennial an important design element. Good seed heads. Medium-height, it forms small clumps that can be scattered to develop a sense of rhythm.

Sun
Hardy to USDA zone 3

Lobelia cardinalis

Vivid scarlet summer flowers on tall, narrow stems make this short-lived perennial stand out. It will self-seed on damp soil if there is not too much competition. Sun or very light shade on damp to wet soils.

Sun/light shade
Hardy to USDA zone 3

Lysimachia ciliata 'Firecracker'

Attractive dark foliage on a medium-height perennial that also has small yellow flowers in early summer. A running habit (common to the genus) but rarely a problem among established plants. Grows well on most soils.

Sun/light shade
Hardy to USDA zone 3

Lythrum salicaria

Deep pink spikes in mid- to late summer on a tall perennial that has achieved notoriety in North America for its invasive tendencies, which it never displays in its native Europe. Narrow upright habit, on damp or even wet soils.

Sun
Hardy to USDA zone 4

Miscanthus sinensis

A clump-forming grass with a great many cultivars, varying in height from medium to very tall. Late summer-flowering, with seed heads capable of standing all winter. Sun or very light shade on fertile soils, including damp ones.

Sun/light shade
Hardy to USDA zone 5

Monarda didyma

Monarda are medium to tall perennials much appreciated for mid-summer flowers and for being excellent pollinator plants. Some forms can split up and move around, others are more solidly clump-forming. Sun or very light shade, fertile soil.

Sun/light shade
Hardy to USDA zone 4

Oenothera lindheimeri

A medium-height perennial with a long summer season of white flowers on long, rangy stems. Very heat- and drought-tolerant; hardy but surviving winter best in warm summer climates.

Sun
Hardy to USDA zone 5

Onoclea sensibilis

A short fern with a running habit that makes it invaluable for creating a spontaneous, natural look among other plants in damper soils. Yellow autumn colour. Thrives on most soils, with the exception of dry ones.

Sun/light shade
Hardy to USDA zone 2

Origanum vulgare

Short perennial with late summer flowers that are an incredible magnet for pollinators. Somewhat untidy as a border plant, but good in rough grass on dry, calcareous soils. Clump-forming but does gradually spread. Most soils tolerated.

Sun
Hardy to USDA zone 4

Panicum virgatum

A tall, vigorous, clump-forming prairie grass with late season cloud-like flower/seed heads. Many cultivars, some with red autumn colour. Can overwhelm smaller plants on fertile soils.

Sun
Hardy to USDA zone 5

Persicaria amplexicaulis

Medium-height perennial that usefully forms clumps with dense ground-covering foliage and a long season of late summer flower; several different colour varieties. Needs fertile soils; not good in drought.

Sun/light shade
Hardy to USDA zone 4

Phlomis fruticosa

An evergreen, medium-height shrub with a rounded, relatively open habit, flowering in early summer; enjoys a longer lifespan than many Mediterranean-region plants of this type. Tolerant of dry and calcareous soils.

Sun
Hardy to USDA zone 8

Phlomis russeliana

A medium-height, evergreen perennial that makes an effective groundcover but also co-exists well with other robust perennials. Early summer flower and attractive weather-proof seed heads. Grows on most soils, but not very dry ones.

Sun
Hardy to USDA zone 5

Phlox spp.

The taller phlox are an important group of mid-summer flowering perennials. There are many cultivars, which vary greatly in vigour – this one is medium-height and a strong clump-former. Needs fertile soils.

Sun/light shade
Hardy to USDA zone 3

Rhinanthus minor

Low to short annual that parasitises grass and so weakens it, potentially allowing many other wildflower species to propagate. Grown easily from seed raked into very short cut grass in autumn; save the seed next year to spread it further. Needs well-drained soil.

Sun
Hardy to USDA zone 3

Rudbeckia fulgida

A short perennial that slowly forms wide clumps, flowering late summer to autumn. Much valued for its relatively low stature. Various forms are available.

Sun
Hardy to USDA zone 4

Salvia nemorosa 'Caradonna'

One of several closely related short- to medium-height perennials (and hybrids between them) that flourish on dry soils, especially if calcareous. Violet-blue flowers in early summer; can repeat-flower later if dead-headed.

Sun
Hardy to USDA zone 4

Salvia rosmarinus

A medium to tall evergreen shrub, popular as a herb. There are many different forms, including prostate ones; taller ones can lose foliage at the base and cannot be pruned back successfully. Tolerant of dry, shallow soils.

Sun
Hardy to USDA zone 5 if well-drained

Salvia yangii

An extraordinarily tough shrub, although nearly always cut down annually and so treated as a perennial. Medium to tall in height, upright habit, flowering usefully in mid-summer. Grows in any well-drained soil, including very poor and dry situations.

Sun
Hardy to USDA zone 4

Sanguisorba officinalis

One of a group of species and hybrids, mostly tall perennials with attractive, divided foliage and flower heads in mid-summer, with later seed heads. Mostly dark red, some pinks and creams. Most soils, damper preferred.

Sun
Hardy to USDA zone 4

Santolina chamaecyparissus

A short shrub with dense evergreen aromatic foliage, flowering in early summer. Short-lived, especially on more fertile soils. Good on dry and poor soils.

Sun
Hardy to USDA zone 7

Silphium laciniatum

An exceptionally tall perennial in flower, with yellow daisies in late summer and autumn. Dramatic foliage, especially when backlit. A surprise plant for prairie-style plantings in fertile soils.

Sun
Hardy to USDA zone 3

Solidago speciosa

One of the best of a varied group of perennials that includes some very weedy species but also many good garden and prairie plants. Tall, late summer to autumn flowering, clump-forming. Grows best in fertile soils.

Sun
Hardy to USDA zone 3

Stipa gigantea

A tall evergreen grass, although only the flowers and seed heads get above knee-height. Flowering in early summer, the seed heads remain good until early winter. Tussock-forming and not spreading. Good on dry and poor soils.

Sun
Hardy to USDA zone 7

Stipa tenuissima

A short grass, the fluffy foliage of which makes it invaluable for a very long 'meadow' season. It is, however, short-lived, though it may (or may not) self-seed predictably; it can be invasive in some regions. Thrives in most soils, including dry, infertile ones.

Sun
Hardy to USDA zone 6

Symphyotrichum novae-angliae 'Violetta'

One of the many daisy family plants known as asters, invaluable for late season colour. This tall to very tall species shows a lot of natural variation, with many garden cultivars. All are good pollinator plants. Likes reasonably fertile soil.

Sun/light shade
Hardy to USDA zone 4

Teucrium fruticans

A very tall Mediterranean shrub growing up to 3 metres (118 in), with silvery foliage and flowers produced during winter and spring. More long-lived than many, able to be pruned in various ways. Tolerant of dry soils.

Sun
Hardy to USDA zone 8

Thalictrum aquilegiifolium

Usefully tall for an early summer-flowering perennial, with elegant foliage and a narrow habit that means it becomes relatively inconspicuous after flowering. Dislikes heat.

Sun/light shade
Hardy to USDA zone 5

Thymus serpyllum

A very low-growing and spreading shrub, one of many plants conventionally associated with rockeries; can be used for carpeting and blending with other low-growing plants, or even as a lawn grass substitute. Early to mid-summer flowering.

Sun
Hardy to USDA zone 4

Tiarella wherryi

One of several species and varieties of a low to short perennial that combines attractive foliage with spring to early summer flowering. Most are slowly clump-forming and ideal for shade, although not deep shade. Humus-rich, moist soils preferred.

Shade
Hardy to USDA zone 3

Valeriana officinalis

A tall perennial that flowers in early summer; its fugitive running habit sees it popping up between other plants. Best on damp soils in cooler climates.

Sun
Hardy to USDA zone 4

Vernonia noveboracensis

A very tall prairie perennial that is among the last to flower in autumn, very good for pollinators. Produces slowly expanding clumps and prefers damper sites.

Sun
Hardy to USDA zone 5

Veronicastrum virginicum

A tall, mid-summer-flowering prairie perennial that stays remarkably good-looking until well into the winter, with firmly upright stems and narrow flowers and seed heads. Grows slowly into clumps.

Sun
Hardy to USDA zone 3

GARDEN DIRECTORY

AUSTRALIA

Phillip Johnson Garden
Woodend, Victoria
Private garden
Plantings along 110 m /360 ft drive,
within 1,300 sq. m / 0.3 acre garden
Climate: Warm temperate with dry summers,
USDA Zone 10a
Designer: Phillip Johnson
www.phillipjohnson.com.au

Stone Hill
Woodend, Victoria
Private garden
6,000 sq. m / 1.5 acres
Climate: Warm temperate with dry summers,
USDA Zone 10a
Designer: Michael McCoy
www.thegardenist.com.au

FRANCE

Cap d'Antibes Garden
Cap d'Antibes, Provence
Private garden
1,200 sq. m / 0.3 acre
Climate: Mediterranean, USDA Zone 9b
Designer: Alejandro O'Neill
www.alejandrooneillgardens.com

Les Cyprès
Villefranche-sur-Mer, Provence
Private garden
3,500 sq. m / 0.9 acre
Climate: Mediterranean, USDA Zone 9b
Designer: James and Helen Basson
www.scapedesign.com

Le Jardin de Berchigranges
Granges-sur-Vologne, Alsace
Private garden open to the public
3 hectares / 7.4 acres
Climate: Cool temperate, high rainfall, 650
m / 2130 ft altitude, USDA Zone 7b
Designers: Monique and Thierry Dronet
www.berchigranges.com

Le Jardin Sec
Mèze
Experimental garden for Pépinière Filippi
nursery
6,000 sq. m / 1.5 acres
Climate: Mediterranean, USDA Zone 9b
Designer: Olivier Filippi
www.jardin-sec.com

GERMANY

ABB Factory
Mannheim, Hesse
Ornamental plantings around industrial
facility
2,000 sq. m / 0.5 acre
Climate: Mildly continental cool temperate,
USDA Zone 8b
Designer: Bettina Jaugstetter
www.jaugstetter-landschaftsarchitektur.de

Hauptfriedhof Ludwigshafen
Ludwigshafen am Rhein, Rheinland
Palatinate
Public garden
2,000 sq. m / 0.5 acre (smaller areas within
cemetery/park complex)
Climate: Mildly continental cool temperate,
USDA Zone 8b
Designer: Harald Sauer

Schau- und Sichtungsgarten Hermannshof
Weinheim, Baden-Württemberg
Private garden open to the public
1.8 hectares / 4.5 acres
Climate: Mildly continental cool temperate
with warm summers, USDA Zone 8b
Designers: Urs Walser and Cassian Schmidt
www.sichtungsgarten-hermannshof.de

JAPAN

Tashiro-no-Mori (Tashiro's Forest)
Tokachi, Hokkaido
Private garden
5.6 hectares / 13.8 acres
Climate: Strongly continental cool
temperate, USDA Zone 6
Designer: Yukiyo Izumi

**Tokachi Millennium Forest:
The Meadow Garden**
Hokkaido
Private garden open to the public
1.5 hectares / 3.7 acres
Climate: Strongly continental cool
temperate, USDA Zone 6
Designer: Dan Pearson
www.tmf.jp

THE NETHERLANDS

Groningen City Garden
Groningen
Kempkensberg Building public garden
1.1 hectare / 2.7 acres
Climate: Cool temperate, USDA Zone 8a
Designer: Lodewijk Baljon Landscape
Architects
www.baljon.nl

Hummelo: Perennial Meadow
Broekstraat, Hummelo
Private garden
500 sq. m / 5,400 sq. ft within larger garden
Climate: Cool temperate, USDA Zone 9b
Designer: Piet Oudolf
www.oudolf.com

Lianne's Siergrassen: Prairie Garden
De Wilp
Nursery with prairie garden
3,500 sq. m / 0.86 acre
Climate: Cool temperate, USDA Zone 9b
Designer: Lianne Pot
www.prairiegarden.info

NEW ZEALAND

Mamaku
Auckland, North Island
Private garden
1,000 sq. m / 0.25 acre
Climate: Humid sub-tropical, USDA Zone 10b
Designer: Xanthe White
www.xanthewhitedesign.co.nz

Jo Wakelin Garden
Near Cromwell, Central Otago, South Island
Private garden
2,000 sq. m / 0.5 acre
Climate: Dry continental, USDA Zone 9b
Designer: Jo Wakelin

SPAIN

Water Mill Garden
Rascafría, Sierra de Madrid
Private garden
500 sq. m / 5,400 sq. ft
Climate: Continental, USDA Zone 7b
Designers: Miguel Urquijo and Renate Kastner
www.urquijokastner.com

UK

Barbican Estate
London, England
Gardens around public spaces and private
residences
1,600 sq. m / 0.4 acre
Climate: Cool temperate, USDA Zone 9a
Designer: Nigel Dunnett
www.nigeldunnett.com

The Barn: Prairie Garden
Serge Hill, Hertfordshire, England
Private garden
2,000 sq. m / 0.5 acre
Climate: Cool temperate, USDA Zone 8b
Designer: Tom Stuart-Smith
www.tomstuartsmith.co.uk

Cambo Gardens: The Walled Garden and the Prairie
Fife, Scotland
Private garden open to the public
1 hectare / 2.5 acres (walled garden);
700 sq. m / 7,500 sq. ft (prairie)
Climate: Cool temperate, cool summers,
USDA Zone 9a
Designer: Elliott Forsyth
www.cambogardens.org.uk

Dyffryn Fernant
Newport, Pembrokeshire, Wales
Private garden open to the public
1.2 hectares / 3 acres (cultivated),
within 2.4 hectares / 6 acres
Climate: Maritime cool temperate,
USDA Zone 9a
Designer: Christina Shand
www.dyffrynfernant.co.uk

Gelli Uchaf
(Upper Grove)
Carmarthenshire, Wales
Private garden
6,000 sq. m / 1.5 acres
Climate: Cool temperate, USDA Zone 9a
Designers: Julian and Fiona Wormald
www.thegardenimpressionists.com

Great Dixter House
and Garden: Meadows
Northiam, East Sussex, England
Private garden open to the public
0.75 hectare / 1.9 acres within larger garden
Climate: Cool temperate, USDA Zone 9a
Designers: original layout by Edwin Lutyens,
planting by Daisy Lloyd, Christopher Lloyd
and Fergus Garrett
www.greatdixter.co.uk

Grey to Green City Garden
Sheffield, South Yorkshire, England
Ornamental plantings in public spaces
1.3 km / 0.8 mile pedestrian highway
Climate: Cool temperate, USDA Zone 8b
Designer: Zac Tudor and Sheffield City
Council landscape team
www.greytogreen.org.uk

Hailstone Barn
Cherington, Gloucestershire, England
Private garden
1,200 sq. m / 0.3 acre
Climate: Cool temperate, USDA Zone 8b
Designer: James Alexander-Sinclair
www.jamesalexandersinclair.com

James Hitchmough Garden
Sheffield, South Yorkshire, England
Private garden
500 sq. m / 5,400 sq. ft
Climate: Cool temperate, USDA Zone 8b
Designer: James Hitchmough
instagram.com/jameshitchmough

The Lookout
Lympstone, Devon, England
Private garden
0.8 hectare / 2 acres
Climate: Maritime cool temperate, USDA
Zone 9a
Designers: Jackie and Will Michelmore

Oudolf Field:
Hauser & Wirth Somerset
Bruton, Somerset, England
6,500 sq. m / 1.6 acre
Climate: Temperate oceanic, USDA Zone 8
Designer: Piet Oudolf
www.hauserwirth.com

Oakwood at RHS Garden Wisley
Wisley, Surrey, England
Royal Horticultural Society garden open
to the public
1.8 hectare / 4.5 acres within larger garden
Climate: Cool temperate, USDA Zone 8b
Designer: George Fergusson Wilson,
managed by curator Matthew Pottage
www.rhs.org.uk/gardens/wisley

Stansbatch Barn
Near Hay-on-Wye, Herefordshire, England
Private garden
800 sq. m / 0.2 acre
Climate: Cool temperate, USDA Zone 8b
Designer: Catherine Janson

Trentham Gardens:
Lakeside and Woodland
Stoke-on-Trent, Staffordshire, England
Private garden open to the public
Planted areas along 3 km /
1.9 miles of paths within 120 hectare /
297 acre park
Climate: Cool temperate, USDA Zone 8b
Designer: Nigel Dunnett
www.trentham.co.uk/trentham-gardens

Wildside
Near Buckland Monachorum, Devon,
England
Private garden
1.6 hectare / 4 acres
Climate: Cool temperate, USDA Zone 9b
Designer: Keith Wiley
www.wileyatwildside.com

USA

Chanticleer: Bell's Woodland
Wayne, Pennsylvania
Public garden
1.6 hectare / 4 acres
Climate: Humid continental, USDA Zone 9a
Designer: Chris Woods and Przemek Walczak
www.chanticleergarden.org

Fort William Park: Children's Garden
Cape Elizabeth, Maine
Public garden
6,000 sq. m / 1.5 acres
Climate: Humid continental, USDA Zone 5B
Designer: James McCain
www.jamesmccaingarden.com

Federal Twist
Stockton, New Jersey
Private garden
6,000 sq. m / 1.5 acres
Climate: Warm temperate, USDA Zone 7a
Designer: James Golden
www.federaltwist.com

High Line
Manhattan, New York City, New York
Public garden
2.3 kilometres / 1.4 miles
Climate: Humid continental, USDA Zone 7b
Designer: James Corner Field Operations,
Diller Scofidio + Renfro, and Piet Oudolf
www.thehighline.org

Innisfree
Millbrook, New York
Public garden
75 hectares / 185 acres
Climate: Humid continental, USDA Zone 6b
Designer: Lester Collins, with Walter
and Marion Beck; Curator, Kate Kerin
www.innisfreegarden.org

New York Botanical Garden:
Native Plant Garden
Bronx, New York City, New York
Public garden
1.4 hectares / 3.5 acres
Climate: Humid continental, USDA Zone 7b
Designer: Sheila Brady, of Oehme van
Sweden Associates
www.nybg.org

Prairie Garden
Lakeville, Connecticut
Private garden
6,000 sq. m / 1.5 acres
Climate: continental, USDA zone 5b
Designer: Larry Weaner
www.lweanerassociates.com

Bernard Trainor Garden
Monterey County, California
Private garden
6,000 sq. m / 1.5 acres
Climate: Mediterranean, USDA Zone 9b
Designer: Bernard Trainor
www.groundstudio.com

Von Schlegell Garden
Portland, Oregon
Private garden
4,000 sq. m / 1 acre
Climate: Borderline Mediterranean, USDA
Zone 8a
Designer: Sean Hogan
www.cistus.com

BIOGRAPHIES

The individuals included here have been particularly influential within the naturalistic planting movement, not necessarily because they are all garden people, but because they have helped to raise the consciousness of both practitioners and the general public. While not a comprehensive list, these individuals have encouraged others to think about the value of native plants, to consider the importance of designed landscapes for biodiversity and to use conventional garden plants in different ways, and they have broadened the palette of what we plant in our gardens and expect in our landscapes.

Beth Chatto (UK)

Gardener, nursery owner and writer, Chatto (1923–2018) introduced to the English-speaking garden public the idea of matching plants to their environment, building on her husband Andrew's extensive research into ecology. Part of an élite artistic circle, Chatto's plant selection was influenced by the painter Cedric Morris. Her garden in Essex became a test bed for her ideas. It is still a very popular destination garden, along with its accompanying nursery. The nursery's stands at London's Chelsea Flower Show from 1970 onwards, along with Chatto's prolific writing and lecturing, did much to promote a naturalistic garden aesthetic and an ecologically-aware planting style.

Nigel Dunnett (UK)

Professor of Planting Design and Urban Horticulture at the University of Sheffield, Dunnett has tended to focus on the functional aspects of naturalistic planting – green roofs, rain gardens, sustainable drainage – as well as working on planting for more general public projects. The Barbican estate in London is an example of a complete re-thinking of green space in a high-density residential environment.

Olivier Filippi (France)

A nursery owner, Filippi has a deep understanding of the Mediterranean region flora and how it may be used in gardens and landscapes. A methodical practitioner and recorder, he seeks to share his experience of dry habitat gardening through writing and photography. His publications and the enormous plant range of his Le Jardin Sec nursery has enabled a wide range of design practitioners and others to start to develop planting combinations for private and public projects across the region.

Karl Foerster (Germany)

Nursery owner, plant breeder, writer and broadcaster, Foerster (1874–1970) played an important role in promoting perennials in Germany, and in introducing grasses into cultivation. During the 1920s and 1930s he was part of a liberal intellectual circle that included many leading cultural figures – it was named the Bornim Circle, after the village where he lived. His multicultural approach to plant selection stands in stark contrast to that of Willy Lange (1864–1941), whose habitat-inspired plantings were influential but whose politics has led to his being discredited. Foerster's work was not naturalistic in any real sense, but he is widely seen as the movement's founder.

Henk Gerritsen (The Netherlands)

Designer, gardener, artist, writer, Gerritsen (1948–2008) was a key collaborator with Piet Oudolf during the 1990s. His Priona Garden was hugely influential in developing and popularizing naturalistic planting styles, initially largely through the photography of Marijke Heuff, which highlighted the seed heads and dying foliage that gardeners normally hide. Priona combines wild plantings with clipped foliage and a variety of artistic interventions. A gifted and witty writer, Gerritsen collaborated with Piet Oudolf on a number of books on perennials.

Richard Hansen (USA)

A hugely influential German horticulturist, Hansen (1912–2001) founded in 1947 the Sichtungsgarten Weihenstephan, a public garden attached to an educational institution north of Munich, which was also intended to be the locus for research and the dissemination of results to professionals and the general gardening public. In the 30 years he headed the institution, Hansen developed a systematic approach to planting design that focused on developing plant communities, thereby enabling landscape architects and others to develop complex sustainable and long-term plantings.

James Hitchmough (UK)

Professor of Horticultural Ecology at the University of Sheffield, Hitchmough has promoted naturalistic design throughout his career, developing seed mixes for large-scale public projects, which he has achieved through directing postgraduate students, thus building up an impressive body of evidence-based methodologies. His consultancy work and collaborations in China will probably be his greatest legacy.

Lady Bird Johnson (USA)

A former First Lady (wife of President Lyndon Johnson), Johnson (1912–2007) was one of the United States' most active campaigners for native plants. In 1982 she founded the National Wildflower Research Center near Austin, Texas, for research into and promotion of native plants in designed and managed landscapes, including roadsides. The planting of highways, initially with colourful annuals and later with more complex combinations of perennials, has become an increasingly prominent part of the American landscape.

Wolfram Kircher (Germany)

Professor of landscape management at the Fachhochschule Sachsen-Anhalt in Aschersleben, eastern Germany, Kircher has played a key role in developing three cutting-edge vegetation technologies: green roofs, natural swimming pools and mixed planting systems. All of these can be seen as aspects of 'applied ecology' – the successful use of plants based on an understanding of their ecological functioning, often at their limits of tolerance, for both functionality and aesthetics.

Rob Leopold (The Netherlands)
Gardener, seedsman, writer, philosopher, Leopold (1942–2005) was an innovator in many areas. He is remembered as a highly effective networker who did much to make key connections between enthusiastic gardeners and growers during the 1980s and 1990s. Founder (with Dick van den Burg) of the seed company Cruydt-Hoek in 1978, he invented the concept of mixed annual seeding, as well as promoting the native wildflowers that increasingly now adorn the country's roadsides for much of the summer.

Darrell Morrison (USA)
A retired Dean of the School of Landscape Architecture at the University of Georgia, as well as a practitioner in the field, Morrison has been one of the most influential advocates for the use of native plants in landscape design, as well an influential educator in naturalistic design principles.

Lorrie Otto (USA)
A Wisconsin resident, Otto (1919–2010) was an active conservation campaigner and one of the first to challenge the statutes, once common across the United States, against growing anything more than a couple of inches (5 cm) tall on private front lawns. She was instrumental in setting up The Wild Ones, an organization dedicated to garden and landscape biodiversity, chiefly through the use of native plants.

Piet Oudolf (The Netherlands)
With a style that combines modernism and plantsmanship, Oudolf has raised planting design to rock star status, also – crucially – achieving respect from the contemporary art world. The New York High Line project of the early 2000s sealed his status. Unlike many other garden designers, most of his significant work is public, including modern parks, regeneration projects and the gardens of art museums. A garden designer all his life, he became interested in using perennials during the 1980s; finding sources of supply difficult, he set up his own nursery in the Dutch countryside. His plant selection and the growing number of high profile projects he carried out brought about a huge shift in, initially, the Dutch nursery industry, and then across Europe and North America. His focus on perennials does not exclude woody plants, but these are largely there, perhaps inevitably, to frame complex perennial combinations. His planting focuses mostly on the latter part of the growing season,

with a strong winter presence. Although not in any sense an ecological designer, his introduction of a strongly naturalistic aesthetic has enabled more dynamically ecological work to achieve acceptability.

William Robinson (UK)
An Irish gardener, Robinson (1838–1935) became one of the most innovative and influential garden writers and magazine editors of the late Victorian and Edwardian eras. *The Wild Garden* (1870) was a polemic proposing the emulation of natural beauty in the garden, as opposed to the hothouse-fuelled formality that dominated horticulture at the time. Ecology was little understood, however, and the book's immediate practical impact was limited; nevertheless, it has been inspirational to later gardeners. Robinson can be seen as the 'father' of wild-style planting in the English-speaking world.

Amalia Robredo (Argentina)
A garden and landscape designer and a teacher of landscape, Robredo has been an influential and pioneering promotor of the use of native plants in gardens and other designed landscapes in South America. She has played a key role in the evaluation of native species for horticulture.

Cassian Schmidt (Germany)
Director of the Schau- und Sichtungsgarten Hermannshof in Weinheim and Professor of Plant Use at Geissenheim University, Schmidt leads research into planting mixes, mostly for public use. He has made the Hermannshof garden into a showpiece of contemporary thinking about planting design, with a huge range of plant types that, unusually, are of equal interest to the professional and the amateur gardener.

Ernst Silva Tarouca (Austro-Hungarian Empire)
An aristocrat, politician and amateur dendrologist of the German-speaking Austro-Hungarian Empire, Silva Tarouca (1860–1936) lived at Pruhonice, now in the Czech Republic; the garden is much restored and still botanically very diverse. He experimented widely with naturalizing plant species in different habitats. After the demise of the empire, he worked with Camillo Schneider on an influential encyclopedia that illustrated many of his ideas on wild planting.

Sarah Stein (USA)
Initially a writer of children's books, Stein (1935–2005) enjoyed a second career as an influential writer and promotor of garden biodiversity, which she dubbed 'ungardening'. This occurred in the 1990s, just when naturalistic planting and the native plant

movement were making the transition from minority interest to something more popular.

Jac Thijsse (The Netherlands)
Nature writer, teacher and conservationist, Thijsse (1865–1945) co-founded *De Levende Natuur* (*Living Nature*) magazine and played a major role in educating the Dutch public on gardening and nature matters. Thijsse was one of the first in his country to argue for the protection of nature for its own merits. In 1925, for his sixtieth birthday, he was offered some land for the construction of an 'instructive park', which he planted up in a series of habitat zones. It was later to be named Thijsse's Hof, and it became the blueprint for a network of *heemparks*, parks and community gardens planted almost entirely with native plants. *Heemparks* are central to what is today a very well-organized movement integrating home and community gardeners, designers and professional landscape managers.

James van Sweden (USA)
Architect and landscape architect, Van Sweden (1935–2013) founded with Wolfgang Oehme the landscape practice Oehme van Sweden Associates; from the mid-1970s they radically changed planting design in the United States, focusing on broad masses of perennials and ornamental grasses. Oehme was a horticulturist from East Germany, whose teachers had trained under Karl Foerster. Their very different personalities complemented each other, and they developed a design approach for both public landscapes and private gardens that proved highly effective. While their work is only very rarely ecological, they broke the arguably ossified mould of garden and landscape design in the US, opening the doors to the current generation of design practitioners.

Larry Weaner (USA)
A practising landscape architect who established his practice in 1982, Weaner will perhaps be best remembered for inspiring a paradigm shift in the way that native plants are used, bringing together aesthetics and a strong sense of ecological development. He stresses the interlinking of design and management, arguing that the selective encouragement or discouragement of particular species can be used as design tools.

Keith Wiley (UK)
Former Head Gardener at The Garden House, Devon, before setting up his own garden business, Wildside, in 2003, Wiley has become known for a highly individual approach to planting design. This is based on a strongly artistic methodology, which he has promoted through books and lecturing.

FURTHER READING

Andre Baranowski (foreword by Dorothy Kalins), *Garden Wild*. New York: Rizzoli, 2019

Gilles Clément, *Le jardin en mouvement*. Paris: Sens et Tonka, 2017

Nigel Dunnett, *Naturalistic Planting Design: The Essential Guide*. London: Filbert Press, 2019

Rory Dusoir, *Planting the Oudolf Gardens at Hauser & Wirth Somerset: Plants and Planting*. London: Filbert Press, 2019

Olivier Filippi, *The Dry Gardening Handbook: Plants and Practices for a Changing Climate*. London: Filbert Press, 2019 (first edn London: Thames & Hudson, 2008)

Olivier Filippi, *Bringing the Mediterranean into Your Garden: How to Capture the Natural Beauty of the Garrigue*. London: Filbert Press, 2019

James Golden, *The View from Federal Twist: A New Way of Thinking About Gardens, Nature and Ourselves*. London: Filbert Press, 2021

Richard Hansen, *Perennials and their Garden Habitats*. Portland, OR: Timber Press, 1993

Laurie Hégo, Joëlle Le Scanff-Mayer and Gilles Le Scanff-Mayer, *Le jardin de Berchigranges*. Stuttgart: Ulmer Verlag, 2008

James Hitchmough, *Sowing Beauty: Designing Flowering Meadows from Seed*. Portland, OR: Timber Press, 2017

Ian Hodgson, *New Wild Garden: Natural-style Planting and Practicalities*. London: Frances Lincoln, 2016, 2021

Phillip Johnson, *Connected: The Sustainable Landscapes of Phillip Johnson*. Sydney and London: Murdoch Books, 2014

Noel Kingsbury, *Natural Garden Style*. London: Merrell Publishers, 2009

Noel Kingsbury, *The New Perennial Garden*. London: Frances Lincoln, 1996

Noel Kingsbury, *Seedheads in the Garden*. Portland, OR: Timber Press, 2006

Noel Kingsbury and Piet Oudolf, *Oudolf Hummelo: A Journey through a Plantsman's Life*. New York: Monacelli Press, 2015, 2021

Noel Kingsbury and Piet Oudolf, *Planting: A New Perspective*. Portland, OR: Timber Press, 2013

Noel Kingsbury and Piet Oudolf, *Designing with Plants*. London: Conran Octopus, 1999, 2008

Christopher Lloyd and Fergus Garrett, *Meadows: At Great Dixter and Beyond*. London: Pimpernel Press, 2016

Piet Oudolf and Rick Darke, *Gardens of the High Line: Elevating the Nature of Modern Landscapes*. Portland, OR: Timber Press, 2017

Piet Oudolf and Noel Kingsbury, *Planting Design: Gardens in Time and Space*. Portland, OR: Timber Press, 2005

Piet Oudolf with Noel Kingsbury, *Piet Oudolf: Landscapes in Landscapes*. New York: Monacelli Press, 2011

Dan Pearson with Midori Shintani, *Tokachi Millennium Forest: Pioneering a New Way of Gardening with Nature*. London: Filbert Press, 2020

Thomas Rainer, *Planting in a Post-Wild World*. Portland, OR: Timber Press, 2015

Tim Richardson and Tom Stuart-Smith (preface by Piet Oudolf), *Tom Stuart-Smith: Drawn from the Land*. London: Thames & Hudson, 2021

Alessandro Rocca, ed., *Planetary Gardens: The Landscape Architecture of Gilles Clément*. Basel: Birkhäuser Verlag, 2008.

Claire Takacs, *Dreamscapes: Inspiration and Beauty in Gardens Near and Far*. Richmond, VIC/London: Hardie Grant Publishing, 2018

Claire Takacs, *Australian Dreamscapes: Movement, Light and Colour: The Art of Planting in Gardens Inspired by Nature*. Richmond, VIC/London: Hardie Grant Publishing, 2019

Bernard Trainor, *Ground Studio Landscapes*. Princeton, NJ: Princeton Architectural Press, 2019

Larry Weaner and Thomas Christopher, *Garden Revolution*. Portland, OR: Timber Press, 2016

Keith Wiley, *On the Wild Side: Experiments in New Naturalism*. Portland, OR: Timber Press, 2004

INDEX

Page numbers in *italics* refer to illustrations

318

ACKNOWLEDGEMENTS

I am very grateful for the collaboration of all the garden owners, gardeners, managers and designers whose work is featured here. This book is a celebration of your efforts and of your courage as innovators. Thank you to Victoria Clarke, who had the vision to recognize the importance of our work and to take this on as a publishing project; it has been wonderful seeing how she and her colleagues at Phaidon have shaped images and text into a magnificent book. Thanks are due to Paco Lacasta for creating the book's stunning design, and to Diane Fortenberry for her sensitive editing of the text. My wife, Jo, has had to put up with the endless progress reports and moans inevitable in any publishing process, the things that authors' partners always get to hear first. It has been a privilege to collaborate with Claire Takacs, whose photographs for this project are amazing and with whom I look forward to working again. I would like to pay tribute to Ros Wiley, wife of Keith Wiley, who died during the book's early stages of development. Ros was a crucial contributor to the making of the extraordinary garden at Wildside, one of the most visionary in the book, as well as being one of the very few people who have been able to represent the feel of naturalistic planting in her work as an artist. **NOEL KINGSBURY**

Thank you, Noel Kingsbury, for 13 years of thoroughly enjoyable collaborations and connections with inspiring gardeners around the world, and for opening my eyes to what really good planting is. Thank you, Juliet Roberts, then editor of *Gardens Illustrated*, for this life-changing introduction. Thank you, Phaidon – it was my dream to be published by you, and the perfect culmination for Noel's and my work together. Thank you, Victoria Clarke, our brilliant editor. Your level of care and expertise are unparalleled. Thank you, Paco Lacasta, for the most beautiful design, for your patience and for a cover I cannot stop looking at. Thank you to all of the gardeners and designers in the book. It's been an extraordinarily memorable journey to spend time in your gardens, and with you. **CLAIRE TAKACS**

Phaidon Press Limited
2 Cooperage Yard
London E15 2QR

Phaidon Press Inc.
65 Bleecker Street
New York, NY 10012

phaidon.com

First published 2022
© 2022 Phaidon Press Limited

ISBN 978 1 83866 105 2
ISBN 978 1 83866 530 2 (signed edition)

A CIP catalogue record for this book is
available from the British Library and the
Library of Congress.

Commissioning Editor: Victoria Clarke
Project Editor: Victoria Clarke, with
assistance from Diane Fortenberry
Production Controller: Sarah Kramer
Design: Lacasta Design

Printed in China